Praise for
Lessons from the Titans

In every era, it is always tempting to believe that the fundamentals have somehow changed. This book provides perceptive analyses of the enduring lessons from some of the most important companies in our nation's history. Leaders of today and tomorrow, across all industries, will do well to learn how to apply these fundamentals to their own time.

—Wes Bush
former Chairman and CEO of Northrop Grumman
and Director of General Motors and Cisco

Highly instructive. Every business executive, investor, and student of leadership should read this book. *Lessons from the Titans* shows us that excellent CEOs lead organizations that win and thrive because they implement great processes around operational excellence.

—Inge Thulin
former Chairman and CEO of 3M and Director of Merck

An engrossing read with many lessons to mull over for senior executives and emerging managers alike. This book reminds us that sustainable success depends on operational and financial discipline.

—Nick Santhanam
Senior Partner and Head of the Advanced Electronics
and Industrials Practice at McKinsey & Company

Few have the years of experience and insight into industrials that Scott, Carter, and Rob do. They've written *the* book on building great operating systems, disciplined capital deployment, and process capability to sustain long-term, consistent, top-quartile performance.

—Kirk Hachigian
former Chairman and CEO of Cooper Industries and
Director of NEE, PACCAR, and Allegion

With credibility built over 60 years of collective industry experience, the authors bring a unique inside view of what it takes to succeed in business. *Lessons from the Titans* is a must-read about the importance of innovation, competitive edge, disciplined investment, and leadership.

—Stephanie Link
Global Research Director and Portfolio Manager
at Nuveen and CNBC contributor

Business success still depends on keeping the organization focused on profitable growth through continuous operational improvement. *Lessons from the Titans* doesn't just explain how; it shows you these principles in action.

—Ed Breen
Executive Chairman and CEO of DuPont and Director of Comcast

LESSONS FROM THE
TITANS

LESSONS FROM THE TITANS

WHAT COMPANIES IN THE NEW ECONOMY CAN LEARN FROM THE GREAT INDUSTRIAL GIANTS TO *DRIVE SUSTAINABLE SUCCESS*

SCOTT DAVIS
CARTER COPELAND
ROB WERTHEIMER

NEW YORK CHICAGO SAN FRANCISCO ATHENS LONDON
MADRID MEXICO CITY MILAN NEW DELHI
SINGAPORE SYDNEY TORONTO

2 3 4 5 6 7 8 9 LCR 25 24 23 22 21 20

ISBN 978-1-260-46839-7
MHID 1-260-46839-9

e-ISBN 978-1-260-46840-3
e-MHID 1-260-46840-2

Design by Mauna Eichner and Lee Fukui

This publication is designed to provide accurate and authoritative information in regard to the subject matter covered. It is sold with the understanding that neither the author nor the publisher is engaged in rendering legal, accounting, securities trading, or other professional services. If legal advice or other expert assistance is required, the services of a competent professional person should be sought.

—From a Declaration of Principles Jointly Adopted by a Committee of the American Bar Association and a Committee of Publishers and Associations

Library of Congress Cataloging-in-Publication Data

Names: Davis, Scott (Scott Reed), author. | Copeland, Carter, author. | Wertheimer, Rob, author.

Title: Lessons from the titans : what companies in the new economy can learn from the great industrial giants to drive sustainable success / by Scott Davis, Carter Copeland, and Rob Wertheimer.

Description: New York : McGraw-Hill, [2020] | Includes bibliographical references and index.

Identifiers: LCCN 2020012125 (print) | LCCN 2020012126 (ebook) | ISBN 9781260468397 (hardcover) | ISBN 9781260468403 (ebook)

Subjects: LCSH: Success in business—Case studies. | Corporations—Case studies. | Technological innovations—Management—Case studies. | Strategic planning—Case studies.

Classification: LCC HF5386 .D323 2020 (print) | LCC HF5386 (ebook) | DDC 658—dc23

LC record available at https://lccn.loc.gov/2020012125

LC ebook record available at https://lccn.loc.gov/2020012126

McGraw Hill books are available at special quantity discounts to use as premiums and sales promotions or for use in corporate training programs. To contact a representative, please visit the Contact Us pages at www.mhprofessional.com.

CONTENTS

ACKNOWLEDGMENTS

Each of us has a story to tell of someone who took a chance on us at some point in our careers. Research departments on Wall Street are notoriously difficult to get into and even more difficult to advance in once there. It takes commitment and sponsorship to get very far. We were each amazingly lucky and grateful to be emerging analysts who were mentored by some of the most talented writers and thinkers in the business—people like Alice Schroeder, Steve Girsky, Mary Meeker, Chuck Phillips, Henry McVey, Byron Wien, Barton Biggs, Stephen Roach, and Jennifer Murphy. They were all top-ranked analysts in their field at a time when competition among analysts was amazingly high. And they each had impressive second careers once their analyst days were over. Management at senior levels was equally inspiring: Mayree Clark, Dennis Shea, and Andrew Jones from the Morgan Stanley research department; Stu Linde from the Lehman Brothers research department; Ruth Porat from investment banking; and Morgan Stanley CEO John Mack each stand out. These were leaders from a different era. Expectations for tangible results were beyond high, but mentorship and coaching were equally intense. We are each thankful for the experience they gave us.

When we started this project, we had no idea the magnitude of the challenge we were walking into. Starting a new business, analyzing companies during this wild period in history, and writing a book all at the same time is a bit crazy. And the reality is that many companies don't want their story to be told. We learned that humility in a culture and among its leaders extends even into retirement, perhaps even unto death. One of the great lessons of this project is that successful people and successful businesses usually prefer to be out of the limelight. In that context, we are grateful to the family of Brian Jellison, who allowed us to tell his story, and to the leaders who worked beside him at Roper. Same with Danaher, which has an amazing story, and we are thrilled that the company trusted us to tell it.

To our colleagues at Melius Research, a simple thank you falls short of expressing our gratitude. Not only are Jake Levinson and Ryan Eldridge exceptional analysts, but both proved invaluable in helping each chapter come to life. The rest of the Melius team provided regular feedback, often telling us hard truths about our early drafts, which was incredibly valuable throughout the process.

To those who helped write, edit, and go through countless rewrites and re-edits, we cannot say thank you enough. Our agent, John Butman, kept us focused and humble. His unexpected passing in March of 2020 is still hard to accept. We consider ourselves fortunate to have had access to his talents, even if only for a short time. Our collaborator, John Landry, was professional and steady and helped guide a project that was sprawling and ambitious.

To our clients, none of this would have been possible without you. Thank you for the faith that you have in us and the advice we provide. In the spirit of this book, we endeavor to get a little bit better every day. Melius, the name of our analytics firm, is Latin for "continuous improvement," and we try to live those principles with enthusiasm. We endeavor to learn from both our mistakes and our successes and to turn those experiences into useful work each and every day for you.

We'd also like to thank a key partner, Casey Ebro, our editor at McGraw Hill, for taking a chance on us. We were first-time writers with a book concept that could have easily been ignored. We are indebted to you, Casey, for your guidance and belief in us.

For me, my last thank you is the most important of all. My wife and business partner, Liz Davis, is not just an amazing wife and mother; it turns out she's also an exceptional editor. She spent day after day helping each of us recover from one bad draft after another until we started to find competence. And her patience and enthusiasm for the project from day one proved invaluable. Both Liz and I are lucky to have supportive parents and family members who have done nothing but prop us up from day one.

This project involved another level of time and commitment for all of us. It wasn't isolated to the office. Carter is thankful for the never-ending support of his wife, LoraMarie, his four wonderful children, and his parents, who have been a constant in his life and career. Their love and encouragement are the source of his unbounded optimism. He is also indebted to his mentor, Joseph Campbell Jr., whose training on how to be a humble but curious analyst, doting father, and thoughtful human being helped shape him into the person that he is today.

Rob is grateful for the support of his family throughout the project. Weekend editing sessions provided an opportunity to show the kids that the process of writing, rewriting, and doing it all again is not just something taught in school.

INTRODUCTION

Even before the coronavirus pandemic exposed flaws in government planning and tested the limits of modern medicine, the world had already become frighteningly out of balance. Tweets had taken over from substantive conversation and "news" had become unapologetically biased. High debt levels and rising leverage risk was something only old people talked about. Massive transfers in wealth, led by cheap money and various asset bubbles, were bringing us to the verge of revolution. And political extremism was gaining ground in many countries around the globe. A world that counts $15 trillion in negative-yielding government debt as not enough is a different world from the one we grew up in. And now a recession has put many businesses on the brink of collapse, even businesses that were not all that long ago thought of as invincible.

In the stock market, investors have spent much of the last decade bidding up technology giants to levels that make sense only if these firms face limited competition and amazing profitability for decades. Market share has become the primary goal in a winner-take-all economy. Far beyond Silicon Valley, companies have been spending heavily on growth and paying little attention to how they'll actually make money once they get there. With all the talk about disruption and market dominance, you might think the laws of business had been repealed. It's as if the hard-learned lessons from the 2008–2009 financial crisis have already been long forgotten, even as we encounter a new crisis that could have even deeper impacts.

In this new world, companies are increasingly difficult for investors to value. Determining which ones are truly built to last has taken a back seat to dreams of market disruption and domination. WeWork's near collapse in late 2019 serves as a stark reminder of this challenge, Uber's extreme volatility is another, and Tesla is a notable addition to this roller coaster ride. And the extreme stock market volatility that has defined 2020 so far has brought many sectors to Depression era–type valuation levels while barely touching others. Overall, this backdrop can only be characterized as unstable equilibrium.

Truth is, we may not know for a decade whether Google is built to last, whether Apple can thrive without its visionary founder, or whether Facebook is just a fad. It will take another five years to see if Tesla's innovations can stay ahead of the onslaught of new electric-vehicle launches soon to hit the market. In a world moving toward "natural and fresh," it's hard to know if fake meat is a step backward or a game changer. Or if the megamergers in healthcare and consumer goods will create efficient scale or just feed bloated bureaucracies. All these companies are just as susceptible to faltering as past giants that enjoyed similarly glittering reputations. Today's disrupters will face their own disruption risks in time.

We wrote this book because, as Wall Street analysts, we've seen firsthand how fleeting success can be. In fact, we've seen far more failure than success. And we think that trend is about to get much worse. In the decades after World War I, the average age of a company in the S&P 500 was 60 years. Today, it's less than 20 years and projected to decline every year for the next decade. Some of these companies disappeared because they were acquired; some just flat-out died. Either way, the common thread is a failure to sustain the excellence that got them into the S&P 500 in the first place. So why can't large, wealthy organizations maintain their competitive advantages? The most common explanation by the pundits is disruption, which is exceedingly hard to predict and most likely a convenient excuse. The reality is more complex and humbling. Companies usually fail because of the incompetence and arrogance of a complacent management team, not because they struggled to predict the future.

Predicting the future may itself just be an exercise in futility. The coronavirus pandemic is a clear example of the random walk we take each day. And this is not a new phenomenon. When we were growing up in the 1980s, futurists predicted the widespread adoption of electric cars by the late 1990s. In fact, GM launched a concept electric car with the EV1 all the way back in 1996. Decades later, we are still in the early stages of adoption, with headlines that highlight the rapid pace of potential disruption. Really? Thirty years later. If this pace of disruption has caught auto leaders or investors by surprise, they most certainly must have been out of touch in more ways than we can imagine. Meanwhile, few expected the computing power we have today and the pervasive impact of the internet and smartphones. Netscape cofounder and Silicon Valley investor Marc Andreessen noted in 2011 that "software is eating the world." That prediction sure seems accurate. Few could have dreamed of the impact that software has already had. But that prediction was ignored by most and stands out as being unusually prescient. Even the best CEOs are kidding themselves if they think they can consistently predict more than a little bit forward.

So it's important that senior managers focus on what they actually can control: fostering a humble culture that encourages continuous improvement, holding the line on corporate costs, driving toward manufacturing excellence, encouraging extreme customer focus, establishing a disciplined capital allocation process, moving a portfolio toward higher-return assets, all while setting the incentives needed to keep employees focused on the task at hand. These are the factors that differentiate the winners from everyone else.

The reality is that nearly all companies have access to the tools necessary to advance their businesses even while being disrupted. In a world where capital is cheap and readily available, even a slow management team can likely find the resources needed to make major business model shifts; and this is true whether that's using the power of M&A to accelerate a new path or investing heavily in the existing core. We've seen success in each. But the key is to invest, not just stand around watching others take the lead. In most industries, companies falter not because there was a sudden break in products or markets, but because those companies failed to keep up with faster-moving rivals. Complacency, arrogance, empire building, and grandiose visions are common characteristics of failure. In fact, we've seen elements of each of these in every single failure we've analyzed.

In this context we believe that greater focus should be applied to the basic old-fashioned principles that we observe in the best-run companies. These principles exist, they are time tested, and our aim is to share them with you.

WHY INDUSTRIALS ARE THE PERFECT SECTOR TO ANALYZE

As veteran analysts, we've had a front row seat for the market's two-decade-old obsession with disruption, digital transformation, market dominance, and cultish leadership. But as the era of the "new economy" shows early signs of maturation, the question becomes, What companies will endure and continue to grow—and how? The answer comes from an unlikely place: the big industrial companies that have chugged along successfully, many of them for decades. They are the market's original tech sector. (See Figure I.1.) They were once young high-flyers, not much different from many of the tech wonders of today. Each was spawned in some manner from a singular disruption, the dream of an entrepreneur, or some other key competitive advantage. GE goes back to the inventions of Thomas Edison, Boeing to the origins of flight, Honeywell to the thermostat, and Stanley Black & Decker to hardware starting in the 1840s. But after that disruption phase, each of these companies was tested in ways their founders never imagined. High profits always attract new entrants, and perversely those entrants are often advantaged by the ability to copy others' successes, all with the benefits a clean sheet of paper and fresh capital can offer. More important, each of these companies had to survive periods of poor leadership, grandiose visions, and the inevitable loss of focus that infects an organization when systems and processes are not encouraged.

Despite these challenges, the companies we highlight survived the peaks and valleys of business realities, and most thrived. With iter-

Figure I.1: **Industrials were the original technology and growth sector.**

Dow Jones Industrial Average Constituents	
1896	
American Cotton Oil Co.	Laclede Gas Co.
American Sugar Co.	National Lead Co.
American Tobacco Co.	North American Co.
Chicago Gas Co.	Tennessee Coal, Iron & Railroad Co.
Distilling & Cattle Feed Co.	U.S. Leather Co.
General Electric	United States Rubber Co.
2020	
3M	JPMorgan Chase
American Express	McDonald's
Apple	Merck
Boeing	Microsoft
Caterpillar	NIKE
Chevron	Pfizer
Cisco Systems	Procter & Gamble
Coca-Cola	Travelers
Dow	United Technologies
Exxon Mobil	UnitedHealth Group
Goldman Sachs	Verizon Communications
Home Depot	Visa
IBM	Walgreens Boots Alliance
Intel	Walmart
Johnson & Johnson	Walt Disney

Source: Dow Jones, Bloomberg

ations of both failure and success, they developed the most advanced business systems on the planet. The very best defied the odds and became exceptional. The truth is that their secrets are hardly secrets at all—continuous improvement, rigorous benchmarking, disciplined investment, principled leadership, solid business systems—but these practices have been long forgotten, ignored, or dismissed by the businesspeople hypnotized by the Google-Amazon-Apple dream. These industrial companies are the inspiration for our work.

There's a reason we talk about the Dow Jones Industrials—these companies dominated the stock market for much of history. Industrial companies have carried out or suffered more disruptions than any other. This year's coronavirus pandemic is just the latest one. These companies make industrials the perfect sector to study, with data on great successes and even greater failures that go back for north of a century. These companies had celebrated successes like diesel locomotives, jet engines, grain harvesters, factory robots, and x-ray machines. They had seemingly magical market positions, but most of them squandered that advantage. Arrogance led to wasteful investment decisions, poor labor relations, and countless scandals. Air and water pollution flowed from their greed. Domestic and overseas rivals offered lower costs and higher quality, and many of these one-time leaders refused to adapt and change. The ones that learned to overcome these challenges and thrive, however, make for fantastic study.

Most of the failures in American business are subtle. The companies merely fade away, usually merged into a bigger entity that is happy to take on an installed base, customer list, some technology, and talent—all for a fire sale price. These companies don't get categorized as failures in an absolute sense. In fact, the executives normally walk away richer and are celebrated. But without that sale or merger, their future was heavily in doubt. They count into the thousands, just in the industrial sector alone. And while we have looked at more than a hundred years of data, we realized that we didn't have to go back that far. The reasons for failure and the formulas for success haven't really changed at all. Whether it be 1950, 1980, or 2020, they are pretty much exactly the same.

If we back up a bit, what is interesting and perhaps ironic is that the pattern of struggling/failure that turns into sell/merge has fed the M&A appetites of many of the most successful entities for decades. Warren Buffett was an early M&A value-based pioneer, and much of private equity exists today on the back of that strategy. The very process of buying someone else's management screw-up, and then fixing, closing, or selling what you don't want, has helped more than a fair share of companies to show profit growth well above that of peers and to compound returns.

The industrial sector has had years to perfect this strategy, and as a result it has shown rising margins for decades, despite increased global competition, relatively limited organic growth, and countless disruptions. (See Figure I.2.) In fact, the industrial sector joins the tech sector in being the only other S&P 500 sector to show rising profit margins for each of the last five decades. Ironically, the oldest and the newest S&P sectors have been succeeding, but for different reasons. Industrials gobble up the weak, improve their operations, and control their mature markets via consolidation, while tech focuses on disruption and wins by creating virtual monopolies in new markets. This is a clear example of two industries at very different stages of maturity. But it wasn't always that way. Since industrials were the original tech, it would seem logical that the lessons from their survival could be immensely valuable to today's tech world. Eventually, tech will have to move past this early disruption phase to something more sustainable. And that's why the case studies in this book are so valuable. The lessons are striking, and they are also timeless.

Figure I.2: **Industrials have expanded their net profit margins for decades despite rising global competition.**

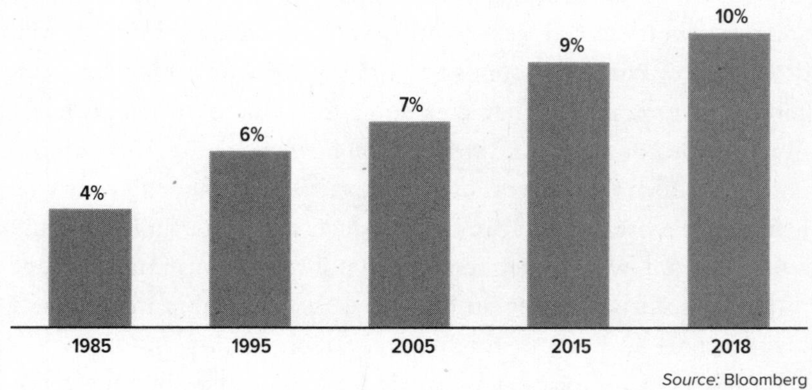

Source: Bloomberg

Because we've been analyzing industrials for decades, we know why GE faltered and how Honeywell saved itself, despite the odds in 2001 that suggested just the opposite; how Danaher became one of the most successful companies in history by reinventing itself over and over; and how Stanley Black & Decker used both manufacturing excellence and focused innovation to succeed in one of the most competitive segments on the planet, hand tools. We study risk management, and few firms have experienced the prideful highs that retreated into humiliating lows like Boeing. And we dig into the power of compounding by sharing the story of two amazing value creators: Roper and TransDigm.

We draw on a century of company data to see what patterns persist. We have a statistical sampling of winners, losers, lost souls, and comeback stories. The surviving industrial companies have found a way to thrive after decades of competition, cyclical swings, and geopolitical shifts, and their resilience has something to teach the rest of the economy. The challenges don't end once you've disrupted your industry; you just get new ones.

WHAT WE LOOK FOR

We spend tremendous effort looking for signs of arrogance; it's the most common attribute of failure, even rising above complacency, and those who succeed seem to find a way to encourage humility. We describe how business systems and rigorous benchmarking can keep companies grounded so they keep doing the work to sustain the business over the long run. And we focus on how companies that continuously improve their operations generate the cash flow necessary to invest even more creatively in new products and opportunistic acquisitions. And how they are then able to use continuous improvement processes to drive higher profits and cash from those incremental investments—in a very methodical, repeatable fashion.

Like many business books, we do fixate on culture but not in the same context as popular literature. A healthy and supportive culture is absolutely critical to any company's long-term success. But we've found it to be a by-product of actions and incentives, not a driver. Said a different way, it can't be force-fed from the top. It's not about words—it's about actions. Most companies that talk about culture don't have one, at least not a good one. Culture doesn't come from a mission statement or a CEO's webcasted lecture. Culture is encouraged from the top but is actually built from the bottom—on the factory floor or in the cubicles where the actual work gets done. The safety and well-being of employees must be its foundation. The customer centricity in the sales and marketing organization is the next building block. Is the R&D organization dedicated to solving today's customer problems and the day-to-day blocking and tackling that goes along with that mission? Are employees focused, motivated, empowered, and committed to continuous improvement? Do leaders benchmark to best in class and accept the challenge if their company begins to fall behind? Is being ethical a basic minimum expectation? Does bad news travel faster than good, and do leaders rally to solve the problem, or do they waste energy assigning blame? While it's convenient to talk about culture from the corporate office vantage, it's meaningless if managers don't live it at the most junior levels and if it hasn't permeated through to the lowest rung of labor.

Where the top of the organization influences culture is on actions and incentives. CEOs who behave badly typically run organizations that . . . behave badly. Compensate folks to do the right thing, and that good behavior will likely become the norm. Financial incentives do matter. There is no right or wrong culture; we've seen successful companies with quite different approaches that work. Ping-Pong tables and nap rooms may help set the casual tone for some organizations but could have just the opposite impact for others. What matters is whether those approaches fit the company's leadership, capabilities, and challenges.

As for disruption, we've seen plenty of it, both in the companies we study and in our own workplaces. One of us saw his firm, Lehman Brothers, go from Wall Street darling to bankruptcy in six months. The other two watched as their employer, Morgan Stanley, came within a few hours of its own death, surviving only because of government support and a last-minute lifeline investment by a Japanese bank. Before the 2008 crisis we lived through the tech bubble of

1999–2001, when analysts were stars with limos lined up to ferry even the most junior employee home. By 2004 we were barely employed. Today's coronavirus crisis offers a completely different challenge that has brought more than a fair share of disruption risk and a narrative that is far from complete.

Still our experience of studying companies over decades has convinced us that disruption gets too much attention, and although "death" often seems to happen quickly, it rarely does in reality. The Wall Street firms that fell apart in 2008 had elevated risk levels for many years prior. Public filings were pretty clear; debt levels were skyrocketing. Today's pandemic came on suddenly, but warnings of such an event have been out there for decades. Most governments just chose to ignore the risk and failed to prepare. So while disruption gets the headlines and attention, everyday blocking and tackling is far more critical: business systems that keep entities focused; benchmarking that never allows entities to stand still and can humble even the best operators. We're especially impressed with the power of compounding—even 1 to 2 percent annual improvements add up. A steady improvement in the efficiency of operations provides rising cash to invest in future growth, which in turn can raise the returns on your operations further. It's a virtuous cycle that gives companies the flexibility to pivot around disruption or any other challenge—the "flywheel effect"—the term that Jim Collins successfully promoted with his excellent work in the 2001 bestselling book *Good to Great*. (See Figure I.3.)

HOW WE MEASURE SUCCESS

Ideally, we'd measure success using a broad set of metrics, financial and nonfinancial. However, the nonfinancial ones can be impossible to measure with any accuracy, carry a lot of discretion, and have variable relevance to different industries. For example, employee engagement, the overall employee experience through a career, customer satisfaction, the product's value to society, and community and environmental

Figure I.3: **The modern-day "flywheel."**

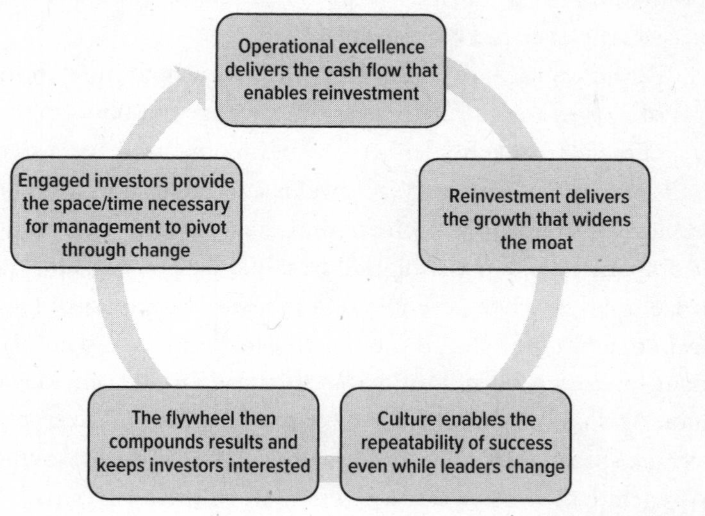

Source: Melius Research

metrics are important, but can we effectively utilize them? We struggle with this on many levels. The reality is that successful companies have created opportunities for employees and often pay quite well, but most of them have also exported jobs to low-cost regions. The net impact on society isn't clear, but survival in many sectors has required a complete change in cost structure. Apparel after the 1970s is an example: remain in the United States and most certainly go bankrupt or move manufacturing overseas and stay alive. Not the easiest decision, but few are better served by a company that dies while standing on an outdated principle.

Employee engagement may be all the rage; yet the data aren't public so we can't work with it—and we'd be skeptical of management's discretion around the scoring. Most factors get manipulated as soon as they're added to a bonus algorithm.

In any event, we have little choice but to define success by financial metrics, and we've found that stock market returns over time correlate higher to survival than any other metric. In the long run, the stock market is a fair referee. Capital flows to value-creating entities and drains from value destroyers. In the short term there is hype and speculation, but in the long term the correlation between enterprise success and stock market returns is high.

While we use shareholder returns as a way to measure the success of a company's strategy over time, we are not blind to the interests of a wider stakeholder set. The best companies seem to balance it all quite well. Ultimately, survival is critical. It does little good for employees, suppliers, customers, and their respective communities if a company fails. For the big failures, like Enron, Arthur Andersen, or Lehman Brothers, the loss of a job was accompanied by a sharp decline in résumé value, loss of healthcare benefits, and empty retirement funding promises. A kick in the head, on top of a kick out the door. And more often than not, companies that can't keep pace with average shareholder needs eventually fail. Once they lose the ability to generate the cash necessary to reinvest in their assets, their people, their suppliers, and their customers . . . it's game over in a downward spiral.

Until a better measure is found, shareholder value and its hypercorrelation to survival will reign as our metric of choice. We don't ignore other stakeholders, and in fact at times we'll emphasize the importance of one over others, but only when it's crucial. The successes of key stakeholder groups are not mutually exclusive. The reality is that companies that find long-term success nearly always focus intensely on customer needs, treat suppliers as partners, consider employees as their biggest asset, and invest in their communities. We find little evidence to the contrary. But shareholder value must be front and center. Without some semblance of continuous value creation in the entity, underinvestment is all but guaranteed, and then all other stakeholders are doomed.

On the qualitative side, much of what we look for relates to efficiency in operations, combined with strong tactical and strategic decision-making. Often these are improved through acquisitions and focused R&D spend. We look for compensation schemes that align with the interest of owners and for investor relations teams that excel at communicating with shareholders. We find that effective communication prompts longer-term strategic decisions and buys management the critical time needed to execute a plan. All good things take time. In fact, the companies we highlight in this book required up to seven years to fully execute their strategy. Any business plan that has teeth will require consistent focus, and that's probably the hardest part. Sticking with a strategy through the ups and downs of a business cycle while also dealing with the "whack-a-mole" daily distractions requires tremendous focus.

WHO WE ARE

We are Wall Street analysts who spent most of our careers at bulge-bracket investment banks, recently breaking out of the fold to form our own equity research, data analytics, and consulting firm. We each have long experience following industrial companies of many types and sizes and their publicly traded stocks. As analysts, our job is to dig deep into the businesses within a company, offer a detailed earnings analysis, value the entity, and ultimately rate the stock as a buy-hold-sell versus peers or the market overall. Some critics say we are just overpaid journalists, while others cite conflicts of interests that can cloud judgment. These points have some truth; as in any other profession, there are some strikingly bad participants. But there are also the exceptional. And each of us has had the luck to work with some of the most gifted analysts on the planet. In any event, the power that analysts hold remains outsized. An influential one can kill a merger deal, impair an IPO, and influence massive board-level changes. And this power typically gives us near speed-dial access to top executives at many of the largest companies on earth. Executives often discuss their ideas, plans, concerns, and visions with us: some in public, some in confidence, and often one-on-one for hours. We've seen some exceptional tacticians and some brilliant operational minds—as well as the opposite of both—in enough iterations to fill more than one book.

NAVIGATING THE BOOK

Most of the case studies here began as tech-driven growth companies from generations past. They dealt with the realities of ruthless competition, shortening product cycles, and wild swings in business conditions. They went through periods of empire building and unfocused management. Eventually they developed tools to ensure survival.

Many of their competitors don't exist anymore; they went bankrupt or were absorbed by winners that managed profits and capital more effectively. The tools needed to ensure survival evolved and sharpened over the years: There was a time in industrial America when a simple, competent command and control management system was enough to bring success. And there have been times when sharp, painful cost-cutting was required to stay in the game. Changes in global trade or competitiveness often required aggressive action. It's clear that is no longer enough; at the least much more discipline is required.

The clearest lesson from our century-long database is that undisciplined operations don't work. They don't work for core operations, where sooner or later the inefficiency of having too little or too much product drags profit down. They don't work for acquisitions either. Managing by heroic CEO decisions and forecasts is a doomed strategy. We've seen hundreds of billions in value destroyed by management teams trying to outguess the business cycle and growth in end markets. Sooner or later, management guesses wrong and gets behind the curve.

Drawing on a century-plus data set, we identify the companies with sustained success and the metrics that correlate to their success. We explain what organizations can do to move those metrics in the right direction and the trendy avenues they should avoid. We explain the importance of having a business system to control costs, focus employees, and channel cash toward profitable growth. And we reiterate the importance of benchmarking at all levels of the organization, where appropriate.

Most of the book consists of case studies of companies struggling to maintain their market positions over time—with both failures and successes. The case studies show the human factor that every corporate leader must grapple with.

Chapters 1 and 2, on General Electric, are foundational chapters. The story begins with GE's creation more than 125 years ago but focuses mainly on the last four decades. CEO Jack Welch carried out a remarkable vision for reinvigorating the conglomerate, but then opened the door to the arrogance that eventually led his successor, Jeff Immelt, down a disastrous path. While these and other chapters offer colorful details on individual leaders, the stories emphasize the need for discipline, often with the help of proven business tools, to prevent people from getting caught up in the enthusiasms of the moment.

From there, we move to a company that struggled to regain profitability and eventually, if fitfully, succeeded. But it then squandered so much of that progress. Boeing, in Chapter 3, became a duopoly in 1997 alongside Airbus, dominating the world market for passenger jets. Yet results were mediocre at best, until the company eventually learned to focus on a simpler and less risky business model and product offering, not on the technological extremes its wide-eyed engineers and leaders once sought. We then dig into Boeing's terrible mistakes with the 737MAX model as an example of arrogance creeping into an organization in which shortcuts are taken, just when success seems unstoppable.

With the company impaired by the grounding of its largest and most profitable product, the near stoppage of air travel in early 2020 brought the company to its knees. A clear lesson of extremes, a company on top of the world in one year and at the bottom of the abyss in the next. A mere millisecond in historical standards but one that will redefine one of the world's beloved industries. The learnings are remarkable.

Danaher, in Chapter 4, adapted Lean manufacturing to both its operations and its acquisitions, aggressively channeling cash and debt leverage to acquire high-potential assets. It redefined itself over and over to a set of assets that could be optimized under its powerful business system. Its move into healthcare could not be more timely given today's challenges. Chapter 5, on Honeywell, illustrates a company that had lost its way and nearly faltered, but was saved by an unconventional CEO who brought accountability and meaning back to the firm, with impressive results. We contrast these two success stories with United Technologies, in Chapter 6, which narrowly pursued a single metric, growth in earnings per share, beyond the point of usefulness. United Technologies had the right idea, but its system couldn't adapt as the company changed over time.

Caterpillar, in Chapter 7, is another interesting case study: a company that has spent more than its fair share of time on top of the world, dominating markets for construction equipment thanks to its advanced products and powerful dealership network. Yet it went through an extended period of extreme volatility as it struggled both to forecast and to manage the wide swings in demand, swings that were intensified by a rapidly globalizing economy. With new management, it has adopted Lean manufacturing and other systematic disciplines to keep costs down and get itself back on the right path.

Next we cover two companies with a razor-sharp focus on adding value, which resulted in outsized returns for investors. In Chapter 8, we describe how Roper transformed itself from a maker of industrial pumps to a supplier of business and infrastructure software by relentlessly moving cash to better opportunities. In Chapter 9, we recount the story of TransDigm and how it embraced the concept of compounding, using leverage and M&A to roll up niche aerospace parts suppliers. It achieved sky-high profit growth from its disciplined pricing and cost initiatives. Each of these stories generated exceptional results for shareholders and seemingly endless opportunities for employees and other stakeholders.

Next, in Chapters 10 and 11, we tell two stories with unique lessons. Stanley Black & Decker, once dominant in hand tools, saw its margins disappear, but it regained its position with a combination of Lean and renewed, but focused, innovation. The Stanley story shows how companies can enforce a business system while simultaneously transforming their industry. United Rentals, on the other hand, does no manufacturing of its own; it buys heavy equipment from others and rents to its construction and industrial customers. After years of rolling up parts of a poorly disciplined and fragmented industry, it dedicated itself to systematically delivering value to customers, both operationally and in its capital allocation. The results have been transformational, with growth in the upper deciles of the S&P growth index, sustained for a decade. That's in an industry perceived to be completely undifferentiated, with limited technology. Our conclusions found in Chapter 12 go deeper into the common lessons learned from these case studies and include additional real-world applications.

Perhaps what is most exciting about this project is that these companies have tremendous stories and yet go largely unnoticed. The lessons from these industrial titans are invaluable. Because if GE can fail, then pretty much any company can. If Boeing, as America's largest exporter, can go from an enviable profit machine to a company seeking a government handout in less than a year, any company can. And in the same context, if Danaher can win by focusing on manufacturing excellence and cash generation, then so can you. This book—a hard-headed explication of what companies can do to thrive and prosper in the coming environment—will equip you with the insights, strategies, and tactics to ensure that you count your organization among the winners in this new economy.

CHAPTER

1

GENERAL ELECTRIC

PART I

The Jack Welch Years and the Cash Flow Machine That Created the Largest Company on Earth

BY SCOTT DAVIS

Our first case study is the biggest story of them all, the amazing and disheartening narrative of a signature American company that rejuvenated its business a number of times and then faltered, in one of the largest erosions of shareholder and reputational value in history.

General Electric (GE) reached the pinnacle of capitalism in the 1990s. In 1999, *Fortune* called CEO Jack Welch the "Manager of the Century." With a $600 billion market cap in 2000, it became the most valuable company in the world, about 20 times the size of other large companies at the time, like 3M or DuPont. GE came back to earth when the tech bubble burst in 2001, but it held onto its reputation as one of the best-managed companies in history, a reputation that ebbed and flowed through a spectacular crash in 2008, a short-lived resurgence by 2015, and then a stunning free fall in 2017–2018 to a value of around $50 billion in April of 2020. A once nearly $60 stock price fell to near $6 at the bottom, a shocking 90 percent drop over 18 years. It was a decline that ended with the loss of tens of thousands of jobs, the elimination of the dividend, and a full-blown SEC fraud investigation.

GE's fall has provoked a strong emotional response from nearly everyone with a stake in the company. Some view it as a poster child for corporate greed, others as a failure of SEC oversight. The truth is more complicated, but the lion's share of the blame has fallen on long-time CEO Jeff Immelt, combined with inadequate board oversight.

This chapter focuses on the spectacular rise of GE under CEO Jack Welch from a middling old industrial company in the early 1980s to America's most admired company by the late 1990s, whose size in today's dollars is comparable to behemoths such as Microsoft, Apple, Amazon, and Google (Alphabet). (See Figure 1.1.) Chapter 2 chronicles the spectacular fall from grace under Jeff Immelt from

Figure 1.1: **GE's market-cap equivalent at its peak was larger than most of today's hot tech names.**

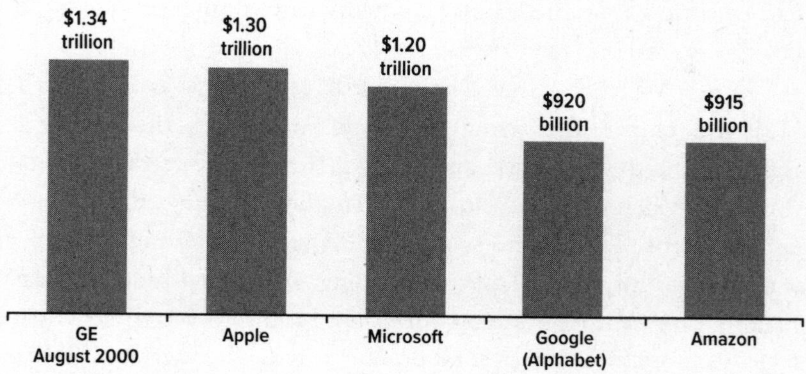

Note: GE assumes the same relative size as a percentage of the S&P 500 at peak, adjusted for 2019 year-end S&P 500 market capitalization. In other words, GE's August 2000 peak is converted to 2019 dollars. Apple, Microsoft, Google (Alphabet), and Amazon are as of December 31, 2019.

Source: Bloomberg

2001 to his firing in 2017 and extends to the company's continued challenges today.

GE'S EARLY DAYS

GE began with the 1892 merger of the two leaders in electricity-generating equipment, Edison General Electric and Thomson-Houston Electric. In the 1920s through the 1940s under longtime CEO Gerard Swope, GE invested in management and mastered the manufacturing and installation of equipment that was, at the time, about as high tech as it got. Electricity was still new in the world, and the growth was tremendous. The young company expanded into new areas, especially lighting and household appliances, while also moving aggressively into mining and rail markets. It became an industrial powerhouse that succeeded in most areas it tried, for the better part of 50 years.

The company found new challenges in the 1960s and 1970s from growing competition, both domestic and from overseas. By then, GE had become a slow and clumsy company, careful to get things right, but slow to respond to changing markets.

When Welch became CEO in 1981, his goal was to trim the bloat and return GE to its nimbler roots. At the time, the press typically referred to GE as "the lumbering giant," not exactly the reputation that Welch wanted to sustain. Welch was a young (mid-forties) and aggressive leader who saw much bigger potential. His first five years were spent cutting layers of management and pushing decision-making down through the organization. He also invested heavily in factory automation and pushed productivity onto the factory floor, a campaign that culminated in the 1990s with the aggressive adoption of Six Sigma (a system for extreme quality control). (See Figure 1.2.)

Meanwhile he pushed his executives to boost market share and find new areas of growth. Divisions had to be number one or number two in key markets to be kept in the mix. Welch exited slower-growth, more competitive businesses like mining and replaced them with higher-growth, often higher-tech areas such as specialty plastics. He wanted businesses with the potential for concentrated market share. His motto became "Fix it, close it, or sell it."

To win the organization over to his agenda, Welch beefed up rewards, with stock options his preferred currency, and encouraged risk taking. Those who missed their numbers went on probation and were fired if they fell short again. Those who met or exceeded the numbers saw a sizable pay bump and a faster career track. For the rest of the organization, he instituted forced ranking, with the bottom 10 percent of employees let go each year. By 1986 the company had fired over 100,000 employees, a quarter of the workforce, and despite the warnings of critics, revenues actually grew through this turmoil. No restructuring of this scale had ever been done in American history; it was thought to be impossible. (See Figures 1.3 and 1.4.)

Figure 1.2: **The Jack Welch years (1981–2001).**

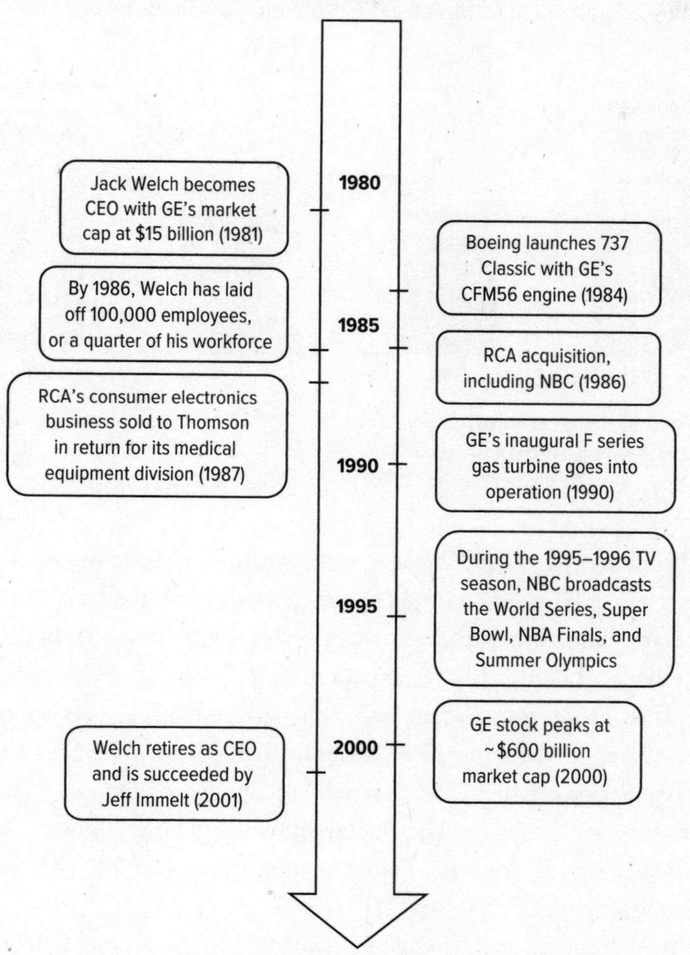
1980
1985
1990
1995
2000
Jack Welch becomes CEO with GE's market cap at $15 billion (1981)
Boeing launches 737 Classic with GE's CFM56 engine (1984)
By 1986, Welch has laid off 100,000 employees, or a quarter of his workforce
RCA acquisition, including NBC (1986)
RCA's consumer electronics business sold to Thomson in return for its medical equipment division (1987)
GE's inaugural F series gas turbine goes into operation (1990)
During the 1995–1996 TV season, NBC broadcasts the World Series, Super Bowl, NBA Finals, and Summer Olympics
GE stock peaks at ~$600 billion market cap (2000)
Welch retires as CEO and is succeeded by Jeff Immelt (2001)

Source: General Electric filings, press reports; Bloomberg

Figure 1.3: **Jack Welch cut head count by 25 percent in his first five years . . .**

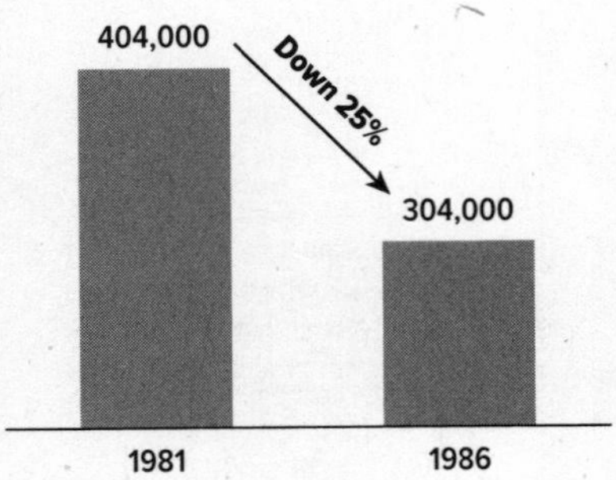

404,000
Down 25%
304,000
1981
1986

Note: Data is pro forma for cost actions and excludes the impact of the RCA acquisition.
Source: General Electric filings

Figure 1.4: **. . . while simultaneously growing revenues by over 30 percent.**

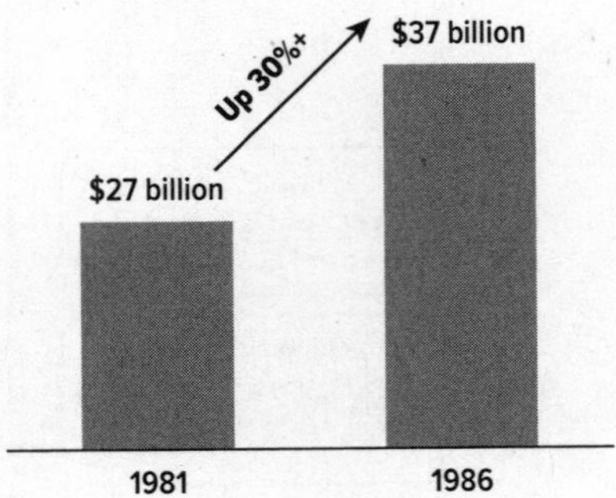

Source: General Electric filings

Not surprisingly, GE became a cutthroat, almost manic organization where paranoia reigned. Management embraced a "work hard/play hard" culture, as employees were given increasingly difficult projects with higher and higher expectations. If you succeeded, you were moved to a different job, usually in a different region, every two to three years. It was a hard life, and families paid the price; executive divorce rates were high. But financial results were outsized, and GE's reputation for exceptional management was growing. GE's stock price nearly doubled during this five-year time frame (up 180 percent), far outpacing the S&P 500 (up 80 percent).

The "Neutron Jack" image is how many people saw Welch in his early to middle years. The focus was on his ruthless management style, passed on to colleagues at GE's famed training center in Crotonville, New York. Just as important to his longer-term success, however, was his creative and gutsy dealmaking. Welch's lean, profitable operations generated a lot of cash, and he reinvested that cash at exceptional returns. A return on invested capital (ROIC) of 20 percent+ on his deals was not unusual, twice what was considered normal. His track record was almost uncanny.

Welch's most important deal was buying RCA in 1986. At $6.3 billion, it was then the largest non-oil deal in history, and it added $8 billion in revenues to GE's existing $28 billion. Ironically, Wall Street didn't love the move. Analysts saw Welch as just a cost-cutter who was stretching beyond his core skills. RCA held everything from mainframe computers and semiconductors to consumer electronics and a huge communications arm. Investors saw the deal as just adding more stuff to an already overly diverse portfolio.

Welch saw an RCA that had valuable assets that he could monetize more easily than perceived. His plan was to break up the company and keep the pieces that he really wanted, notably the NBC television network. In the end, he sold all the noncore assets for a total that exceeded the purchase price, and he left himself the crown jewel, NBC, essentially for free. It was a brilliant move—and an unheard of M&A strategy at the time. Only then did Wall Street see Welch as a complete leader overall, credibility that took seven years to build. This shift in his image occurred only after massive operational fixes, the selling of low-growth assets, and a game-changing acquisition.

The history books miss one critical component of GE's success in that time period. By the mid- to late 1980s, GE was becoming a cash flow machine. Welch taught managers to fixate on every detail. From the productivity of the factories to every contract term, they emphasized cash flow. And that cash flow allowed for five large bets on future growth: (1) air travel, (2) gas-powered electricity generation, (3) global healthcare expansion, (4) television advertising, and (5) financial services. These areas of focus would lead GE to another 15 years of unprecedented growth and success, cementing Welch's reputation as a visionary and helping catapult GE stock to an eye-popping 3,100 percent gain during his tenure. (See Figure 1.5.)

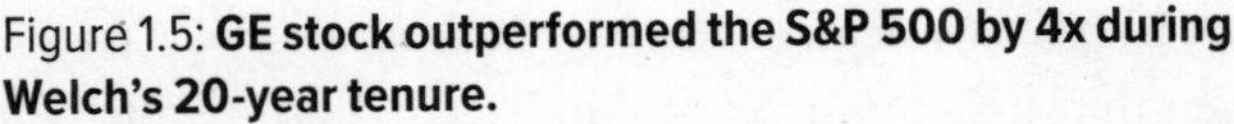
Figure 1.5: **GE stock outperformed the S&P 500 by 4x during Welch's 20-year tenure.**

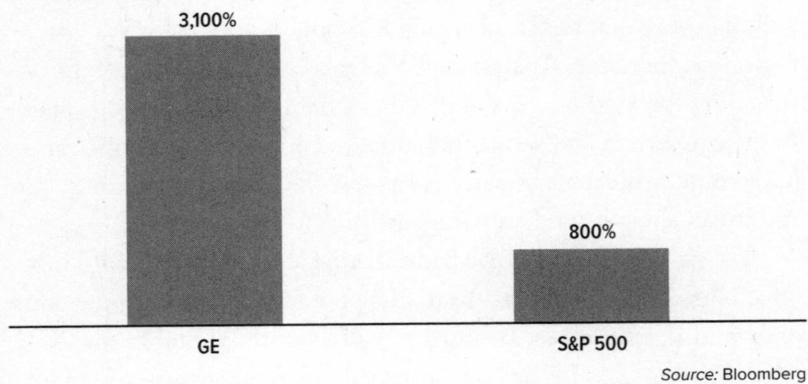

Source: Bloomberg

Big Bet #1: Air Travel via GE's Large Aircraft Engine Franchise

Welch was convinced that future growth in air travel would be driven by two important trends. The first was toward direct point-to-point travel, the most common type of travel that occurs in developed markets today, whereby businesspeople and consumers fly on lower-cost, narrow-body jets (i.e., single aisle) from one city to the next, without connecting to a larger hub. The best early example was Southwest Airlines with its exclusive fleet of narrow-body Boeing 737s. The second trend was globalization; his view was that the world would increasingly need to connect. Welch saw this trend in his own businesses, in which his employees increasingly needed to travel around the world to see customers.

Boeing recognized the same opportunity and was similarly investing in the future, most notably with a substantial upgrade of its 737 model, a midsized plane perfect for the type of point-to-point travel both GE and Boeing expected to dominate in the future. The 737 was then using a jet engine made by Pratt & Whitney, a company owned by the smaller, but still powerful, United Technologies. But Boeing wanted more from its engine suppliers, specifically greater fuel efficiency and noise reduction. GE had the cash flow to invest and the willingness to take on the risk. With little prodding from Boeing, Welch jumped at the opportunity and persuaded Safran, GE's joint venture partner for narrow-body jet engines, to commit 50-50 to the heavy investments required to sharply improve on their existing engine (called the CFM56). That allowed for an even larger development budget, dwarfing the funds available to its key competitor.

Impressed with the result and faced with the reality that Pratt & Whitney showed little interest in investing at the level necessary, Boeing deemed the CFM56 the sole engine for its 737 program. Airbus, the other maker of big passenger jets, made the CFM56 one of two options for its competing A320 narrow-body platform. Today the 737 and A320 together make up 60 percent of all commercial aircraft in the world, and GE's engines are dominant.

Welch's bet was risky because the engine improvements required huge up-front expenditures and had two degrees of uncertainty. First, GE and Safran had to succeed in reaching the fuel efficiency and sound requirements at a manageable cost. Second, they needed a big jump in jet sales to spread out those costs over many units. In fact, they needed to sell thousands of engines over a decade just to break even. In aviation, the product typically sells for low margins (in fact, often at a loss), but the manufacturer makes a lot of money providing service and spare parts over the long life of the engine. If the narrow-body 737 and A320 products had not achieved outsized growth, GE's bet would have failed mightily. And that was certainly possible—most aerospace experts questioned the 737 upgrade. Those who were bullish on air travel expected growth mainly in wide-body airplanes, not single-aisle jets such as the 737. Others expected air travel to continue to be a novelty for the rich. Welch's view was considered aggressive, even crazy.

Instead, the 737 with the CFM56 engine became perhaps the most successful product launch in American history, and more than 32,000 engines have been delivered to airlines around the world. The engine continues to this day to be the most profitable product in GE's most profitable business.

Big Bet #2: Gas-Powered Electricity with GE's F Series Turbine

Welch likewise found great success with the F series gas turbine, also developed in the 1980s. He bet that natural gas would be plentiful and that electric utilities would move away from dirtier coal power—and similar to Boeing's needs, they would want a more efficient product to help justify the shift. Natural gas was seen as a cleaner solution versus coal, and after the 1979 Three Mile Island crisis, nuclear was no longer viewed as an option. Demand for electricity spikes when it is hot in the summer, with the sharp rise in daytime use of air conditioning. Utilities need to generate electricity as cleanly as possible, but they also need to deal with sharp changes in demand—a major technical challenge.

After a massive engineering effort, GE designed the F series power turbine to be both flexible and highly efficient, with high levels of reliability in either mode. Utilities could turn it on in a flash as a "peaker" unit on hot summer days. Or they could run it as baseload power 24/7 in an economical "combined cycle" in which excess heat powered a steam turbine. That versatility, along with increasingly cheaper natural gas, made it cost competitive with coal, and with far less environmental impact. The F series became the gold standard for gas turbines for two decades, and GE gas turbines now generate a third of all the electricity in the world.

To get those advances in performance, GE had to invest heavily up front. Like jet engines, power turbines have low margins up front, but they last for decades with years of high-margin replacement parts and service revenues.

By the time Welch retired in 2001, gas turbines were in extreme demand, and the F series investment paid off to a level never thought possible. The world was investing heavily ahead of what it thought would be a technology/internet-driven boom for electricity. That demand would create a bubble, one never seen before in the utility world, and a subsequent crash that helped define the early years of Welch's successor, Jeff Immelt.

Bet #3: Growth in Healthcare with Medical Diagnostic Equipment

Medical equipment in the mid-1980s was a new industry for GE altogether. The 1986 RCA deal suddenly gave Welch a large consumer electronics business (notably televisions) that was viewed as very attractive by most at the time. But Welch was a contrarian by nature, and this was exactly the kind of business he did not want to be in, one with limited product differentiation and strong global competitors to contend with. Healthcare, in contrast, was a growth business without dominant players, but which needed extensive investment and engineering expertise. Welch figured that if he could dump his flashy consumer electronics business and invest the proceeds at a lower price in healthcare, that would be an ideal portfolio swap.

Within a year of doing the RCA deal, Welch bundled GE's and RCA's consumer electronics businesses and sold them to Thomson, in return for its medical diagnostic business and $800 million in cash. Welch then invested the excess cash in both internal research and bolt-on acquisitions, specifically focused on diagnostics, which became the mainstay of GE Healthcare. That division grew from $1 billion in revenues in 1987 to more than $8 billion in 2001, an astounding 17% annual growth rate. Meanwhile, Thomson struggled for years in consumer electronics against tough global competition, eventually exiting most of the businesses it had purchased from GE at a steep loss. It was a brilliant trade for GE.

Like jet engines and turbines, diagnostic equipment requires large R&D funding, substantial program risk, and a long sales process. MRI, x-ray, and CT machines are minimally profitable on the initial sale but offer highly profitable revenue streams from consumable films and services—just the type of razor/razor blade business Welch reveled in and investors loved.

Bet #4: Growth in TV Advertising via the GE-Owned NBC Network

While Welch had no interest in selling actual TVs, he loved the potential in the NBC asset that he got in the RCA deal. At the time, three networks dominated TV: CBS, ABC, and NBC, with NBC largely viewed as the weakest of the three. Welch's timing could not have been better.

In the mid- to late 1980s, TVs were getting bigger and clearer and had better sound and color. Consumer product companies like Procter & Gamble, Coca-Cola, and General Motors increasingly allocated more to ad budgets. A disproportionate amount of those dollars was moving from radio and print news to TV.

Welch invested heavily in program development to bring NBC back. In the morning, TV news was evolving, and NBC's *Today Show* was growing its viewership with rising stars. Afternoon soap operas pulled in a generation of viewers, game shows gained in popularity, and evenings took off with hits such as *Hill Street Blues*, *Cheers*, *Seinfeld*, and *Friends*. Welch also helped to build a bigger presence in sports. In the 1995–1996 TV season, NBC broadcast the World Series, Super Bowl, NBA finals, and Summer Olympics, the only time in history that a network had that level of dominance. By then, NBC's credibility within the industry had skyrocketed.

As cable became the new growth opportunity, Welch had NBC expand outside of its core. Acquisition of the little-known Financial News Network in 1991 formed a more solid foundation for CNBC, which itself was just two years old at that point. Telemundo brought NBC into Spanish-speaking TV in 2001.

NBC was finding success across multiple avenues. Growth in the industry itself was solid, well above GDP. Pricing was going up each year on a per-ad-minute basis, and cable channels were getting subscription fees. Successful shows were also syndicated at a nice profit. It was an amazing business, and one that came to Welch nearly free via the RCA deal.

With leadership positions in jet engines, power turbines, and medical equipment, Welch created an industrial powerhouse never before seen in American business. Once NBC was added, GE seemed unstoppable—and that's before we take into consideration the large legacy plastics and appliance businesses that had defined the earlier GE. By the late 1990s, GE's size, scale, and power in America was massive by any definition.

Bet #5: Financial Services via GE Capital

GE's lending business dates back to 1932, with a mission to finance GE's consumer products, notably refrigerators, ranges, and washing machines. The GE Capital many think of today was started in 1984 by longtime head Gary Wendt to address Welch's vision that GE could do more financing away from its original industrial core. The vision had two components.

The first relates purely to a cost advantage that Welch saw in his own financing costs. GE's industrial businesses generated lots of cash, and his M&A plans at that point focused on small bolt-on deals, so there was no need to take on debt. Investors wanted to lend to companies like GE, whose AAA rating mirrored that of US government bonds, yet with a higher yield. Welch could therefore borrow very cheaply and compete quite easily against banks whose costs included not only paying depositors, but also maintaining expensive branch networks. And banks were heavily regulated, adding further costs and limiting growth to a narrower opportunity set. GE, on the other hand, had little regulatory oversight. So for Welch in the late 1980s through the 1990s, GE Capital became a powerful growth engine, all done within quite acceptable leverage boundaries.

The second vision related to the reality that as an unregulated entity, GE Capital could lend money, provide managerial expertise, and be quite creative overall in the process. It could lend where banks typically didn't like to go in those days, areas like store-branded credit cards, project and equipment financing, aircraft leasing, railcar leasing, medical equipment leasing, and private equity financing. Anything niche or unique fit the vision. Insurance products were later added to the mix.

It wasn't all perfect, of course. In fact, GE Capital stumbled early on due to the bad decision to purchase Kidder Peabody in 1986—a humbling deal that taught Welch that some businesses just can't be "Six Sigma'd." The world of investment banking was just too far afield for GE. In hindsight, the expansion into insurance proved a bad move too, a big setback for GE after Welch retired. Hindsight will also show that GE Capital may not have been the most ethically managed asset that Welch oversaw. The quarter-to-quarter earnings performance eventually revealed a pattern of abuse, notably one-time gains that juiced earnings. But the investment in GE Capital overall did yield outsized results. By the time Welch retired, about 40 percent of GE's earnings came from financial services, and GE Capital was one of the largest financial institutions in America.

POSTMORTEM OF THE JACK WELCH YEARS

In looking back at the Welch era, what's most impressive is how he executed each stage of GE's evolution at such a high level. If he hadn't first succeeded in structurally reducing GE's cost base, then he might not have gotten board approval for the large, game-changing RCA deal. The success of that acquisition provided the air cover to take the strategic and financial risks inherent in the already ramping new aircraft engine and soon to ramp power turbine program, not to mention the aggressive entrance into healthcare diagnostics and investments made in NBC. He had the foresight to exit a sexy business, like televisions, to expand in the lesser-known business of medical equipment. All of that fed into the expansion of GE Capital, the most controversial part of his tenure. We can debate who was eventually to blame for the near failure of GE in 2008, but it's important to remember that meltdown came a full seven years after Welch's retirement. Welch had arguably expanded GE Capital to its fullest, and growth afterward should have been done with less leverage and risk. Hindsight here is 20/20.

What is also very clear is that Welch had a bold playbook. His vision of factory floor competence boosted margins and cash, even while investing heavily. He expected hard work and exceptional performance from his managers, and he benchmarked diligently as an accountability tool. His playbook also included a heavy emphasis on global expansion and, in his later years, a hyperfocus on the internet as a productivity tool. His initiatives were never optional, but he sold the merits hard. He took little for granted.

In his early years, he endured the extreme unpopularity that comes along with laying off a whopping 100,000 employees, but it's clear he knew he had no chance unless he fixed the bloated corporate structure. His investments in automation and adoption of Six Sigma kept employees focused for north of a decade, and GE became a world-class manufacturer. The reputation of the company rose steadily, and the results for a broader stakeholder group were largely outstanding.

The deals themselves took GE to a different level, but the equal hero here was the operational and management discipline. People forget at times, but Welch was a roll-up-your-sleeves operating guy. His operating reviews were intense. He wanted detail and precision. He had no patience for those who couldn't keep pace. And it was the strength of his operations that gave him the cash, the confidence, and the support of his board to make some pretty big bets on the future.

With all these bets paying off, the 1990s were immensely profitable for GE. Other industrial companies struggled to remain relevant in the new economy of the internet, and yet GE found ways to capture headlines. In the emerging cult of the CEO, Welch became the archetype celebrity leader. He and his senior team also became immensely wealthy. All that success led to a dangerous level of arrogance, which was beginning to show by the late 1990s.

And perhaps this is where the GE story began to fray. After two decades of exceptional returns, GE's culture began to lose focus on what had gotten it to this point in the first place. The company began to revert to its bureaucratic beginnings, ignore its factories, and go after increasingly larger and riskier deals, all with more debt leverage and the help of opaque accounting.

Ironically, the triumphant Welch era ended with an apparent setback: the failed attempt to buy Honeywell in 2000. In a battle of big egos, the European Union rejected the $45 billion acquisition. GE's aggressive public comments and its premature moving of staff into Honeywell headquarters didn't help. Mario Monte, then head of the EU's Competition Commission, may have blocked the merger as much for political as substantive reasons. His decision was later overturned, but it was too late: GE dropped the deal. Whether that deal would have been good or bad for GE, we will never know. But megadeals done in the final innings of a CEO's tenure seem to rarely work. Ego and arrogance appear to play a big role in the outcome.

Welch's final years were far from his best, maybe even downright destructive, but the value creation over time had already cemented his legacy, perhaps overshadowing a company that was beginning to slip. The celebrity that began to follow him served as a distraction for a CEO and an organization that had otherwise remained focused for the better part of two decades. Welch's final move was selecting his successor, a fateful decision that has historians now questioning much of Welch's legacy in its entirety. While Welch remained quiet during most of GE's eventual decline, he would later admit that he was "deceived"—a comment that offers little solace to those who suffered from the largest destruction of shareholder value in American history. Sadly, Jack Welch passed away in March 2020, before he had a chance to comment on this manuscript.

Lessons from the Jack Welch Era

- Attacking the cost base should be the first step in any turnaround.
- Aggressive internal and external investment can coexist.
- Cash flow is the best weapon in an arms race.
- Moving a portfolio toward growth often means exiting popular businesses that are nearing maturity or where competition is rising.
- Reward people according to the strategy.
- Welch fired his bottom 10 percent each year. That's too hard on a culture, but there is likely some level of turnover that makes sense.
- Welch's worst years were his last two to three and unwound some of his legacy. This is common among CEOs. Boards should manage the exit strategy more aggressively.

CHAPTER

2

GENERAL ELECTRIC

PART II

How a Culture of Arrogance Led to the Largest Collapse in American History

BY SCOTT DAVIS

The GE CEO selection process has historically been a grueling multiyear contest pitting business heads against each other in a rather public forum. Welch had delayed his retirement while the Honeywell deal was being reviewed, so the contest to select his successor was particularly intense and long. In hindsight, it may have led to a level of fatigue and burnout that post-Welch management seemed to exhibit at GE.

In any event, a few days before the tragedies of 9/11, Welch hit mandatory retirement and turned over the reins to his chosen successor, Jeffrey Immelt. His parting advice, as Immelt told me some time later, was to "blow it up," which we assume was Welch's way of giving him the green light to chart a new and quite different path. That's essentially what Welch had done when he had taken over in 1981. And by 2001, GE certainly needed a reset.

For one, the market's expectations were out of whack. Profits had ballooned in the late 1990s due to GE Capital's investment winnings, outsized pension investment gains in the bull market, and a bubble in gas power generation. In 2000, the company had an eye-popping P/E ratio (price to earnings ratio) of 40x, more than double the market's average over time (at 17x in early 2020). And if you adjusted out the unsustainable part of the earnings algorithm (i.e., pension and one-time gains), that ratio was likely closer to 60x—insanely expensive for a mature company. The GE that Welch had created was not sustainable, and with the stock market falling back to earth, Immelt needed to take the up-front hit. (See Figure 2.1.)

Figure 2.1: **The Jeff Immelt era and beyond (2001–2019).**

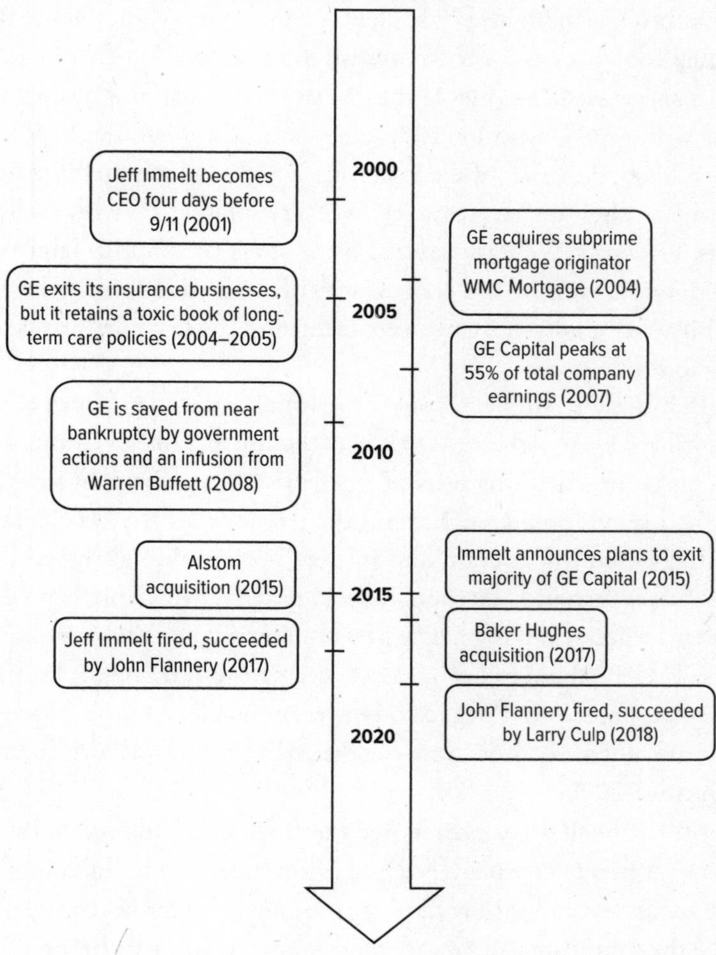
2000
Jeff Immelt becomes CEO four days before 9/11 (2001)
GE acquires subprime mortgage originator WMC Mortgage (2004)
GE exits its insurance businesses, but it retains a toxic book of long-term care policies (2004–2005)
2005
GE Capital peaks at 55% of total company earnings (2007)
GE is saved from near bankruptcy by government actions and an infusion from Warren Buffett (2008)
2010
Alstom acquisition (2015)
Immelt announces plans to exit majority of GE Capital (2015)
2015
Baker Hughes acquisition (2017)
Jeff Immelt fired, succeeded by John Flannery (2017)
John Flannery fired, succeeded by Larry Culp (2018)
2020

Source: General Electric filings, press reports

More specifically, GE Capital needed to shrink, or at least decrease risk with lower debt leverage. Unlike the industrial businesses with technological and scale superiority, GE Capital had few sustainable advantages other than low-cost borrowing. The supernormal profits were attracting powerful rivals, and regulators were increasingly loosening the reins on banks, allowing them to expand into these niche areas.

At the same time, while Welch had invested heavily in his factory assets through the mid-1990s, they began to fall behind by the time Immelt took over and needed a fresh round of investment. After his initial successes in engines and turbines, Welch had not pushed forward with next-generation technology, and R&D had not kept pace. This is likely the result of the hyperpressure he had put on his managers to beat their quarterly targets. Welch's infatuation with earnings beats, his rising P/E ratio, and also the stock price in his later years was notable, even by the crazy standard set in the days of the tech bubble. As a result, shortcuts were taken and the GE core was beginning to rot.

In hindsight, Immelt should have immediately dampened expectations. He even had a ready excuse: the horrors of 9/11 hit a week into his tenure, sparking fears of recession and a cutback in air travel. GE had provided the engines on the jets that hit the World Trade Center, leased the aircraft, and insured both buildings. Freed from Wall Street pressures, he could have slimmed down Capital and done the hard work of forging a new path. But he did neither.

GE Capital did sell some assets early on, but it bought far more. It was expansion that began to border on reckless, but few cared to notice. By then, investors were caught up in the housing-driven boom of the mid-2000s.

Still, Immelt was a hard-nosed executive who had risen to the top of a no-nonsense company. For him to get caught up in the company's past successes shows how hard it is for any prosperous company to make the transition to a new market context. If we justly praise Welch for transforming a company that was still profitable, then we can't so easily expect Immelt to "blow up" the most admired company around. Eventually Immelt did make fairly drastic changes to GE, although usually too late.

More interesting than what Immelt kept is what he changed. Where Welch, trained in engineering, had focused on operational details and gotten into the weeds at plants, Immelt was from sales and had little interest in factories. He had a more affable, positive manner and spent more time on people than process. He wasn't interested in systems. Immelt used to claim that he knew his top 600 executives in some level of detail. But factory visits became less common, and business reviews lacked the intensity of the Welch era. GE was becoming a much softer company. Some of that was needed in a world that was also softening, but the pendulum swung too far, and the culture began to have conflict. Welch-era managers were taught accountability, and results were the scorecard. Newer managers focused on big ideas. Most were caught in the middle and struggled to know what to focus on. Immelt also seemed caught between two conflicting worlds.

Immelt saw GE's size and influence as bigger than just an average company—he saw the political power, the influence on policy and trade, and the impact his words could have on a world far wider than GE's reach. By 2002 his power was perhaps beyond compare in American business today. And that type of power invites all kinds of challenges—arrogance for one, but outsized demands on your time for another. Pretty easy to lose focus with that context. Something the CEO of a complex company can ill afford.

As for the outsized power, that wasn't so crazy back then. The largest corporate CEOs were celebrities, household names with reputations fed by their broad media appeal. And GE was top of that list. GE had a factory or sales office in nearly every major congressional district in the country. It was one of America's largest exporters, an important military supplier, and one of the biggest unionized employers. Its products kept the electricity on in people's homes, powered aircraft, presented the news via NBC, and ran diagnostic testing in most American hospitals. The lending arm touched nearly everyone who had a store-branded credit card, which was most households at the time. The world now has Google, Apple, and Amazon to look up to, but GE was equivalent to a combination of all three. When my boss at Morgan Stanley asked me in 2001 if I'd like to take over responsibility for analyst coverage of GE, I could hardly control my excitement. It was a massive promotion and a career-changing event.

The early Immelt days did show promise, and having trained under Welch, Immelt tried to continue his predecessor's disciplined accountability while pushing his big-ideas agenda. But over time

Immelt's softer edges defined the culture. No more mandatory firing of the bottom 10 percent or "Fix it, close it, or sell it." Instead of bold up-front bets that went against the grain, Immelt took the long view on conventional ideas. Welch had pushed R&D to develop products within its core, products that could be commercialized within five years. Immelt had a wider lens and favored scientists with big visions, even if those technologies were 20+ years away from commercialization. Welch wanted no-nonsense, practical people, while Immelt sought optimistic dreamers. In fact, Immelt's entire legacy could be summed up in one word: "optimism." Ironically, that would become his downfall.

GE MANAGES THE NARRATIVE AND EARNINGS TO HIDE ITS FLAWS

Enthralled by the future, Immelt didn't want short-term problems or criticisms to get in the way, and so he doubled down on an unfortunate legacy of Welch: earnings management. In the late 1980s, as GE Capital began its expansion, Welch had discovered that financial services offered a lot of discretion in declaring gains and losses. When GE's core businesses had slow quarters, he could balance them out with strong results from Capital and vice versa. Welch's earnings management became famous, even applauded, despite the clear ethical lapses guaranteed to occur with such discretion. Immelt continued and possibly even expanded the practice. After multiple years of crisis that have now defined his legacy, this earnings management arguably crossed well into the unethical.

To win at this earnings game, GE cut back on disclosures—details that analysts relied on in order to navigate this increasingly complex company. At Morgan Stanley, we struggled to find any consistent way to model out the company's earnings or even compare its risk profile with others. The reported numbers were constantly changing, and it took multiple days or weeks just to reconcile the differences, if you could at all. And just when you felt like you were looking at solid financial comparisons, the company would alter its disclosure, and we would have to start all over again.

Money seemed to pass back and forth within GE businesses, for no clear reason special-purpose entities were created, and loans were originated and then syndicated, only to fall off the balance sheet, all while creating some sort of paper profit gain. Complex derivative products were used. Long-term debt was swapped for short-term, fixed-rate debt for floating and vice versa. Currencies were bought and sold, all in the name of "hedging," but there seemed to be no consistency if that was the case. Special leasing arrangements were sometimes used so that even shipping a unit across the street would constitute a sale and revenue booked. Tax gains and losses were created when needed to smooth results. GE would fight the IRS on every penny. Most quarters saw some sort of "tax gain," and that gain was buried in a financial statement category called "other."

It was beyond complex. It was financial engineering at its most extreme—perhaps on a scale never seen before and not since. And there was no one outside the walls of corporate HQ that had any ability to follow all the pieces. Those of us who followed the company for a living were just kidding ourselves that we understood all the financials.

The difficulty we had in modeling out GE wasn't for a lack of talent or resources. We had some of the most qualified finance experts on the planet, used to tearing apart financial statements for sport. But we couldn't make the models work. And we were far from alone. Debt rating experts seemed particularly frustrated. The SEC should have taken notice, but no one seemed willing to take on GE and its powerful lobby.

In today's world, analyst complaints get the attention of auditors and regulators. We saw that in the failed WeWork IPO in late 2019. The system worked to protect investors from misleading financials. But back then, no one was empowered to call out GE's actions. The power in the system was all in the possession of large companies, which had a hand in setting regulations and then abusing them, and any vocal complainants were usually dealt with harshly.

Adding to the difficulty, Immelt reinforced Welch's "Don't question us" mentality. While we celebrate many of Welch's accomplishments, the darker reality included the fact that Welch had built a fortress around GE. Outsiders were viewed with disdain. The arrogance and insularity grew with Welch's public celebrity. The intimidation factor was massive. And though Immelt softened Welch's harder line on outside criticism, he largely looked the other way when subordinates carried on the practice. At GE, protecting Immelt's image and the company itself became more important than any ethical consideration.

As a GE analyst, I knew that the power of GE put my job at constant risk. If the company blacklisted me, I might never find work again. GE's talented, relentless investor relations (IR) team had no interest in letting analysts challenge its public narrative. The scare tactics had few boundaries.

In 2003, I gave the company the courtesy of seeing a draft of a report I wrote that criticized parts of GE Capital and compared its rising risk profile directly with that of banks, notably Citigroup. Sending drafts was a common practice back then to speed up fact-checking. Shortly thereafter, on a summer Sunday afternoon, I got a call on my cell phone. It was a member of GE's IR team. The substance of the call was a demand that I drop the report altogether. If not, the team would use all its power to squash my credibility, including leveraging CNBC anchors (GE owned CNBC within its NBC unit) to attack my findings. The caller also raised the possibility that GE management would elevate its dissatisfaction with me all the way to the top of Morgan Stanley's executive team. I was reminded in that call that Immelt knew all the bank CEOs, having most on speed dial.

Morgan Stanley, to its credit, allowed publication, but only after I had a lengthy back-and-forth over multiple days with internal lawyers and managers, who softened the findings in the report. One of the quieter ways that GE would go after an analyst's credibility would be to question the relevance of the findings and question the quality. If you're managing an equity research department on Wall Street, it's hard to know what action to take when a company calls and says the report quality is low and misrepresents the truth. The "truth" often takes substantial time to surface, and relevance is highly subjective. It's usually just safer to soften the report and move on, which is exactly what GE wanted and almost always achieved.

GE's threats always included some comment about the company's relationship with the firm's investment bankers. After all, for investment bankers, GE's size, debt issuance, and dealmaking made it a virtual ATM machine. An analyst could only get in the way of a never-ending stream of revenues. In fact, for the better part of my first year covering the company, one investment banker called me nearly every day to remind me that GE had the power to destroy me, and if it was up to him, he would advocate for exactly that. In those days, that level of harassment was still allowed, and research had limited power in the organization.

I tried to shake it off, but GE's tactics certainly affected my work. It's hard to stay firm when punched in the face so frequently and violently. At some point you start to give in. By 2004, I upgraded GE stock to a buy rating on a view that margins were set to inflect upward. That served to lessen the harassment for sure. I even got a holiday card from Immelt that said, "I have 19 percent op rate [operating margins] tattooed on my ass." That margin never happened, and the stock call was dead wrong.

Several journalists at major financial publications have shared with me similar stories of GE's pressure over the years. This was particularly true of the *Wall Street Journal*, which always put top talent on the GE beat, usually the kind of reporters that GE did not want—the kind that asked a lot of questions. Over time, I bonded with some of these folks, mostly over GE's severe reactions to anything we would write that wasn't outright complimentary. Legendary *Fortune* magazine reporter Geoff Colvin told me of his astonishment at GE's violent response to a critical report that he wrote on Immelt. He said that GE's response was the most aggressive that he had ever experienced in his very long career in journalism.

All of this ties back to the celebrity status that Welch passed down to his successor. As we know from Welch's divorce proceedings in 2002, even in his retirement, he enjoyed outrageous perks like continued access to GE's oversized fleet of aircraft. Immelt, for his part, embraced the perks with similar enthusiasm. The airplane fiasco reported by the *Wall Street Journal* in 2017, where a backup jet followed him on business trips in case the main jet had problems, exposed just a small piece of the excess. In selling NBC in 2009, for example, he had an entire golf course shut down so he and Brian Roberts of Comcast could negotiate in private while playing. Roberts viewed that as highly unnecessary. Even among large and powerful companies, these types of behaviors are outside the norm.

Immelt despised spending time with analysts and shareholders, a group that he believed lacked the imagination needed to understand his big ideas. He even joked about that part of his job being the least pleasant. Any effort to do so was in the context of "keeping enemies close." In fact, on one particular occasion, he invited me to be a guest of his at the annual College Football Hall of Fame induction ceremony, an organization that he was president of at the time. Sometime before dinner he introduced me to the head of the NCAA, Mark Emmert, as "the most dangerous man on Wall Street." A joke perhaps, but the tone bordered on malicious, and when I laughed, he only glared back, then walked away. It was clear that he feared anyone who could derail his vision, despite the fact that analysts' influence at that time was at a low point, and GE was still a giant, powerful organization. Was he that paranoid, that insecure, or just plain afraid that stakeholders would begin to see that GE was faltering and that he had lost control?

In his earlier days on the job, he was considerably more "Street friendly," and I got a chance to spend time with him in Dallas in 2003. I hosted a meeting where he was invited to speak with a couple hundred of Morgan Stanley's individual investor clients and afterward to sit down more privately with about a dozen local institutional investors. Even though I had set up both meetings, GE told me I could not sit in on the more private one—the company would not risk having Immelt's informal conversations seen in print.

Before the meeting we had a brief chat in the hallway, and I asked about his life as CEO. "Do you wait in line at the hotel check-in?"

"No, my forward team handles it and hands me a key when I walk in."

"Do you use the hotel gym?"

"No, my forward team flies my fitness equipment down and sets it up in my room."

I covered other large companies. None of their CEOs at that time had a security detail, advance teams, or gym equipment set up for them in their hotel suite. As a more experienced analyst today, if I were to hear that, it would set off all kinds of alarms. Back then, as a newer analyst, I just figured it was justified by GE's size, and no expense was too high to make its CEO comfortable.

It's easy to understand how Welch's success went to his head, but Immelt hadn't yet created an ounce of value at GE. The stock had long since stopped its ascension, and the company's credibility was beginning to slide.

Admittedly, the early years after the euphoria of the tech bubble along with GE's outsized reputation would have been a tough situation for any leader, but Immelt didn't rise to the occasion. Instead of Welch's bold, savvy bets, which were financed with the strong cash flow that came from patient attention to costs and productivity, he became fascinated with the hottest new trends, financed largely with debt. After the dark days of 9/11, he went into airport security, but he had no strategy for developing a competitive advantage. He paid a hefty price to acquire a number of subscale security firms that had no real connection to each other, only later to be sold at a big discount and loss to United Technologies. Then he made a play in clean water, but the myriad of acquired assets never quite fit together and were likewise sold at a big loss. This pattern went on and on for the better part of 15 years. Overpay for hot properties that fit the big-ideas concept, capitulate a few years later at a loss, and shrug it all off because GE's size made losses appear small and they could be covered up by gains elsewhere.

His poor timing was almost surreal. In 2007, after arguably the greatest real estate bull market of all time, he went heavily into commercial properties. He also bought a subprime mortgage originator near the housing peak, despite GE having exited a similar business years earlier and despite clear signs of ethical challenges within the industry overall.

Far from improving the acquired businesses with GE's vaunted managerial skills, the company usually made the asset worse. The high prices paid for each acquisition left little to reinvest in the business. And when Welch left, so did much of the factory-level talent that got GE to the top in the first place. Six Sigma was long forgotten, Lean manufacturing a mere brief experiment. Benchmarking against traditional metrics fell off the list and was replaced by a new concept called Net Promoter Score, another flavor-of-the-day hot new metric. All the while, the company's manufacturing quality slipped.

GE Capital kept expanding and quickly passed the 50 percent of profits threshold that most investors viewed as the absolute maximum size from a risk perspective. Deals became even larger and more complex, but Immelt kept investors happy by constantly churning the portfolio. They applauded the exit from insurance in 2004. But little did investors know that GE retained substantial tail-liability risk in several of its deals. Long-term-care insurance had the biggest impact. As losses on those policies piled up, despite the company's best efforts to hide them, GE eventually took a massive $15 billion hit to reserves in 2018—a size that few could have ever imagined possible, particularly given the fact that many investors were led to believe GE had completely exited the insurance business via the IPO of Genworth in 2004 and asset sales to Swiss Re in 2005. (See Figure 2.2.)

THE CULTURAL BREAKDOWN

Where was the rest of the organization, especially the board, as Immelt pursued these costly moves? It seems the GE board was charmed by Immelt. The board members benefited from his Augusta

Figure 2.2: **Capital's expansion began under Welch, but Immelt took risk to dangerous levels, over half of GE's earnings at peak.**

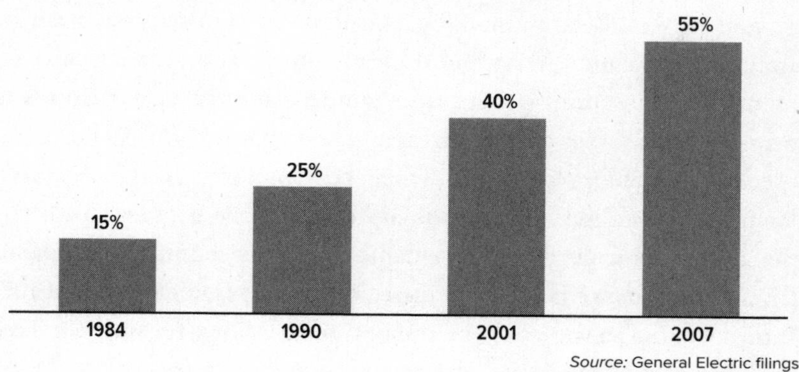

Source: General Electric filings

golf membership and access to GE aircraft, as well as choice seats at major entertainment events, along with attractive compensation packages. The Olympics served as an opportunity for directors and their spouses to "oversee" NBC. Top shareholders were similarly enticed to attend and were given seats on GE's aircraft to make the trip.

Immelt seemed to favor directors with limited experience in GE's core businesses. Most of the board had headline-grabbing names, but few ever actually dug into the businesses themselves or had ever managed something with this level of complexity. He also diluted vocal members of the board by keeping an unusually large board, typically around 18 members, while a normal size would be 12 or fewer. For reference, Apple has 8 board members, while Amazon and Google/Alphabet each have 10. A board size of 18 is considered dysfunctional by nearly every corporate governance expert on the planet.

The board had little incentive or ability to raise objections. Instead, with the stock price in the doldrums, the board sought different ways to justify executive pay. Immelt's annual pay often exceeded $20 million, all while shareholders continued to lose from his poorly timed investments and lack of focus on operations. In total, Immelt was reported to have earned an eye-watering $275 million in compensation over his 17-year tenure, a tenure that twice nearly bankrupted the company.

Immelt's senior team enjoyed similar celebrity treatment. One executive is reported to have had a hair stylist travel with her on the private jet. Another commuted back and forth to his family estate in Italy on GE planes. Most had multiple offices and access to apartments in major cities. Others were compensated far more than their peers in similar roles at other firms and had wide-ranging perks. One executive loaned money to a Brazilian customer that ended up in jail, losing GE hundreds of millions of dollars in the process. Another manager was involved in questionable revenue accounting that led to SEC fines. Finance heads were increasingly rewarded for obfuscation. Internal auditors were paid by the businesses they were entrusted to monitor. Honest reporting was viewed as unimaginative.

These excesses were established early on in Immelt's tenure. When he went into biotech in 2003, he had to convince Sir William Castell, the CEO of Amersham, to sell the company. In return, Castell received not just the job of leading GE's overall healthcare unit and a large salary but also a board seat and outlandish perks such as GE paying for the lease on his Rolls-Royce. Amersham was a rare Immelt acquisition that eventually paid off, but Castell was a terrible leader, and the healthcare business struggled for years until he was finally ousted.

When John Flannery took over as CEO after Immelt's ouster in 2017, he told me a story about when he ran M&A for GE. Immelt walked into his office one day and asked if he was working on any exciting deals. Flannery responded that valuations were high, so they should consider selling some assets now and revisit buying another day. To which Immelt responded, "Don't be a pussy," and walked out. By the time Flannery had taken over from Immelt, it was clear that even he had little respect for his predecessor. He even asked me in an early get-together, with IR staff present, "When did you realize that Immelt was a fraud?" The question nearly knocked me off my feet. GE people, up to that point, had largely protected Immelt. Flannery didn't last long in the seat; the company was too far gone at that point. Hardly his fault—he walked into a buzz saw.

While current GE executives are careful in their criticisms, rightfully focusing on the future, more than one has mentioned to me their surprise that the internal audit staff didn't elevate concerns until well after Immelt was gone. We may never know where, when, and how the system broke down. In the absence of that knowledge, we have no choice but to assign responsibility for GE's decline to the board and its CEO and chairman.

The reality is that every company struggles with the temptation to fudge numbers or, worse, to improve short-term results at the expense of the long term. The good ones have accountability systems that keep most people in line. *There's nothing that destroys a culture faster than wasteful spending and celebrity behavior among the executives.* Every example of corporate failure we know about included exactly that. What employees see, they start emulating. Customers and suppliers eventually see as well, and the brand suffers.

By 2004, with profits no longer keeping pace with those of GE's peers, Immelt worked hard to keep up a positive appearance. Besides buying aggressively and expanding Capital, the company issued earnings reports full of one-time gains and buried restructuring expenses. Losses typically went "below the line" in areas such as discontinued operations. The reality of an asset became secondary to how it could be presented. I asked Immelt in 2005 why he didn't sell NBC Universal (NBCU), still valued at a solid $50 billion, even as it was coming under pressure from declining ratings. He said if the unit wasn't worth more than $70 billion in three years, then he should be fired. In fact, he sold NBCU to Comcast in 2009, four years later, for all of $30 billion. Then Comcast managed to double NBCU's earnings three years later. Even with all the competition out there, NBCU under a different owner is likely worth upward of $100 billion. The context is astounding. NBCU, which equated to less than 20 percent of GE's earnings in most years prior to its sale, is now worth about all of what remains at GE *combined*. GE sold at the absolute bottom, leaving billions on the table. When I later brought up that conversation to Immelt in front of a small group of investors at an annual industry conference, he asked me, "When did you become such an asshole?"

GE'S FIRST NEAR BRUSH WITH DEATH, THE GREAT RECESSION OF 2008–2009

The Great Recession of 2008–2009 brought GE to its knees. GE was harder hit than most companies, due to its outsized exposure to financial services, its record-high debt levels, and a deep recession that was hurting even its strongest businesses. But even before the crisis accelerated, GE showed signs of cracking. On a March 2008 webcast to retail investors, Immelt had actually promised a good start to the year, only to host an earnings call just a month later when the company badly missed its earnings guidance. Then in 2009 he became the first CEO in GE's history to cut its dividend, a devastating blow that he described as the worst day of his life. He had always felt connected to individual retail shareholders, especially GE retirees, which included his father. The share price sank from $40 to nearly $6. GE arguably would have gone under had the US government not come in and insured its short-term debt (i.e., commercial paper), which saved GE along with other financial institutions at the time. Except GE wasn't supposed to be as risky as a bank. And just like most banks in late 2008 and early 2009, GE had to raise equity to firm up its balance sheet—in this case a timely investment by Warren Buffett.

In consistent form, GE fought hard against any accusation that it had lost its edge. In fact, on that April 2008 conference call, in which GE showed its first outsized earnings miss since the events of 9/11, I questioned GE about its struggles, even drawing the analogy of the Chicago Cubs baseball team that had long struggled to win and whose supporters optimistically used to joke, "We'll get 'em next year." My comments were admittedly a little emotional, partially because GE's IR machine had assured investors all through the quarter that the economy was having no adverse impact on its businesses. It was an outright lie, and I found that one to be far more offensive than the usual tales GE would tell, particularly in light of the fact that just a few weeks prior, we had downgraded our industrial sector rating to a "sell" on our own macro concerns, and GE had gone out of its way to tell our clients that we were going to look stupid for the negative call.

Playing into all my greatest fears about the power of the GE machine, the company tried to get me fired that day—because Immelt found my comments "rude, offensive, and unprofessional." I later found out that it wasn't Immelt who made the phone call to complain about my words, but his longtime CFO, Keith Sherin. Sherin was a tough-as-nails sidekick who engineered much of GE's financial complexity. While we fault Immelt throughout this chapter, Sherin played a key role in GE's rising risk profile. I was later told that Sherin agreed to "allow" me to keep my job if I would apologize to him in person. We scheduled a private lunch at GE's NYC headquarters in Rockefeller Center a few weeks after the call. It was a white-gloved, butler-served meal in a conference room on the executive floor, and I'm convinced that we were the only two people on that floor that day.

To be clear, I did not apologize. At that point, cooler heads had prevailed, but my career at Morgan Stanley suffered nonetheless. After that Friday-morning conference call, I spent the weekend fighting to keep my job. Shaken to the core by the reality that after more than a decade of unimaginable hard work and sacrifice as an analyst, I nearly lost it all. I did take a sizable pay cut in the end, which eventually catalyzed the conclusion that I had to leave the firm to restore my career. All because I had the gall to question Immelt's strategies on the day of GE's worst earnings miss in history. This was only months away from the company's near collapse in the 2008–2009 financial crisis.

GE REEMERGES POST CRISIS

After the dividend cut and tarnished reputation in early 2009, Immelt finally started to shrink GE Capital and simplify the overall portfolio. Those efforts gained urgency when the Federal Reserve designated the company a systemically important financial institution—a step that brought the kind of governmental oversight that Immelt hated.

But as he reduced the company's exposure to financial services, he needed something to replace the lost earnings. He settled on two big initiatives: digital transformation and the acquisition of a large French power infrastructure company named Alstom. With digital, Immelt saw enormous potential in the industrial internet and additive manufacturing (also known as 3D printing), and he wanted to supply the software as well as the hardware. He turned the company's small IT support unit into a separate GE Digital division. It had the ambition and budget to become a world-class software house.

The digital foray won the company good press, but it would be many years of heavy investment before anything tangible emerged, and even then, finding new revenues was difficult. Unlike Welch's focused bets, Immelt's digital strategy had no specific digital product in mind, at least not one that customers were currently looking for. Instead it was more of a concept. "GE would become the backbone to the entire industrial internet" sounded sexy, but it wasn't clear that it was necessary or even all that useful. Even with billions of dollars behind the plan, it was pretty much doomed from the start. By the end of Immelt's tenure, nearly all hope of GE ever becoming a legitimate software supplier was gone.

In hindsight, many tech investors note Immelt's lack of knowledge in the tech world, illustrated by his hiring of an executive from Cisco, a hardware provider, to build and run GE's software businesses. His choice of location for GE Digital, San Ramon, California, was just not a place where high-end software code writers either lived or wanted to work. GE was only able to attract B-team programmers and had to pay up even to get those. The world of tech was so foreign to GE's stodgy East Coast heritage that the clash was notable. In our visits to San Ramon, we were always struck by how out of place GE executives seemed. They would get off the plane in San Francisco wearing the more formal classic GE uniform, put on jeans and sneakers, and shazam!—they were transformed into tech guys. Talk about creating cultural confusion. In any event, initiative one failed terribly.

Immelt's second initiative was to acquire Alstom, the big French maker of electric power generators, grid equipment, and power plants.

Alstom was a poorly run rival with margins less than half of GE's, and GE figured that its superior management capabilities could double those margins, all while finding outsized cost synergies in the merged companies. Alstom's number four market share in gas turbines would boost GE's number one share in a business already consolidated down to a few players, Siemens and Mitsubishi being the other big names. On the surface, the deal looked reasonable.

Investors did not know, however, that due diligence had revealed that Alstom was in poor shape, much worse than what anyone inside GE had previously thought, and GE should have walked away. But Flannery, still head of M&A, said later that he knew it would be career suicide to argue against the move. Making matters worse, the EU dragged out approval of the deal for more than a year, all while Alstom's engineering and sales talent fled, new contracts were signed with terrible terms, and finances fell further into the abyss. To top it off, the EU then required GE to sell critical technology to an emerging competitor (Ansaldo) with Chinese ownership (Shanghai Electric). In gobbling up a key competitor, GE was forced to create a new one, which crushed all the benefits of consolidation in the first place. But GE pressed on, even raising its bid to $17 billion ($11 billion of it in cash) in order to beat out a joint bid from Siemens and Mitsubishi. GE also had to promise to protect current jobs in France and create new ones. In protecting those jobs, the crucial cost-cutting part of the deal model went out the window.

GE insiders say that power generation leaders warned Immelt that the deal was doomed, but he went ahead anyway. He may have felt he had little choice. In selling off most of GE Capital, he was eager to reposition around a "new GE," and on paper the strategy made sense. The IR team presented a future 2018 earnings profile of $2.00+ per share, compared with $1.30 earned in 2015 when the target was announced. GE's acquisition of Baker Hughes a year later seemed to provide another tailwind, all assuming that the demand for oil and gas, along with jet engines, healthcare, and, of course, gas turbines, would stay strong. Most analysts and investors, including me, thought this all made sense, pushing the stock up 25 percent in 2016.

With GE's stock rising from its financial crisis low of around $6 to a peak near $32, Immelt regained credibility. He had seemingly engineered the exit from most of GE Capital and replaced those earnings with a higher-quality stream from core operations in power and in oil and gas. The fact that he was willing to bless a $2.00+ earnings profile for the company gave further confidence to that view, suggesting the stock had upside well into the $30s or higher. This was setting Immelt up to retire as the man who got GE through the horrors of 9/11 and the financial crisis of 2008–2009, with investors eventually rewarded with a rising stock price. We just didn't know what many GE insiders knew: Alstom was nearly bankrupt.

HOW WRONG THOSE ASSUMPTIONS PROVED

Critical to the entire $2.00+ EPS (earnings per share) narrative was that the Alstom deal become a resounding success. GE soon discovered the full extent of the troubles at Alstom, but it kept them hidden, figuring it could fix things before losses expanded. But instead of stabilizing operations, the company accelerated its free fall. From then on, GE's earnings and cash flow guidance became optimistic to the point of irresponsible, perhaps even pushing acceptable legal limits. Meanwhile, demand for gas turbines, along with oil exploration equipment, went south as the world economy slowed, and renewables began to rapidly replace traditional gas and coal power generation. Immelt had made an extension of Welch's brilliant trades of the 1980s, but now the timing was badly off. This time, GE was on the wrong side of every bet it made.

By 2019, GE had written off not just the entire $17 billion Alstom deal (valued at zero on the books), but far more and still counting as the business continues to bleed cash today. Instead of $2.00+ of earnings, reality ended up closer to $0.65 (and that's a highly adjusted number with limited cash flow) and with a stock price that dropped from north of $30 all the way back to the financial crisis low of below $7, all coming after two dividend cuts, this time to basically zero. The Alstom deal now ranks as one of the all-time worst acquisitions in history, catalyzing the eventual firing of Immelt in August 2017. Contributing to the debacle was the hidden time bomb in what was left of GE Capital: losses in its legacy long-term-care insurance business.

As of early 2020, the Alstom debacle, combined with the high cost of GE's liabilities, means GE continues to generate almost no cash flow, nearly crippling the company and forcing current management into crisis mode. Immelt had pressed every lever he could to make his actions appear sound. He borrowed money to buy back stock at inflated prices, and he pushed off restating liabilities at higher levels in hopes they would just go away. He put the company in such dire straits that crown jewels such as its fast-growing biotech business were sold just to keep it afloat. (See Figure 2.3.)

Figure 2.3: **Immelt largely unwound the impressive results that GE gained under Jack Welch.**

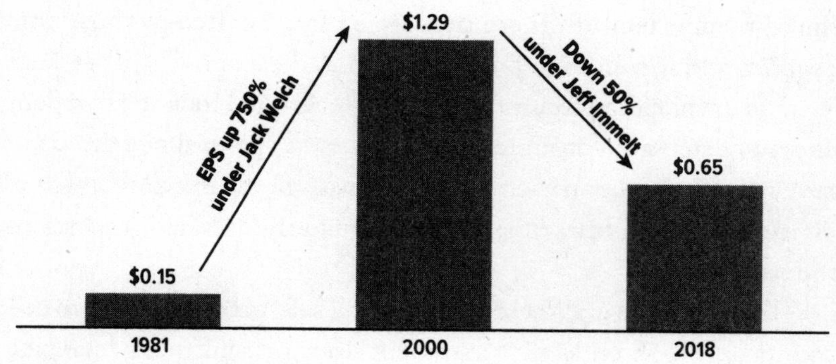

Note: Data is adjusted for stock splits.

Source: General Electric filings

FUDGING THE NUMBERS

It's easy to blame the captain when the ship sinks, but Immelt wasn't the only executive that drove the company toward bankruptcy, not once but twice in a decade. The old-timers talk of a GE that traditionally operated with a conservative, "round-down" culture. Forecasts included cushions to account for weather-related or macroeconomic disturbances. Market share was only one of several goals, and salespeople avoided high-risk customers. They had responsibility not only for landing a deal but executing on it.

That started to change even before Immelt. In the tech bubble years of 1999 to 2001, those who signed a contract were often not the same as those who had to execute on it. A team of dealmakers would come in with rosy forecasts, price a deal around perfect execution, then move on to the next opportunity. A separate execution team then came in and dealt with the realities of the project. Installing a giant power generator, for example, is full of risks, from suppliers to outside engineering partners to geopolitics. A turbine repair under warranty, for example, could cost a few hundred thousand dollars while the turbine remained at GE, but cost many millions of dollars once installed at the customer site. Project delays often came with severe penalties for GE, even if the causes were completely outside of the company's control. Those risks were often ignored by those who negotiated the deals.

Meanwhile the accounting around GE Capital took the company one more step away from reality. Welch even spoke about the art of moving dollars around each quarter to manage the ups and downs of divisional results. Immelt simply deepened the behavior and raised the risk tolerance.

To boost sales and their own bonuses, salespeople gave more discounts and took on shaky customers. They offered more financing with longer terms and smaller down payments. In China, supposedly a GE strength, executives agreed to terms that produced short-term revenues at the cost of intellectual property. Technology "sharing" with local partners became technology theft.

While these troubles took place throughout the company, the power division was the worst offender, especially after 2015 as demand fell. Managers recorded sales on turbines before the units were field-ready. Units were installed with major flaws and did not work to promised specifications. To boost revenue from service contracts, managers used discounts to stuff the channel with as many upgrades as possible.

The result was declining real cash flow, much of it not disclosed in filings until well after the fact. GE's PR and IR teams insisted that things were fine and the company was on track to meet its estimates. Cash, they said, was going to promote growth by extending credit to more customers and to develop new products. Any analyst who tried to probe got a brush-off or worse from Immelt or CFO Jeffrey Bornstein, who had replaced Sherin in 2013. When we wrote in late 2017 that GE should be investigated for deceiving investors and potential fraud, the company responded with a harsh rebuttal that was quickly repeated by more than a few news outlets.

Whether Immelt and his crew committed outright fraud will be determined by the SEC. We don't have nearly enough information to make that judgment. Either way, we are skeptical that they will be held accountable in any real way. More likely, GE itself will be presented with a monetary fine for poor oversight.

As for Immelt, he found a new job and has shown little remorse. Shareholders understand the risks inherent in any investment, but GE was advertised as "safe." Employees were told their jobs were secure. Retirees were told they could count on the dividend, and they favored GE stock in their 401(k) plan. These are the real victims, the ones who deserve to know the truth, the ones asking for accountability.

THE ENDING

By early 2017 there were signs that the great promise of a $2.00+ EPS laid out two years earlier had fallen flat. Even the powerful IR and PR teams were starting to hedge the outcome, blaming lower oil prices, the economy, the French government for Alstom, pretty much anyone or anything they could.

By May, Immelt looked old, tired, and beaten. He was gaining weight and stumbled through his midyear analyst update at the Electrical Products Group Conference, an annual get-together of about 150 influential investors and 25 or so top industrial company CEOs. I was in the front row, perhaps four feet away, and saw Immelt visibly shaking and sweating. I'd never seen him like that. Gone was the confidence he once exuded. On the side of the stage, his usually steady CFO Bornstein sat with his head down, unwilling to make eye contact. The entire experience was surreal. GE executives rip through PowerPoint presentations with ease. But on that day, Immelt could barely change the slides without stuttering. Within minutes my phone lit up with texts from those listening to the webcast, asking, "What is happening?" The press didn't know what to say, how to report what had happened. GE, led by Immelt, was unraveling in front of our eyes.

By July it was clear that Immelt could no longer do his job, and I wrote a draft of a report calling for his resignation. GE became aware of our work from a fact-checking phone call we made and asked us to delay the report for a day, offering a private meeting with Immelt instead. I saw little harm in waiting a day and was still well aware of the power that GE held. Investment bankers were still collecting big checks from GE, and my new employer, Barclays Bank, supported my independence . . . to a point. Anything I wrote that criticized GE needed to be 100 percent accurate. A report calling for Immelt's ouster would be headline news that day, so the work had to be immaculate. I went to hear Immelt's rebuttal.

Visiting the Boston headquarters and sitting in Immelt's private conference room, I was shocked at the conversation—more a confessional than the aggressive and confident Immelt I was used to. A visibly shaken Immelt apologized for how the company had "screwed me," not just for providing the wrong numbers for our analysis, but also for the regular beatdowns from his team. In battle, there are casualties, and it was clear that I was one of many in this war. In a shaking voice, he admitted the $2.00+ earnings guidance provided in 2015 was just a "holding place," that he needed to anchor investors on something hopeful to offset the pain taken in exiting GE Capital. He spoke for a long time without stopping, all while looking down at the table between us. He insisted he and others in the company had no idea Alstom's power division was in such terrible shape. He insisted that all the problems during his tenure were just bad luck, that Welch handed him a "bucket of shit," that he protected Welch's legacy at his own expense. And he further insisted that he got GE through its toughest time period, the financial crisis of 2008–2009. He rambled somewhere between apologizing and not. What was supposed to be a half-hour meeting went on for more than an hour. It wasn't clear what he was trying to accomplish, but he looked like a man living a very big lie and needing to get it off his chest.

From there I sat separately with CFO Bornstein, and the tone was similar. Bornstein had always treated analysts with contempt, usually lecturing us with a scowl. His voice typically boomed. But this time Bornstein blamed the company's failures on the culture's unwillingness to address costs and its bloated ranks. There were fiefdoms all over the world too powerful to break, and there was too much competition among the divisions. He blamed the contest to succeed Immelt for preventing bad news from traveling up and cost mandates from filtering down. He looked lost and weakened. It was clear that his career, as well as that of his mentor Immelt, was over.

I walked out shell-shocked. I had agreed not to write about "anything new discussed in the meetings," which had pretty much made my report obsolete. Everything was new. And any thought of downgrading the stock and advising my clients to sell was out the window. Now I was in possession of material nonpublic information, which carries a legal obligation to maintain confidentially until the information is made public. Both men had all but admitted that GE was in dire straits, that the company had little chance of making earnings numbers, and that the Immelt era was clearly over. At that point, any report calling for Immelt's resignation was irrelevant. He was already gone; just the details of his exit had to be worked out with the board. As we expected, he "quit" a few weeks later, pushed out by directors finally responding to the intense pressure.

Immelt likely knew this was going to happen before we met. I believe he was meeting with me to try to damage-control the narrative of his legacy. Although Immelt always claimed to be thick-skinned, negative press impacted him greatly. He wanted to leave on his own terms, but with the stock in free fall and an activist pushing for change, his fate was already sealed.

John Flannery succeeded Immelt as CEO in August 2017 and immediately instituted a broad review of the company's operations and accounting. On his first day on the job, he called my cell phone, and we spoke for a few minutes. At the end, he said, "I want to be very clear. There will be substantial change. I care about shareholders, and I want an open dialogue with my owners." I met with him one-on-one a few months later, and he had a similar shareholder-friendly tone. But the question he asked me on that day, that I mentioned earlier in this chapter, still haunts me: "When did you realize that Immelt was a fraud?" Without hesitation, I said it was that day in Dallas back in 2003, when he had spoken as if he were already the most accomplished CEO in the world, a renowned leader whose time was too valuable to use a hotel gym or stand in the typically short line at the Four Seasons Hotel check-in counter. He was so caught up in being a celebrity CEO that he forgot he worked for shareholders—and more broadly for stakeholders.

In truth, however, I myself had forgotten that early warning sign over the years. I had allowed GE's leaders and investor relations machine to explain away problems. I tried to stay strong and call out abuses, but after years of intimidation, it was just too much. In the process, I failed many of my clients. I just didn't want to believe that such a great company could allow so many deceptions. These were people I had once greatly admired. The lessons are hard, raw, and humbling. It still feels surreal—a bad dream that I haven't yet awoken from.

POSTMORTEM OF THE JEFF IMMELT YEARS

At its core, GE failed stakeholders because it invested its abundant profits unwisely and took its past success for granted. It relaxed its heretofore impressive management discipline around operations and sales. Then it pushed the envelope of risk higher each year to compensate for the prior year's shortcomings. It also insulated itself from accountability, which is essential to any effective business system.

A contributing factor was that Immelt and his team allowed the company to get too big and complex for effective oversight. (See Figure 2.4.) At their best, conglomerates spread risk, promote global scale, and centralize strong governance, but too often their size breeds overconfidence, and they use their complexity to hide problems. Some conglomerates do succeed (see later chapters in this book), but it takes more management discipline than most companies can muster.

Figure 2.4: **GE's value destruction (in market-cap terms) was nearly two times that of WorldCom, Enron, and Lehman Brothers combined.**

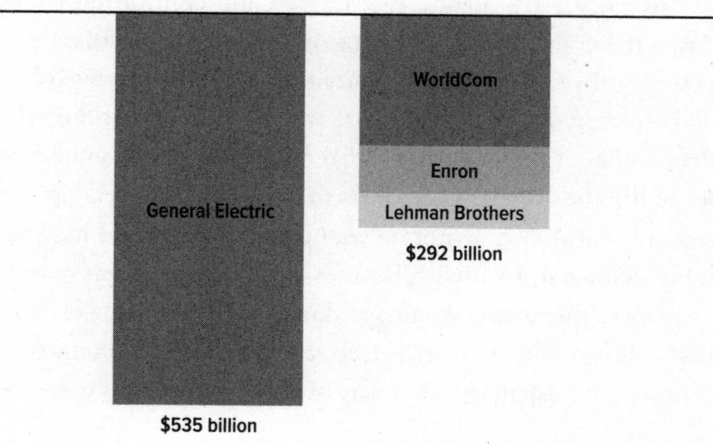

Source: Bloomberg

GE's diversification worked well in the 1990s, but it was a tangled mess soon after. Near the end, and with margins under pressure, GE put almost all its free capital into two areas. Much of it went, reasonably enough, into the thriving aviation division, which rode the continuing global boom in air travel, but the rest went largely to fixing GE Power, ultimately with the Alstom acquisition. That left the healthcare division starved of investment. GE made no real acquisitions in healthcare throughout the 2010s, a decade of major innovations in that industry.

GE was drowning in complexity, which would have made it hard even for disciplined leaders to hold people accountable. KPMG was charging the company $143 million annually in audit fees, involving 21 partners and hundreds of accountants. GE's tax filings ran into thousands of pages. With an engagement that big, as we saw with Arthur Andersen and Enron, it's hard to trust the findings. There are many gray areas and boundaries that can be pushed. It took Flannery several quarters to understand what was actually going on in the company, but by then it was too late, and he was slow to react to a sharply degrading GE. The board fired him for inaction in October 2018. Perhaps it would have been impossible for any insider to unwind Immelt's GE.

In early 2019, new CEO Larry Culp committed to whittling down the company to the core aviation, healthcare diagnostics, and power businesses. He pushed out nearly all the legacy board members and replaced the senior corporate staff. And he has promised to repay debt and get GE back to financial credibility. Those actions may do a lot to dig the company out of its mess—and Culp is a high-integrity leader—but they may not be enough. GE as a brand may be irreparably damaged, even with businesses sold or spun off over the next few years. The financial damage done to the entity makes it less clear that GE can fully weather a deep recession as it has many times in its century-plus existence. That part of the story remains to be seen.

IF IT COULD HAPPEN TO GE . . .

It's easy to present GE's story as a morality tale. Extraordinary success went to everyone's head, GE lost its edge, and the company made things worse by chasing unprofitable short-term fixes. But GE was more than a century old when Immelt took over, and most of its leaders had grown up in the company. GE invested more in management development than most companies, and headquarters actively oversaw the divisions. The company was famous for its systematic approach to business, and it had adapted successfully to previous challenges.

As for Immelt, he was fully a product of "the most admired company in America." He had excelled as head of the healthcare division, and Welch had selected him after a rigorous succession process. Immelt worked hard to envision a new course for the company, including substantial efforts to digitize the businesses. He also had plenty of smart people who could see problems as well as anyone out there. If that kind of organization can fail so dramatically, then every company is vulnerable.

That's especially true of the high-flying tech companies that dominate attention and investment today. We've seen disturbing parallels between their actions, especially on disclosure and accountability, and what we faced with GE. It's human nature: any company that thinks it's special, that the ordinary rules don't apply, will eventually stop doing the exceptional work that brought about its initial success. The distractions of success and celebrity can be overwhelming.

GE's struggles show the difficulty of maintaining focus over decades, especially across CEO transitions. How do you achieve and sustain the discipline necessary to prevent the kind of irresponsibility and arrogance that plagued GE? What kind of leadership, systems, and incentives will focus people on sustained profitability—not on a dressed-up fiction that serves only short-term interests? That's what we explore in the rest of the book and for which we hope to offer insights. Because for every sad corporate failure like GE, there are winners equally worth studying. Taken together, the lessons are extraordinary.

Lessons from the Jeff Immelt Era

- Arrogance is the default culture that follows historical success. Guard against it.
- Benchmarking and accountability are necessary to inject humility.
- CEO transitions are critical to a culture. All eyes are watching actions as much as words.
- Board size and composition matter. Smaller can be better.
- Managing complexity requires another level of skill, which may not be sustainable over time.
- Capital deployment must balance risk versus return; “game changing” is often “game over.”
- Starved factories with a lack of ingrained process are a recipe for disaster.
- Making increasingly bigger bets to “hit the numbers” is a strategy that rarely works.

CHAPTER

3

BOEING

A Struggle to Find Balance in Risk Management

BY CARTER COPELAND

At any engineering-focused organization, risk management and mitigation are guiding principles. Holistically understanding and appropriately balancing the risks associated with a new endeavor are paramount to a project's success. These risks come in numerous forms: technical, contract, cost, schedule, safety, etc., and they all matter. This is especially true at Boeing, the world's largest aerospace company, where the financial bets made on new products are enormous, the technical hurdles are high, and the costs of failure can be catastrophic.

In the last few decades, Boeing went through a transformation. An engineering- and product-centric culture that pushed the boundaries of technology, regardless of financial or business risks, changed to develop a deeper focus on competitiveness and profit generation. The transformation started in the 1990s but didn't take hold until the 2000s. At that point, financial crises made it necessary for new managers to implement meaningful changes in the way Boeing approached the airplane business. Schedule slips and massive cost overruns generated financial losses that, in aggregate, exceeded the company's entire market value. Boeing's long-term health and survival were at stake. Financials were in disrepair, and everything from labor relations to new product development required rethinking.

By focusing on reducing technical and financial risk, the company charted a new path. Each year, financial targets and expectations for future financial performance were ratcheted higher. The stock price followed, making Boeing the most valuable industrial company in the world after decades of being viewed as "uninvestable" by Wall Street. The company's transformation in the 2010s was undeniable. Boeing went from bleeding cash at an unsustainable rate to generating profits at a level that even the most bullish observers never thought was possible. Many of the changes underpinning the company's transformation, such as having a deeper appreciation for emerging global competitors and not taking on new, overly risky projects, were relatively straightforward and easy. Other decisions were tougher, requiring meaningful sacrifices from important stakeholder groups. Reducing jobs, closing facilities, pressuring suppliers for concessions, and pushing off all-new product designs for customers inevitably had cascading impacts. All the financial success came with a cost.

Jobs were lost, relationships with suppliers were strained, and eventually two 737MAX planes crashed, claiming the lives of 346 people. Amid the company's push for lower financial risk and higher profits, it made technical, safety, and public relations mistakes. While attempting to recover from these mistakes, the company maintained an aggressive posture, piling on debt and increasing financial risk. Then, in a stroke of very bad luck, the COVID-19 pandemic brought the company to its knees and on the verge of needing government support to survive.

There is a delicate interplay among a company's various stakeholders, and improperly balancing the competing demands of disparate groups inevitably leads to failure. This is especially true for an aircraft manufacturer like Boeing, whose responsibilities start with the safety of the flying public and extend from the employment of hundreds of thousands of people to its investors and owners on Wall Street. Boeing needs to be safe, technically proficient, and financially viable. The balance remains tenuous, but the company's long-term sustainability hinges on understanding and applying thoughtful focus to the unique needs of each group.

UNDERSTANDING THE AIRPLANE BUSINESS

Aerospace companies and their government sponsors have long pushed the limits of engineering and exploration, often to great technical success. They broke the sound barrier, carried astronauts to the moon, and made the world a smaller place for billions of passengers.

Nevertheless, Boeing, the company sitting atop the global aerospace industry, struggled for decades to consistently make money.

A new airplane costs billions of dollars to develop and remains in service for upward of 30 years. Massive fortunes are at risk, and there is little room for error. For most of Boeing's history, technical achievement was synonymous with financial mediocrity. Cost, schedule, and business risks were usually secondary or tertiary considerations. Innovations in materials, design, and manufacturing processes were often pushed forward without a careful consideration or full understanding of what could go wrong later on in the aircraft production process. Corporate cultures became ingrained with bad habits, and decision-making was driven by internal and external politics more than anything else.

To be fair, the airplane business isn't easy. A manufacturer invests billions of dollars in research and development simply to design a new aircraft and certify it for service. If successful, the company then loses billions of dollars on the first 100 to 200 airplanes as it streamlines complex manufacturing processes and increases volume. After these substantial up-front investments, it then may enjoy several years making billions of dollars when production is mature, pricing is good, and volume is relatively high.

An analysis of a half century of aircraft development programs suggests that bets on new aircraft pay off and make money only half of the time. The other half of the time, poor sales, low production volume, or technical problems and delays lead to significant losses. As a result, until 2010, the industry hadn't consistently generated acceptable levels of profitability. We estimate that from 1970 to 2010, Boeing generated a paltry average profit margin of just over 5 percent in the airplane business.

This historical mediocrity in returns is largely the result of poorly conceived airplane programs dragging down otherwise good ones. An airplane program is a monumental engineering and manufacturing challenge. Engineers design 500,000-pound pieces of equipment that can fly through the sky at 500 miles per hour, and line workers assemble them at a pace as fast as one new plane per day. Organizations of hundreds of thousands of people invest millions of hours and billions of dollars in bringing a new plane to market. At any given time, an aircraft manufacturer only has the organizational bandwidth to produce a few distinct product lines at reasonable volumes. This makes the mix of money-makers versus money-losers incredibly influential to the company's overall level of profitability. For almost the entirety of Boeing's history in the commercial jet business, it had both good and bad programs, due to a culture that focused more on engineering than profitable business.

TWENTIETH-CENTURY BOEING—ENGINEERING FIRST

Boeing has one of the most celebrated engineering cultures in American business history. Walking through an airport, it's not uncommon to see pilots with a sticker on their flight bags stating, "If it ain't Boeing, I'm not going," a marketing tagline reflecting Boeing's desire to manufacture the world's most advanced, highest-quality aircraft.

The Boeing 707 and 747 revolutionized jet travel in the 1950s, 1960s, and 1970s and served as a key source of pride for those who made them. Mainline employees and managers alike saw their engineering capabilities as the unmatched pillar of the company's success. Boeing amazingly launched three clean-sheet aircraft in the 1960s (the 727, 737, and 747), a feat of developmental engineering that no other aircraft manufacturer has ever approached. Engineering triumphs like these helped solidify Boeing's leadership position. However, it sometimes seemed that revolutionary engineering accomplishments were the sole goal of the company, regardless of the financial risks inherent in achieving them. That began to change following the company's merger with McDonnell Douglas in 1997.

Following the McDonnell Douglas deal, Boeing became the undisputed leader of the market for commercial aircraft, with ~70 percent global market share of passenger jets delivered. Yet even with a dominant market position, the company struggled to make money. In fact, during the year of the merger with McDonnell, the new Boeing

Commercial Airplanes (BCA) division failed to deliver a profit at all, as it struggled to bring a new variant of the popular 737, known as the 737 Next Generation (NG) to market. The launch and subsequent ramp-up of the new product was beset by delays that ultimately required a halt in production.

When the merger closed, McDonnell CEO Harry Stonecipher joined as Boeing's president and COO, a job intended to be a preretirement placeholder for the 61-year-old. The son of a Tennessee coal miner, this hard-nosed engineer turned out to be the right executive to steer Boeing through its problems with the 737NG program. He was as tough as they come and immediately clashed with Boeing's engineering- and product-centric approach to running the business.

During his first visit to Boeing's Everett factory, Stonecipher looked at a 747 being manufactured for Air India and asked, "How much do we make on that plane?" He was told that the question was not answerable on an individual plane-by-plane basis. He waited months for a better answer and never got one, later proclaiming, "Only one man, the CFO [Boyd Givan], knows how much it costs to build a jetliner, and he isn't talking." The 747 was an immensely important product for Boeing, representing nearly half the company's profits at the time. Yet at the highest levels of the organization, managers didn't have the detailed understanding of the program's unit economics that normally would be prevalent at a mature manufacturing company. Not knowing how much money the company was making or losing on each customer's aircraft demonstrated a lack of financial rigor that he found simply unacceptable. The complexity and scale of aircraft manufacturing leave little room for error, and a program's success or failure cannot be left to chance. Stonecipher pushed Boeing's overall CEO, Phil Condit, to fire both Givan and Boeing Commercial Airplanes CEO Ron Woodard in an effort to drive better risk-adjusted focus and discipline across the organization. BCA clawed its way back to profitability a year later, but the underlying issues were far from fixed.

Boeing's experience with Stonecipher was emblematic of what many outsiders observed over the years: For Boeing, it was all about the airplanes. The engineers responsible for designing the aircraft, along with the line workers responsible for building them, effectively ran the company. Stonecipher contended that the organization needed to be run more like a for-profit enterprise. For the company to be sustainably successful, it needed to have a healthier balance of engineering and financial discipline. Big product bets would always be at the heart of the airplane business, but Stonecipher tried to get the company to evaluate those bets alongside the risks associated with them. This required a more detailed understanding and tracking of the financial implications of engineering and manufacturing decisions. Stonecipher initiated this process, but meaningful changes didn't come easily or immediately.

Boeing endured a nasty strike later in Stonecipher's tenure, due largely to strained labor relations that many associated with his internal efforts to wrest some control of the company from the engineering group. Interestingly, the strike wasn't conducted by the IAM, the company's blue-collar union of aircraft assemblers, but instead by its engineer's union, SPEEA. This was unique, as labor relations with SPEEA had traditionally been amicable. However, the late 1990s had proved tough for the engineers. Struggles on the 737NG necessitated more of a focus on day-to-day manufacturing operations rather than new airplane designs, and research and development funding came down accordingly. This didn't sit well with the engineering crowd, many of whom were simultaneously feeling their status as elite professionals in the Seattle economy wither away with the tech industry's meteoric rise. In the eyes of the engineers, Stonecipher was the poster child for a management team that no longer understood or appreciated how Boeing did things.

Years after Stonecipher's departure, a leader within Boeing's Commercial Airplane segment complained to me that he believed much of the Boeing workforce thought "it was their God-given right to make airplanes, and that's become a big problem over the years." While Boeing enjoyed an undisputed leadership position for much of the twentieth century, that position wasn't set in stone. What many at Boeing failed to fully appreciate at the turn of the century was that the dominant market share the company had enjoyed for the previous four decades was about to be challenged in a major way by the company's European counterpart, Airbus. While many in the Boeing enterprise still look back on the Stonecipher era as a period of cultural pain, others came to appreciate that Stonecipher was one of the first to see the changing demands on the company's performance that were arising due to competition. Like it or not, Airbus was emerging as a major global competitor that would force Boeing, an organization that had grown very set in its ways, to meaningfully change its behavior. (See Figure 3.1.)

THE RISE OF AIRBUS, BOEING'S FIRST REAL CHALLENGER

Airbus was formed in the early 1970s through an affiliation of cross-country European aerospace companies in a large-scale partnership called a GIE (groupement d'intérêt économique, a unique form of partnership under French law). This structure allowed for the pooling of economic and manufacturing interests, and it suited the goals of subscale planemakers in France, Germany, and Britain looking to better compete in the global market. As aircraft manufacturers in the United States were gaining significant scale in the 1960s and 1970s, European countries needed to work together. Out of this mutual interest and agreement, Airbus was born.

The company's formation and initial product introductions were reasonably successful, and yet Airbus didn't gain real momentum in the aircraft industry until 1985. That's when Jean Pierson, a colorful, chain-smoking Frenchman who once worked on the famous Anglo-French Concorde program, dared to challenge Boeing's market dominance.

Pierson oversaw more than a quintupling of Airbus airplane orders during his 13-year tenure as CEO, along with the launch of the successful A320 and A330 programs, planes that sought to beat out Boeing's offerings at the time. Pierson's Airbus grew to supplant the only other US aircraft manufacturer of significance, McDonnell

Figure 3.1: **Boeing's history (1967–2019).**

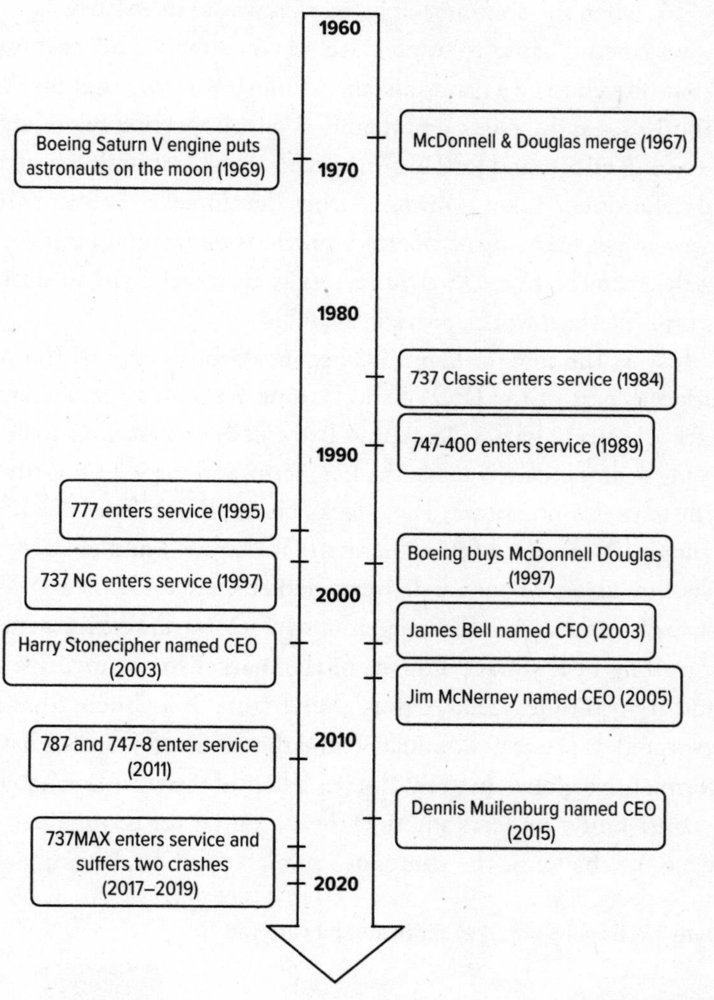

Source: Boeing filings

Douglas, essentially forcing the merger with Boeing. This merger cemented the global duopoly that exists today.

Boeing spent much of Pierson's tenure either dismissing Airbus as a competitive threat or complaining how European government assistance allowed it to exist in the first place. This is rather amusing, as Boeing had gained its leadership in commercial aircraft with the

US government's purchase of a militarized variant of Boeing's first jet, the 707, when the commercial jet market was in its infancy.

As Boeing came to appreciate all too slowly, underestimating Airbus proved to be a giant mistake. While it was true that the Airbus of the 1980s and 1990s cared mainly about supporting regional manufacturing efforts and jobs in Europe, in doing so it built a significant and defensible market position. Airbus developed a family of aircraft more diverse than any of Boeing's previous global competitors. And its sales focus on non-US airlines, just as air travel demand shifted to the non-Western world, proved valuable.

Just as the new millennium began, Airbus came to the public market as part of the IPO of the European Aeronautic, Defense, & Space Company, or EADS. Airbus had credible aspirations to become Boeing's competitive equal in the long term, and the 9/11 tragedy indirectly gave it momentum. The attacks on the World Trade Center hit Boeing's US-centric backlog harder than Airbus's, and in subsequent years Boeing ceded annual delivery market share to the Europeans. In just six years following the merger with McDonnell, Boeing went from controlling nearly three-fourths of the market to occupying a slight minority position versus Airbus. (See Figure 3.2.) Boeing has never recaptured its previous dominance, and the market for aircraft has been a competitive global duopoly. Boeing believed it was untouchable, and by consistently underestimating the potential for anyone, let alone Airbus, to challenge the company's market position, Boeing enabled

Figure 3.2: **Boeing's market share steadily eroded.**

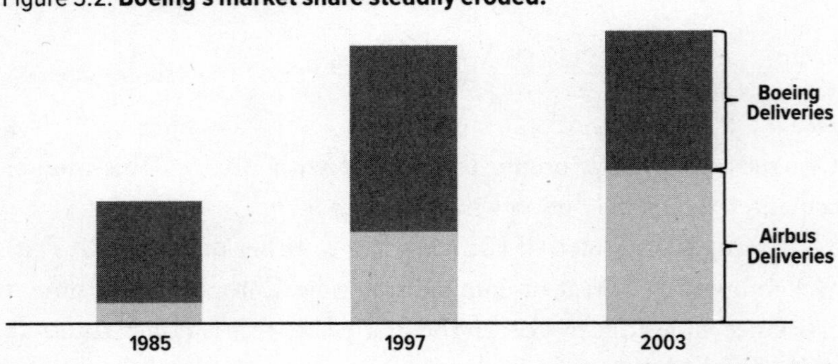

Source: Boeing and Airbus filings

a formidable competitor's rise. In the years that followed, Airbus and Boeing looked to new product offerings to amplify their growth and solidify their relative competitive positioning.

NEW MILLENNIUM, NEW COMPETITION

Think of competitive offerings for airplanes as coming in the same sizes as T-shirts: XS, S, M, L, and XL. (See Figure 3.3.) The small end of the market encompasses planes that regular travelers fly on most often, shorter-haul aircraft with one aisle and 3 to 5 hours of flight

Figure 3.3: **Airplane sizes fall in categories similar to shirt sizes.**

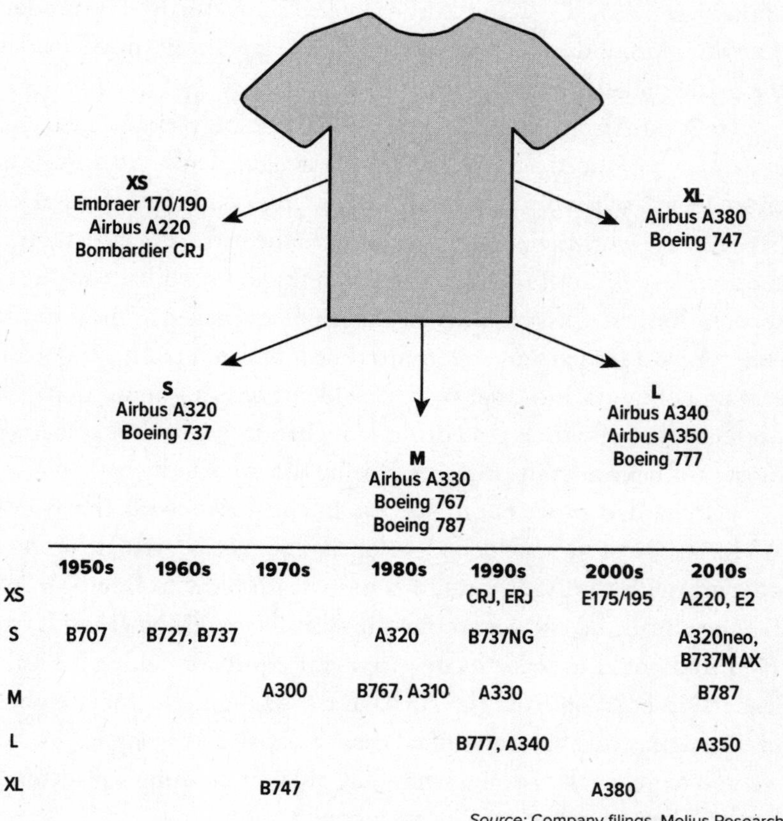

	1950s	1960s	1970s	1980s	1990s	2000s	2010s
XS					CRJ, ERJ	E175/195	A220, E2
S	B707	B727, B737		A320	B737NG		A320neo, B737MAX
M			A300	B767, A310	A330		B787
L					B777, A340		A350
XL			B747			A380	

Source: Company filings, Melius Research

time. At size medium and larger, aircraft have two aisles and can fly 10 to 15 hours or more over long distances, and in this end of the market, product classes are defined by total seating capacity.

Throughout the 1970s, 1980s, and 1990s, Boeing enjoyed a monopoly position in the XL end of the market. Boeing's XL offering was the 747, the double-decker dubbed the "Queen of the Skies." It was used to shuttle 400+ passengers for up to 16 hours, often between some of the world's largest cities.

The double-decker 747 entered service in 1970 and went through several upgrades, the most notable being the 747-400 derivative in 1989. The -400 was a popular plane with no direct competition and decades of manufacturing experience and cost reduction. It helped fund the successful launch of the size-L 777 and offset the struggles of the size-S 737NG. When Airbus looked across the Boeing product portfolio, Airbus decided that a competitive response at the XL end of the market made the most sense.

In 2000 Airbus launched the A380, the largest passenger aircraft ever produced. With two full passenger decks spanning the entire length of the aircraft, the A380 aimed to carry 500+ passengers between the world's booming megacities. The extra size also allowed for a variety of new amenities like swanky onboard bars and even showers for first-class passengers. The plane was hailed as the ultimate step forward for passenger comfort, but it also offered high-density seating configurations that were capable of ferrying more than 800 passengers at one time. As Airbus launched this assault on Boeing's most profitable aircraft platform, Boeing did not sit idly by.

Airbus had experienced success in the 1990s with the A330/A340 family of aircraft, a codeveloped size-M and size-L product offering, with the A330 dealing a near death blow to Boeing's 767. Boeing already had newer products in sizes S (the 737NG) and L (the 777), and opted to focus its development efforts on taking back the leadership position from the A330 in the M segment. The members of the engineering team amplified these competitive dynamics, as they wanted to get back to doing what they did best, pushing the technology envelope in new airplane development.

Major technology shifts in the aviation world happen at a decadal pace, and in the early 2000s there were several vectors of technology that warranted exploration. High oil prices, as well as emerging competition from upstart airline competitors known as low-cost carriers (LCCs), had Boeing's customers clamoring for greater fuel efficiency. Their concerns brought to the fore a new material used mainly in military aircraft and spacecraft production. The new material was carbon fiber reinforced polymer composite (CFRP), or just "composite." Composite's strength-to-weight ratio was significantly greater than that of traditional materials like aluminum, which translated to significant weight savings and by extension to fuel savings. Boeing decided to manufacture an airplane that was thinner, stronger, and up to 25 percent lighter than metal by building it entirely out of composite.

Boeing initially called the new aircraft the 7E7, with the "E" standing for efficiency. Innovation efforts didn't stop with the aircraft structure. Boeing also elected to make the 7E7 the world's first aircraft using all-electric subsystems rather than hydraulic or pneumatic. This drove further weight savings and greater power efficiency from the engines, adding to the fuel savings. The 7E7, later rebranded as the 787 Dreamliner, was precisely the sort of technology moon shot that defined the engineering-centric culture of Boeing's past. It was billed as a superefficient enabler of point-to-point connectivity for airlines, packed with every bit of cutting-edge technology that the company could imagine.

In addition to the grand scale and innovative technologies embedded in the all-new 787, the manufacturing plans involved a great deal of geographic fragmentation. The company outsourced production around the globe, often to greenfield sites that had never constructed anything for an airplane. To make the production system work, Boeing built a small fleet of modified 747 freighter aircraft (called Dreamlifters) to fly giant sections of the aircraft to Seattle for final assembly. Boeing's engineers were reinventing not just what airplanes were built with, but also how they were built. Like everything else on the 787, it sounded like a good idea on paper, but it would prove otherwise. (See Figure 3.4.)

Figure 3.4: **The 787 global outsourcing was unprecedented.**

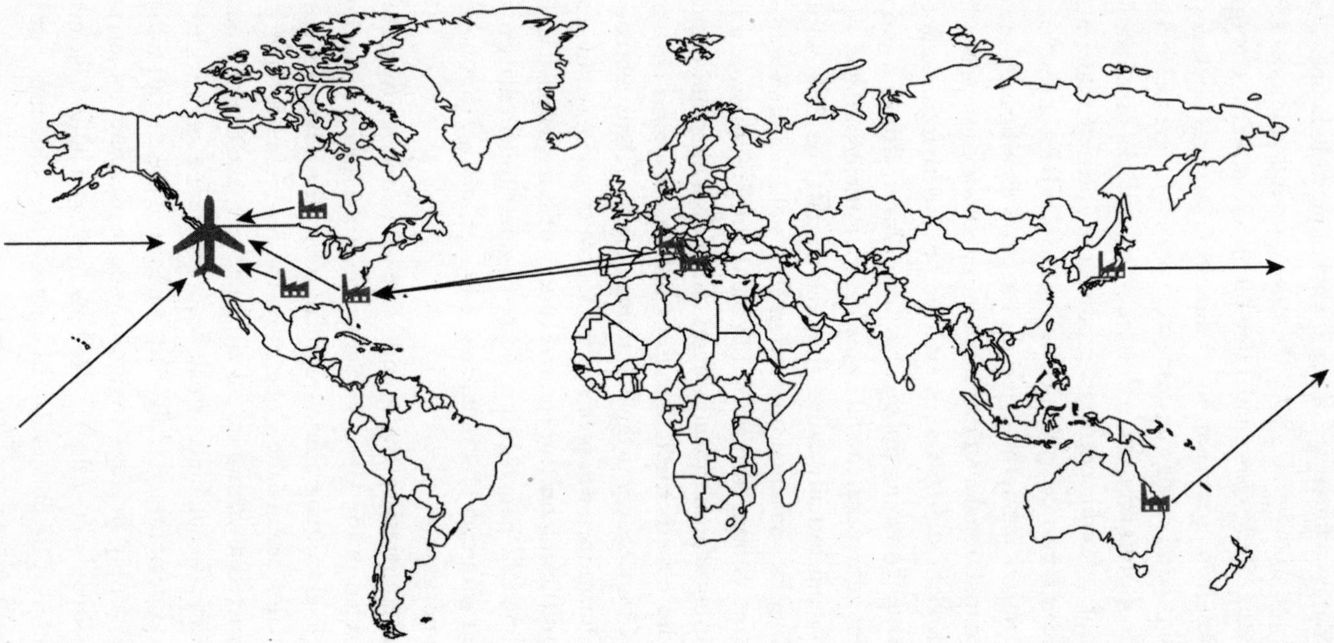

Source: Boeing filings

THE 787 DEVELOPMENT BEGAN TO UNRAVEL

The Beijing Olympics were scheduled for summer 2008, and Boeing wanted the 787 to shuttle passengers to the event from the farthest reaches of the globe. If that wasn't a frivolous enough target for such a major project, someone in the marketing department determined that the perfect date for rollout of the first "completed" aircraft was July 8, 2007, or 7/8/7. Boeing organized the program's schedules and timelines around these events, whether realistic and achievable or not.

The 787 did indeed roll out on 7/8/2007 to throngs of observers in Everett, Washington, but the plane was far from complete. Some fuselage sections didn't fit together properly, parts of the wings were made of painted wood, and the plane lacked a working electrical system. A CEO of a major 787 supplier told me years later, "When I saw light shining through unfilled holes in the fuselage, I knew this thing was an unmitigated disaster waiting to happen." Nevertheless, the schedule was the schedule, and Boeing admitted nothing in the way of problems or delays. That first airplane was built, taken apart, and rebuilt three times. It cost more than $1.2 billion by the time it was "done," well more than 10 times its intended selling price.

The 787's first flight was supposed to happen in August 2007 (shortly after the 7/8/7 rollout), but it didn't occur until December 2009, more than a year after the Beijing Olympics. Boeing announced eight delays to the program's schedule, and the first deliveries to customers didn't happen until 2011, three years later than planned. Aircraft up to the sixty-sixth off the line were referred to internally as the "terrible teens" because they required so much fixing that they weren't all delivered until seven years later, in 2018. Like stubborn kids, they took a long time to leave home. (See Figure 3.5.)

Figure 3.5: **The 787 was delayed eight times.**

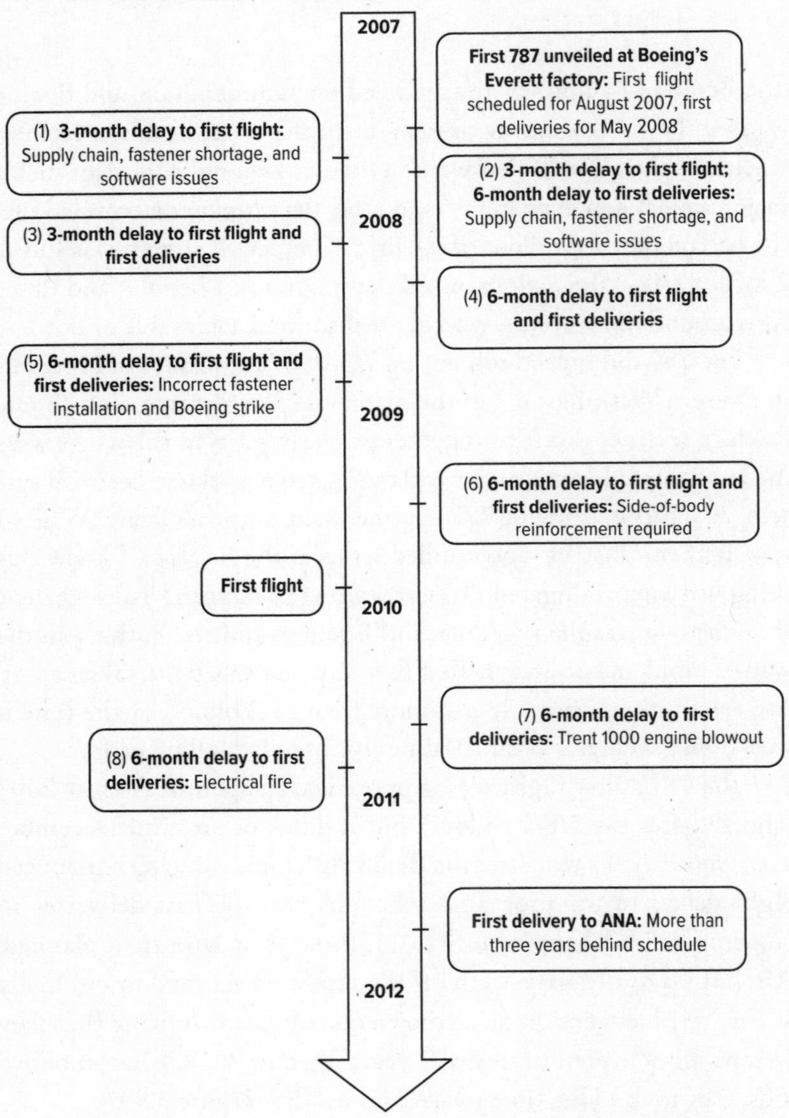

Source: Boeing filings, press reports

Boeing ultimately spent $20 billion on R&D for the 787, but that was just scratching the surface of how much money went out the door before things got under control. Besides the R&D expenditures associated with the program, the company lost an additional $28 billion manufacturing the 787 before the first profitable plane rolled off the line in 2016. This brought total cash out the door to roughly $50 billion, making the 787 investment a bet that was twice the size of the company's entire market value at the time of its launch in 2003. Despite significant technological advances, robust sales, and a product that ultimately was well received by the customer, the 787 was by far the biggest financial failure in the company's history. Along the way, it ended the careers of numerous executives and put the company's financials under enormous strain.

To make matters worse, while the 787 development was ongoing, the company decided to launch an update to its aging 747, called the 747-8, to counter the A380. It featured a longer fuselage and took on the 787's new GEnx engines from GE to improve fuel efficiency. In hindsight, this was purely a vanity project aimed at stealing some market share back from the A380, and it failed miserably. The 747-8 program faced manufacturing delays of its own, which was a particularly embarrassing outcome since the -8 variant was a relatively simple update of a plane the company had been building for over 30 years. The program was an inefficient use of Boeing's engineering, manufacturing, and financial resources at a time when the 787 was bleeding massive amounts of cash. Boeing aircraft margins fell from ~10 percent in 2005–2006 to ~3 percent in just three years, and the company's total cash flow fell by more than half, with no signs of pending improvement. As a result, efforts to reverse course and improve financial performance became necessary to ensure that the company would remain a going concern.

DIAGNOSING WHAT WENT WRONG

In the midst of these crises in 2010, I attended a breakfast with Boeing's then-CEO Jim McNerney, who joined the company in 2005 after serving for two years on the company's board. McNerney was a high-level thinker who was well equipped to conceptualize the causes of the company's recent failures. I asked him bluntly what he thought had gone so wrong, and he candidly said the company had too often pushed technology development much further than customers were willing to compensate Boeing for. In the case of the 787, manufacturing a composite airplane cost significantly more than the company ever imagined, and the technical risks that BCA was willing to take to deliver maximum fuel efficiency were a stretch too far. If that weren't enough, outsourcing massive parts of the production served as the death blow for the program's financials.

In McNerney's view, customers were willing to pay for the improved performance of new aircraft if it translated to fuel savings or greater range, but they certainly weren't going to help foot the cost of development overruns. In fact, they expected exactly the opposite—they wanted to be compensated for delivery delays due to poorly executed development efforts or technological overreach. McNerney coalesced Boeing around a new strategic direction, one he later coined, "de-risking the decade." Up to that point, risk mitigation and financial stability weren't high on the list of priorities. The company's culture assumed that if you designed a great airplane and sold it well, everything else would take care of itself. This long-held mentality led to a major misalignment between internal and external stakeholders and to a decision-making process around everything, from product development to how employees and managers were paid, that created incongruent outcomes. Strikes and labor unrest were common, financial performance was poor, and financial charges were commonplace. No one had a good sense of what the company's level of profitability could be; there was no benchmarking of significance. McNerney sought to reverse these trendlines on numerous fronts.

The de-risking began with a focus on working through money-losing contracts without signing up for any new risky work. Then the company went through broad-based "should-cost" exercises that evaluated functional elements of the Boeing cost structure in painstaking detail, and for the first time it benchmarked the elements against outside data. Corporate incentives also underwent a sweeping overhaul to focus on manufacturing, financial execution, and alignment with total shareholder return. These efforts to contain cost, limit risk, and benchmark and incentivize appropriately, all while constantly examining results and refining the strategy, reoriented Boeing around a new set of guiding principles.

Boeing's focus on de-risking and operational improvement seemed well timed, as Airbus, under new CEO Tom Enders, was engaged in a similar exercise. Airbus had its own near-death experience with the A380, and the wild currency swings of the 2000s left Airbus searching for competitiveness and sustainable profitability as well. This simultaneous risk-adjusted approach to management was best evidenced by the decision of both companies to simply re-engine their two most profitable airplanes rather than design entirely new ones.

In 2010, Airbus and Boeing both had two main profit centers in the airplane units, their single-aisle offerings (A320 and B737) and their twin-aisle offerings (A330 and B777). In the years leading up to this point, Airbus had responded to the 787 by launching an all-new aircraft, the A350XWB, which kept the engineering team busy. Having already developed the 787, Boeing was exploring the idea of allocating its future research and development spending on a new single-aisle replacement for the 737, called the NSA, or New Small Airplane.

Enders and the team at Airbus realized that they needed to stretch the engineering resources of the firm beyond what was prudent in order to fully respond to Boeing if it launched the NSA. Simultaneously, they figured out that by putting newer, more fuel-efficient engines on the A320, they could achieve a significant amount of any efficiency gains the NSA promised for a fraction of the development cost, all while leaving enough engineering resources in place to de-risk the development of the A350. The A320neo (short for "new engine option") was born.

Airbus sold the A320neo at a pace that took the aviation world by surprise, amassing more than 1,000 aircraft sales in just over six months. Boeing initially dismissed the need to respond to the A320neo's success until longtime Boeing customer American Airlines was on the verge of signing an order for 500 A320neos. Overnight,

Boeing scrapped the NSA concept and agreed to launch a re-engined version of its own 737, salvaging half the American Airlines order in the process.

In the years that followed, both companies expanded the re-engining effort to their profitable widebody aircraft (A330 and B777). Unlike the well-trodden "lose billions and maybe make billions" path of clean-sheet aircraft development, re-engining saved billions in up-front development expenses when cash was a scarce commodity due to the failures of the 787, 747-8, and A380. It allowed Airbus and Boeing to continue to sell their mature products at higher volumes and higher prices over a longer period of time.

The re-engining decisions were emblematic of the industry's newfound appreciation of pursuing bigger profits while taking less risk. It was a stark change from behaviors of the past, but following a lost decade of financial performance in the 2000s, the change in strategic direction was both inevitable and well placed.

LOWER RISKS, HIGHER PROFITS

When I began covering the aerospace sector in the early 2000s, then-Boeing CFO James Bell cited a 10 percent operating margin rate as an aspirational goal for the company. Bell's logic was that since 10 percent was the best the company had ever generated in the past, it must represent the upper bound for the future. However, on the back of McNerney's de-risking focus in the early 2010s, Boeing concluded that the mid-to-high-teens margins achieved by other best-in-class industrial peers were achievable. The company instituted new approaches aimed at driving further improvement in sustainable profit margins.

Under McNerney's watch, Boeing launched several initiatives focused on improving cost competitiveness. Realizing that outside suppliers dominated the company's cost structure and that supplier's margins were 50 percent higher in many cases, the company created "Partnering for Success," or PFS. Under PFS, Boeing aggressively pushed suppliers to lower prices or risk being cut out of future platforms. Privately, supply chain partners referred to the initiative as "Pilfering from Suppliers," but they grudgingly went along with the effort. After all, Boeing controlled the intellectual property and took the lion's share of development and production risk. (See Figure 3.6.)

Figure 3.6: **Boeing profitability establishes a new normal, approaching supplier levels.**

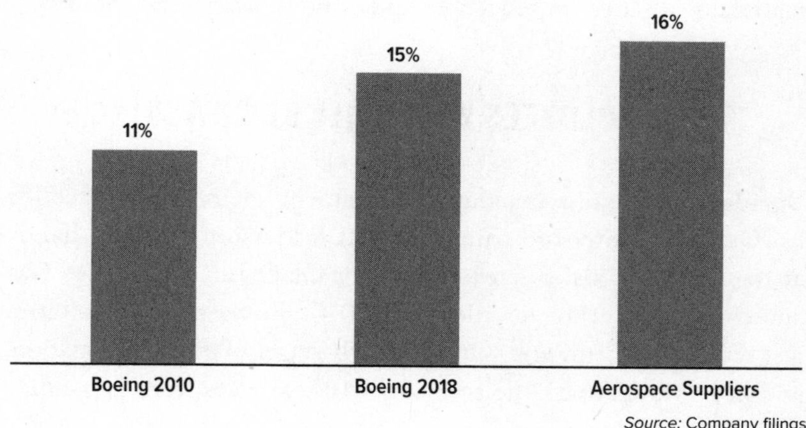

Source: Company filings

Inside Boeing's factories, the company used cross-site comparisons of manufacturing operations called "Champion Times" to rapidly improve productivity. It granularly compared common manufacturing jobs performed at different sites and calculated which workers performed the job in the shortest amount of time. Then it studied the specific behaviors that generated the best outcomes and implemented best practices across the organization in order to replicate them. Furthermore, it invested aggressively in robotics and automation technology, taking people out of the manufacturing organization in certain areas.

As this new path forward for Boeing emerged, financial progress followed. After losing billions of dollars that would never be fully earned back on the first 500 to 600 planes, the 787 went from severely loss-making to breakeven. At the same time, sales volume on the highly profitable 737 rose by a third, absorbing more fixed costs, with productivity gains expanding margins further. Demand for single-aisle airplanes boomed alongside the rapid growth of the global middle class, and strong demand drove higher aircraft pricing. Efforts to reduce supply chain costs hit the bottom line, and the company worked hard to limit growth in fixed costs. Boeing earnings were on a path to doubling or even tripling by the end of the decade.

However, somewhere along the path to great financial success, the company began to lose sight of creeping risks. Those risks would have materially negative consequences for key nonfinancial stakeholders.

"THE EMPLOYEES WILL STILL BE COWERING"

Boeing always had a mandatory retirement age of 65 in place for CEOs, a rule intended to ensure that leadership changed hands at regular intervals. But when Boeing CEO Jim McNerney was approaching 65 in the middle of the 2010s, he wasn't ready to retire just yet. The company was still in the early stages of its transformation, and 2016 would mark the company's 100-year anniversary, a milestone he wanted to reach.

Around that time, as part of the company's newfound religion on cost control, McNerney and his team were looking to secure deals and concessions not just from suppliers but also from employee unions. These deals were initially aimed at improving Boeing's long-term cost competitiveness. The negotiations were contentious and unpopular, but they were necessary to get the company on more solid footing. One of the company's chief risks was out-of-control costs from pension plans put in place decades earlier. Boeing's pension plan was the second largest in America at the time and was underfunded by ~$20 billion. Every year, pension benefits owed to workers ballooned. Stemming the tide of pension cost growth was essential to getting the long-term cost structure under control.

An opportunity to address the pension problem eventually presented itself. On the back of the successful launch and early sales of the 737MAX, Boeing repeated the re-engining strategy with the

777 program, formally launching the 777X. This updated version of the plane would feature new composite wings and larger, more fuel-efficient engines. The plane's design was settled on rather quickly, but where the new version of the aircraft would be assembled remained an open question.

The existing 777 assembly line was just outside of Seattle and seemed the logical choice for the 777X. But Boeing's recently acquired nonunion site in South Carolina was an attractive alternative. The company would use this alternative production site as a bargaining chip in labor negotiations.

A contract negotiation with Boeing's largest union, the International Association of Machinists & Aerospace Workers (IAM), was ongoing, and Boeing wanted the workforce to give up pension benefits for future employees in exchange for keeping 777X work in Washington State. The strategy worked and helped to address the single largest cost problem on Boeing's hands. Yet it strained relations between management and the unions.

While he never said it outright, I always took away from my conversations with McNerney that labor relations were strained for good reason. After all, in 2008 the IAM had gone on strike in the middle of the biggest economic malaise since the Great Depression. It was a bold and poorly timed move by the union, as the economic downturn was compounded by mounting production struggles with the 787. This was almost certainly something that McNerney never forgot.

Not long after the labor deal was done, Boeing's board of directors granted McNerney's request to stay beyond the mandatory retirement age of 65. When he confirmed this extension on the next earnings call, he noted that he was staying longer and that "the heart will still be beating, and the employees will still be cowering." He later apologized, but the message was loud and clear.

McNerney's statement was symbolic of the contentious relationship with labor that resulted from actions taken to help the company recover from the 787's failures. Tough decisions often require sacrifice, and a hard-nosed approach with lingering impacts on various stakeholder groups needs to be thoughtfully considered. This fracture with labor is the first major instance that I can recall when the needs and desires of other key stakeholder groups appear to have been completely forgotten or ignored.

This example may have just been a one-off occurrence, but it certainly stood out as clear evidence that management wasn't messing around. As leadership of the company transitioned from McNerney to Dennis Muilenburg, there were budding signs of stress with other stakeholder groups. McNerney moved to the chairmanship of the board as Boeing approached its hundredth anniversary, with the company's financials delivering consistent improvement. Muilenburg was forced to figure out how to make them even better.

A NEW BOSS PUSHES FOR HIGHER HIGHS

Dennis Muilenburg was promoted to chief operating officer just before Christmas of 2013, coming from leading Boeing's defense business. The first 15 years of his career were spent at the Boeing Commercial Airplanes unit, as an engineer and program manager, making him well seasoned in all things Boeing. With this promotion he became the heir apparent to McNerney.

Muilenburg's most recent success came from overseeing a dramatic cost-cutting effort across the 60,000-person Boeing Defense enterprise, an approach called "market-based affordability." While externally the Boeing defense business wasn't getting the same attention as the commercial airplane unit, internally Muilenburg's success in rapidly reducing costs wasn't going unnoticed. While he was viewed by some of the other executive leaders as aloof and not fully in sync with the needs of the wider organization, his star was undeniably on the rise. McNerney admired his "can-do" attitude and saw Muilenburg as an executive who would push the organization to achieve higher financial highs.

In the commercial airplanes segment, some in the leadership ranks believed that if Muilenburg pursued a similar effort to aggressively reduce head count in their unit, it would prove more problematic. For these managers and employees, the integrity and achievability of the aircraft production plan were paramount, especially given the lessons learned on the 787 in the preceding years. Schedule and customer satisfaction needed to be the primary objective. This tension would prove important later on.

By the time Muilenburg moved to the CEO role two years later, it was becoming clear that expanding margins and growing cash flows were the company's principal financial opportunities. Boeing's decision to forgo building completely new aircraft designs, and instead focus on fixing its money-losing programs, meant that a dramatic improvement in profitability was effectively locked in for the coming years.

Muilenburg announced a commitment to increase operating profit margins from ~9 percent to "mid-teens," along with a plan to grow cash flow every year for the foreseeable future. Wall Street fell in love with the message, and the stock rose by ~40 percent during Muilenburg's first two years as CEO. While much of the success was based on structural improvements across the business, head-count reductions were also a contributing factor. The workforce declined by 13 percent in total and by 15 percent in the commercial airplanes unit. But unlike the cuts at Muilenburg's defense unit in prior years, when sales were declining, the head-count reduction in commercial airplanes occurred while volumes were rising. (See Figure 3.7.)

Figure 3.7: **Boeing's head count fell by 20,000+ even as sales grew.**

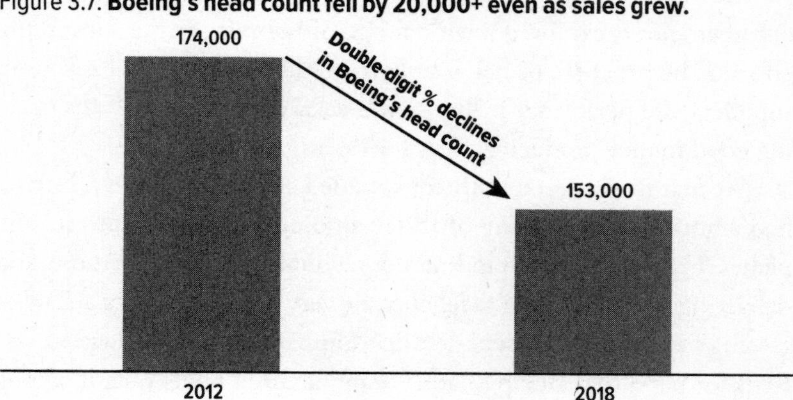

Source: Boeing filings

By the time Muilenburg reached his third year at the helm, the financial performance was so good it was almost unbelievable. During one quarterly earnings release in the summer of 2017, Boeing indicated that it expected to beat its full-year cash flow plan by $2 billion, while reiterating its previous commitment to grow cash flow every year. The baseline for 2017 and every year after moved up by $2 billion, and shares rose by roughly 80 percent in the subsequent year. Boeing became a must-own stock. Muilenburg was named *Aviation Week's* Person of the Year and was featured on the cover of *Bloomberg Markets* magazine with the title "Up, Way Up."

IF A LITTLE IS GOOD, MORE MUST BE BETTER, RIGHT?

In the wake of Boeing's success in expanding profit margins and cash flows, there was a palpable desire to determine what else could be achieved in the future through an expansion of similar efforts. The company launched PFS-2, asking suppliers not just for lower prices but also for more lenient payment terms in new contracts. The move effectively leveraged Boeing's negotiating power to shift more value away from the supplier base and into Boeing's pockets and further fueled the cash flow growth it had promised investors.

Tensions between Boeing and the company's supplier base grew; yet the company pushed forward, undeterred. As a mechanism for enforcement, it explored a wide range of manufacturing insourcing efforts. The prospect of being able to credibly take work back from suppliers and perform it in-house was a serious threat for firms making good money producing parts for Boeing.

At first the insourcing threat sounded strategically savvy. Boeing had a good understanding of the technology that went into its airplanes. However, understanding the technological specifications and delivering manufacturing excellence are very different things. Many of Boeing's suppliers had spent decades optimizing their production systems for parts that Boeing hadn't manufactured on its own in a long time, if ever.

In 2017 I toured one of the sites performing insourced work for the 737MAX that on earlier 737 versions was done by an external supplier. At the end of the tour, I was shown a chart detailing that Boeing's cost per part was at least 30 percent below the prices offered by suppliers A, B, C, and D. One of these suppliers was the previous manufacturer. This seemed odd, as the legacy supplier would have the benefit of decades of manufacturing experience for a component that Boeing only recently started building. This conclusion defied common sense and the well-understood and time-tested principle of manufacturing learning curves.

In a later discussion with a retired Boeing executive, I asked how the math in this insourcing example might be possible. He said that it couldn't be and that the company was simply fooling itself, likely altering the cost calculations in such a way to prove to itself that insourcing must be better. The supply base had to be cheaper on an honest, apples-to-apples basis. But if Boeing convinced itself otherwise, that's all that mattered. The company could decide to insource work even when it didn't make sense to do so. This only served to strain supplier relations even further.

Boeing's aggressive posture didn't stop with unions and suppliers. It expanded into the political realm in 2017 when the company pushed the US government to levy massive tariffs on a new regional jet known as the C-Series being introduced by Canadian competitor Bombardier. The effort was widely seen as an attempt to kill off the program before it gained commercial momentum. In the end the effort backfired: the pressure sent the C-Series program into the waiting arms of Airbus, which acquired the rights to the new aircraft in 2018. Under Airbus's ownership, the competitive threat posed by the program only increased.

Throughout the Boeing enterprise, the increasingly contentious relationship with numerous stakeholder groups was bringing unintended consequences. Financial performance was still improving faster than expected: margins in the airplane unit eclipsed 15 percent by the fourth quarter of 2018, and annual cash flow had grown by about two-thirds since Muilenburg took over. Yet there was creeping evidence that Boeing was starting to lose sight of the holistic approach to risk management that had driven the company's recovery from the struggles of the 2000s.

CRACKS BEGIN TO FORM

The A320neo aircraft, the principal competitor of Boeing's 737MAX, was certified for commercial use in late 2015. This was more than a year ahead of when Boeing's plane would be certified for passenger service. This put pressure on Boeing to ramp up production of the MAX as quickly as possible to keep up with its primary competitor. As such, the 737MAX production plan envisioned the steepest ramp-up in the company's history.

The 737MAX received certification in March 2017, but unlike the smooth production increases executed in prior years, Boeing struggled with the MAX ramp-up. Some believed that the aggressive head-count reduction efforts intended to boost profitability had gone too deep, putting unnecessary stress on the system at precisely the wrong time.

Just before the production ramp-up began, Boeing hired an outsider from GE named Kevin McAllister to serve as the CEO of the Commercial Airplanes unit. He was known as a "customer guy," brought in to help Boeing achieve its longer-term commercial ambitions. He wasn't the factory floor guru that the organization really needed as it increasingly struggled to meet the demands of the MAX production schedule.

Under McAllister's watch, dozens of planes stacked up outside the factory awaiting engines and other parts. Production discipline slipped, both inside Boeing's factories and at suppliers. But given the increased tensions between Boeing and the company's supply base, the path toward fixing the situation became more defined by finger-pointing than partnership. During this time, attention that McAllister should've been devoting to the factory floor was spent advocating for a new aircraft program with questionable returns.

McAllister was pushing for Boeing to formally move forward with an all-new plane called the Next Midsize Aircraft, or NMA. The plane was intended to serve a segment of the market that the current offering of small and medium-sized planes did not fully cover. But the business case for the product was weak. It was challenging to confidently see how the plane could ever be profitable, let alone generate anywhere near the same level of profitability of Boeing's existing portfolio of aircraft. At the very least, its launch would certainly add more risk to the overall system, a system that was already showing signs of strain.

Budding problems weren't confined to the airplane business, as the company's defense business was beginning to struggle as well. The last remaining troubled contract from the 2000s, one that required Boeing to deliver aerial refueling planes to the US Air Force, was becoming a bigger and bigger problem. The company struggled to get work completed on the first wave of production aircraft. Over a three-year stretch, it took a financial write-off on the program in 9 of 12 quarters. There was no program anywhere else in the entire US defense industry with such a consistent string of negative financial charges.

Luckily for Boeing at the time, the upside elsewhere in the business was so strong that investors looked past the tanker charges and other issues as one-offs to be ignored. Cash flow continued to grow handsomely as the 787 program turned the corner and began to produce profits. The stock went even higher. In the eyes of investors, Boeing could do no wrong. (See Figure 3.8.)

Late 2018 represented a peak in Boeing's aggressive posture in going after new business. In an unprecedented move for a major defense contractor, Boeing won two competitions to build military aircraft by bidding to lose money, insisting that it would "make it up on volume" in the future. In my career, I'd never seen a company take a financial charge on a program that it had yet to start work on.

At the time, the company made it clear that it believed that the success of the commercial airplane franchise allowed it to cross-subsidize defense bids in a way that was strategically unique and valuable. To me, it seemed unnecessarily risky. However, all these creeping signs of lost risk management discipline would fall from focus when a bigger emergency occurred.

Figure 3.8: **Boeing cash flow grew from $3 billion to $15 billion.**

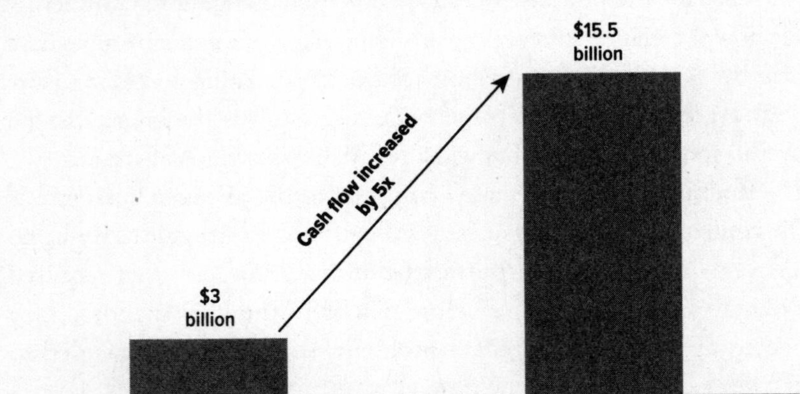

THE MAX CRISIS SUDDENLY CHANGES EVERYTHING

In 2019, following two crashes of the 737MAX, Boeing found itself in a full-blown crisis when it was revealed that a new automated flight control system was the common link in the accidents. The system, known as MCAS, was new to the 737MAX and was foolishly designed to engage based on the input of a single external sensor, something rather uncommon in the aerospace engineering world, which values the safety benefits of redundancy. When engaged, the system pushed the plane's nose downward to prevent the plane's angle of attack from getting too steep. However, if engaged at low altitudes, it proved to be dangerous. Furthermore, the system was included without explicit instructions to MAX pilots about how it worked. In both accidents, a failure to disable the MCAS system's forceful nose-down commands resulted in both aircraft crashing, claiming the lives of 346 passengers and crew.

Following the first of the two crashes, Lion Air Flight 610, Boeing was publicly dismissive of any major issues. Yet behind the scenes, the company was preparing a software modification for MCAS. Evidence of improper maintenance on a key sensor and potentially falsified service records by Lion Air made it difficult to single out Boeing's flight control software as the singular root cause of the crash. However, when the second plane, Ethiopian Airlines Flight 302, went down four months later, alarm bells began sounding in the ears of 737MAX operators, global regulators, and the flying public. At least initially, the company maintained a defiant posture in the face of criticism and calls for the 737MAX to be grounded from service.

The MAX was grounded first by China, then in every other region of the world except the United States; Boeing pushed the FAA hard to keep the plane in service until satellite data provided enough evidence to indicate that there was a common link between the two crashes. Boeing's insistence that the plane was completely safe was tone-deaf to the concerns of the flying public and grossly inaccurate.

Once Boeing finally relented, nearly 400 MAX aircraft were grounded around the world. In the months that followed, a Department of Justice investigation surfaced internal communications that revealed unacceptable levels of pressure on employees to bring the MAX to market as quickly and as cheaply as possible to compete with the A320neo. Furthermore, the MCAS system was exposed as irresponsibly conceived and poorly integrated into the training regimen of MAX pilots. Critics blasted the company's insistence that iPad training, rather than time spent in a simulator, was sufficient. Yet Muilenburg remained bold and dismissive and struggled to connect with the broader public in a way that demonstrated believable remorse.

Crashes of new aircraft types have happened in the past, but none of them have happened in the social media era. The proliferation of the internet created a world where the flying public has endless access to the details of the accidents, and informed and uninformed opinions are readily available in every corner of Twitter and Facebook. Historically, Boeing communicated only on a business-to-business basis with its airline customers. The 737MAX crisis forced the company to rapidly change and to address passengers directly on new communication channels. This represented a completely new challenge for Boeing, one that its executives botched. At best, they were caught flat-footed, and at worst they were incapable of appreciating the severity of this new risk to the business. The flying public was a key stakeholder group whose safety and confidence they weren't treating with the appropriate level of care and concern.

When the grounding began, Muilenburg assumed that a return to flight would happen in relatively short order, when the software update being contemplated after the Lion crash was completed. Muilenburg insisted at the company's annual shareholder meeting that the single-sensor determination was "consistent with [the company's design] processes." However, as the FAA and other global regulators scrutinized not only the MCAS recertification and the single-sensor determination, but the aircraft more broadly, the timeline for the MAX's reentry grew increasingly uncertain. Boeing instructed suppliers to keep producing parts, and MAX production continued even as the timeline began to slip. Hundreds of finished airplanes worth more than $10 billion were placed in company parking lots, awaiting recertification and delivery to customers.

Surprisingly, as pressure on the MAX recertification mounted, Muilenburg was still spending time working on future business projects like the NMA and an exploration of the urban air mobility market through a partnership with Porsche. It wasn't the behavior of a CEO well versed in how to handle a crisis. In fact, it was just the opposite. His lack of engagement with the FAA during this time led to a reprimand by the regulator, a message to Boeing and to the broader public that the MAX's timeline for certification wouldn't be dictated by anything other than the principles of flight safety. Shortly following this event, the *Wall Street Journal* reported that the meeting between Muilenburg and the FAA where this message was delivered was the first face-to-face encounter he had with the regulator during the entire grounding. The lack of personal connectivity was shocking.

The company booked billions of dollars in financial charges related to the MAX grounding, covering both the costs of lower factory productivity and compensation to airlines that couldn't use their airplanes. Like the 787 did just a decade before, the MAX ultimately brought with it lessons that will shape the company's future.

With Muilenburg catching the ire of the FAA, the Boeing board of directors, frustrated by his ineffective management of the crisis on multiple fronts, fired him, but arguably long after the board members should have. Board chairman David Calhoun was appointed as the firm's new CEO. Initial efforts under Calhoun's leadership seemed to represent a reversal of the company's stance on numerous fronts. Boeing quickly backed away from any appearance of forcing the FAA's hand on recertification by setting a more conservative timeline for the MAX's return to flight. Additionally, in a complete 180, it recommended simulator training for all MAX pilots to ensure MCAS familiarity. The NMA project was dropped as part of a broader rethinking of what future product development processes should look like, and PFS was eliminated from the vocabulary of those in supply chain–facing roles. Boeing realized the need to focus on rebuilding trust with the stakeholder groups (regulators, employees, suppliers, the flying public) that had taken a backseat to shareholders for an extended period of time. Sadly, these actions were lost in the noise of the COVID-19 global pandemic, which only two months into Calhoun's tenure called the company's future into question.

To continue to produce MAX aircraft during the grounding, Boeing took on billions of dollars in debt and swung from a position of net cash to a position of net debt for the first time since the 787 crisis earlier in the decade. Funds supported ongoing MAX production in the supply chain and payments to customers for delivery delays. The company essentially made a bet that when recertification occurred, cash would quickly begin to flow and debt could be repaid.

The COVID-19 outbreak put unprecedented pressure on global air travel. Airlines swiftly cut capacity by 80 or 90 percent in some cases. With no one flying, airlines had little or no cash coming in, and cash payable to Boeing was suddenly in question. In hindsight,

Boeing's bet on a quick recovery was incredibly unlucky and ill-advised, and it left the company seeking government support, something unimaginable when the company's stock was soaring to all-time highs just before the MAX crisis only a year earlier. The swing from the world's most valuable industrial company to one whose liquidity and solvency were being questioned in such a short period of time is still mind-boggling.

While almost no one foresaw the extent of the impact that a global pandemic could have on the market for airplanes, it undoubtedly will redefine how everyone evaluates the future. And just like the crises that preceded it, it will forever reshape how the company and all its stakeholders evaluate risk.

POSTMORTEM

Over much of the last three decades, Boeing has struggled to effectively balance the needs of key stakeholder groups, overemphasizing the importance of one or two for extended periods of time. An internally focused engineering- and product-centric culture attained impressive technical achievements, gained outsized market share, and ushered in a period of unprecedented air travel safety. But a lack of financial rigor created an inefficient organization prone to massive economic losses. Market share eventually eroded, and financial health deteriorated under the weight of poor execution and ill-advised development programs. The company was forced to shift its focus to risk mitigation and improved financial performance.

Through a series of deliberate and well-thought-out actions, Boeing improved efficiency in its factories, retired program risk, mitigated development risk, and reclaimed economics that had been lost to the supply chain. It was a real success story. However, an outsized focus on delivering higher financial highs eventually frayed relationships with suppliers and employees and played a role in the tragic loss of 346 lives. Then, a still-aggressive approach to recapture what was lost ran into the most severe crisis in the industry's history. These mistakes were born not of nefarious intent, but rather of a complacency that emerges when an organization experiences success and doesn't rebalance itself to ensure it is effectively satisfying the needs of all stakeholders. Safety, quality, and profits aren't mutually exclusive, but consistently delivering on all of them over the long run requires vigilance and constant recalibration. To be truly successful in the future, Boeing has to find a way to successfully manage all these needs simultaneously.

That's also true for many companies in the tech world. Most of them are engineering- and product-centric, and as their markets mature with slower growth and normal profitability, they'll have to confront the same challenge of ensuring profitability without jeopardizing safety and customer value. Additionally, while Big Tech doesn't grapple directly with safety risks and the loss of human life, issues of customer privacy and social influence are similarly meaningful and only growing in significance. Drawing the lines on customer data use and weighing them against the pursuit of profit and higher share prices is a similar evaluation. It's inevitable that the influence of nonfinancial and nonemployee stakeholders will only continue to rise in the future. And the industry is not immune from its own megacrisis. In fact, cybersecurity threats for Big Tech could prove to be the equivalent of a global pandemic for industrial firms and travel-focused companies.

Boeing's task in the 2020s is now unprecedented. Successfully recovering from the fallout of the COVID-19 pandemic dominates the focus in the short term. Finding a stable financial position and building a sufficient cash buffer for future crises will inevitably be a primary focus for several years. However, this effort has to come alongside managing safety and quality risks first, while not losing discipline on the cost, schedule, and development fronts. New products will be required in due course, but they can't come at the expense of long-term cost competitiveness and financial viability. Similarly, relationships with suppliers and labor have to be carefully structured to ensure operational and financial success without causing disruption. One thing is for certain: more crises lie ahead. The question is whether

Boeing's century-old franchise can evolve to manage the crises of the future without forgetting about balancing and sustaining the gains from the past.

Lessons from Boeing

- Most companies grasp the importance of innovation and growth, but many underestimate risk.
- Success often drives arrogance and/or complacency. Stay focused.
- The severity of most crises is underestimated; crisis management is best done in advance.
- Innovative companies run the risk of favoring engineering over financial viability, but being too financially focused is an easy way to lose sight of other important variables.
- Both the number and the importance of key stakeholder groups always grow over time.
- Overemphasis of one business objective runs the risk of underemphasis of others.
- Some leaders are better equipped to manage certain risks and stakeholders than others. Boards need to act decisively when executives are not equipped to handle a crisis before it spirals further out of control.

CHAPTER 4

DANAHER

Process-Driven Reinvention

BY SCOTT DAVIS

Once a company achieves initial success, no matter which path taken, it faces a new challenge. People relax and allow bad habits to creep in. They erect bureaucracy, lose focus, and leak talent. Performance suffers and culture degrades, but by the time leaders or investors notice, it's often too late.

Danaher may be the best example of a company fighting to resist this complacency creep. Cofounders Steve and Mitch Rales could easily have lost focus, having become billionaires many years ago. But they pushed forward, reinventing the company with a remarkable and inspiring passion for continuous improvement and compounding value. The result may be the most process-driven culture of any company in America.

In early 2020, Danaher was nearing $20 billion in revenues with a market value of $115 billion. Instead of declining into bloated maturity, it built an immensely profitable set of businesses that sell into some of the highest-growth niches in healthcare and water testing/treatment. And although its global franchises employ 60,000 people, with sharp employment growth over time, head count in Washington, DC, headquarters isn't much larger than it was decades ago, still just about 100 people.

The story of Danaher is first and foremost one of constant reinvention. It has fully exited nearly all its initial industrial assets and even spun off its dental platform—a testament to its leaders' determination to gravitate capital toward higher-return opportunities while fading those in the maturity curve. In the process it created several valuable "mini-Danahers," notably Fortive ($25 billion market cap), which houses Danaher's original industrial assets, and Envista ($5 billion market cap), which has the dental assets.

Not only is Danaher willing to become smaller to refocus its portfolio, but once it believes that an asset no longer fits in its long-term plans, it finds a better owner for it—even if the asset is still growing and creating value. This is in sharp contrast to the traditional conglomerates of the past. Its installed base of testing equipment requires a constant stream of Danaher-supplied consumables. It has a high-margin, high-return, low-cyclicality portfolio that most companies would dream about, one that fits the Danaher Business System (DBS) extraordinarily well.

Perhaps what's less understood is how central the Danaher Business System has been to this reinvention. In simple terms, DBS is a set of constantly updated best practices that functions as a playbook for all employees. It provides day-to-day structure, with clear definitions of what matters and how it will be measured. The tools keep employees focused, but less on a specific goal line and more on continuous improvement, people measuring what matters and improving on those metrics a little bit every single day. At its core DBS comes from Lean manufacturing, and it extends from the factory into all other critical functions, including sales/marketing, procurement, and engineering, up into the corporate office and R&D labs.

DBS defines the culture of Danaher. Its excellence is best illustrated through the company's ability to maximize cash flow, profit margins, and the customer experience. DBS creates process where it's needed, freeing up time for the most value-added functions. It also provides the company with differentiation in its M&A and portfolio decisions. Once people are brought in, Danaher teaches them how to be more productive, more focused, and more customer-centric. DBS pushes the organization out of its comfort zone. Employees are empowered to achieve autonomously, equipped with mandatory tools. Lean manufacturing becomes a religion to follow. Wasteful processes are tossed aside. Expectations rise. Those who embrace this rigorous culture thrive; others are filtered out. The metrics are clear, with no place to hide.

The end result is a stock price that continues to rise, an energized and cared-for employee base, products that increasingly solve some of the most important problems in healthcare, and value for all stakeholders that ranks near the top of almost any metric. Danaher is a truly amazing success story in American business, and one that has largely gone untold—and without question a company that today's tech giants can learn from.

FROM REAL ESTATE TO MANUFACTURING—THE EARLY DAYS

The Rales brothers founded Danaher with a strategy akin to today's private equity firms, in that they believed in buying and improving existing businesses, rather than seeding them from scratch. They were young men with limited experience in any real business, and they had limited access to capital. In hindsight they must have had guts. It was long before failure was considered "a learning experience."

They started in real estate where they saw the power of compounding and leverage. By the early to mid-1980s, real estate investing had become very popular, while manufacturing was considered to be on a path to extinction, catalyzed by rising Japanese competition and unfavorable US labor relations. Despite that, they saw a bigger opportunity in manufacturing.

While fishing one summer day on the Danaher Creek in Montana, they set an early vision of what a modern-day industrial company should look like: one in which improving profitability was critical and business goals were closely aligned with the realities of a company using leverage to grow. Rising cash flow would pay off debt levels while supporting the underlying growth needs of the asset.

With limited bank debt funding, they initially bought cheap manufacturing assets of variable quality. The first deal was in 1981 with MasterShield, a sub-$10 million vinyl siding company. Then came Mohawk Rubber, a small tire company, in 1983. At about that same time the Raleses bought DMG, a bankrupt publicly traded REIT that had dated back to 1969. The two industrial assets were then merged into the public entity which was renamed Danaher.

The first official deal under the Danaher name was done in 1986 with Chicago Pneumatic, a much larger multi-asset holding company that included a promising business called Jacobs Engine Brake. Jacobs's main product is the "Jake Brake," that grumbling sound you hear from a truck as it goes downhill, using the engine and exhaust system to assist the braking mechanism in slowing down these heavy vehicles.

Fortunately for the Raleses, the general manager of the Jake Brake operation was a forward-thinking engineer, a perfectionist who took great pride in his job. This manager, George Koenigsaecker, had served as a Green Beret in Vietnam, and after the war he spent time in Japan working for a Japanese and American joint venture. While there he became infatuated with Japanese manufacturing philosophies, particularly the Lean and kaizen approaches. He eventually returned to the United States, settled in Bloomfield, Connecticut, and took a job at Jacobs.

As the Jake Brake grew in popularity, Koenigsaecker rose to head the Bloomfield facility. He became frustrated with its low productivity, subpar product quality, and delays in getting product to customers. He believed the company needed a desperate change or it would fail. In 1988, as he struggled to control Jacobs's spiraling problems, he learned that two architects of the Toyota Production System were in nearby Hartford for a guest lecture. Their names were Yoshiki Iwata and Chihiro Nakao, two of the most well-regarded factory experts in Japan. Koenigsaecker attended their lecture and convinced them to meet for dinner. He desperately sought their advice, and as the wine poured, the men became curious about this mess of a factory they were hearing about. Though they spoke little English and traveled with a translator, the two men and the general manager hit it off immediately. They decided to visit the factory that same evening. The Japanese men were shocked at the poor workflow and bloated inventory levels. Even more surprised were the night-shift folks, a rough-and-tumble crew.

Throughout the night, the crew watched the Japanese men move equipment around and suggest improvements, often mocking the American factory setup. After resting for a few hours back at their hotel, the experts returned and were impressed by how the Americans had immediately put their suggestions into place. Rather than fight the changes as Koenigsaecker had anticipated, the factory workers embraced them. Many of the adjustments were recommendations the workers had previously made, only to be ignored by traditional line managers. In those days, American manufacturing was rigid, with assembly lines set up from engineering blueprints, not optimized around actual workflow and experience. Engineers controlled the factories, while workers lacked the power to change much of anything, even though they were the ones who most easily saw the flaws in a design. By accident or not, Danaher had learned the lesson that employee empowerment was powerful, decades before this concept became popular in the corporate world.

Right away the factory saw improvements in cost and quality. Employees who once felt muzzled and marginalized began suggesting further improvements—and the changes were electrifying. Workers who once slogged and frowned through the workday suddenly were moving quickly, smiling and engaged. Delighted, Koenigsaecker formally employed the Japanese experts on a consulting project for one week a month until Jacobs had set Lean and continuous improvement principles fully into its culture. Customer relationships were repaired, and Jacobs was saved.

The Rales brothers and newly hired CFO Pat Allender were so impressed by the jump in productivity and quality that they quickly sought to adopt the techniques across all their facilities. They assembled their first-ever meeting of all Danaher executives and had Koenigsaecker present a full business case for the new principles. Thus, the Danaher Production System was born, the predecessor to the more evolved and broader Danaher Business System. Its basic principles, rooted in Lean and continuous improvement, are fundamentally unchanged today.

The concepts are simple but require constant tweaking and experimenting. Everything depends on the organizational push for small improvements every day—not big goals with giant leaps, but small changes that all employees can rally around, with a commitment to measurement and tracking. Doing this correctly and over time is challenging. Even kanban, which is just a factory scheduling system to track workflow and ensure daily management, can be hard to implement at an existing factory. While standard practice in nearly all factories today, back in the 1980s, kanban was rare outside of Japan. Even today it's often used incorrectly. It requires a healthy level of humility and amazing focus at all levels of an enterprise.

That's why it's so much harder to perfect than many realize. The smallest quality control problems—a defective part from a small supplier, an equipment failure on the factory line, or even a simple mistake made by a tired worker—can wipe out much of the profits and cash flow of an entire shift, day, month, or even quarter. It takes great discipline and commitment to develop a culture of excellence, one that executes at the highest level. Over time those small improvements add up to massive change.

DRIVING CASH FLOW

From the beginning, the Rales brothers and their young but rising-star finance chief (Allender) were adept at cash management, managing their debt levels and bank relationships. In fact, cash flow was what most attracted the Raleses to Lean in the first place, because it freed up cash stuck in inventory and exposed inefficient arrangements with suppliers and customers. In the 1980s companies in America were just beginning to focus on "new" metrics, like ROIC (return on invested capital). With less inventory, faster cycle times, less rework, and lower warranty costs due to higher-quality products, factories could substantially boost their returns on capital. Rising cash flow and rising ROIC were nearly perfectly correlated.

Even though Danaher was a young company in the late 1980s, it was already a half decade ahead of its American and European peers—and closing the gap with Japanese competitors.

With the unexpected success at Jacobs, the Raleses aimed for bigger acquisitions where Lean could be applied. But banks were naturally risk averse, and debt markets on Wall Street were still emerging, which brought Danaher into the world of junk bonds. After an introductory meeting with junk bond king Michael Milken, the Danaher team decided that junk bonds would supply the next stage of growth.

In the late 1980s, junk bonds fueled both growth successes and debt excesses—and Milken was the gatekeeper. Companies now had a new tool to fund aggressive plans. Investors rushed to the higher yields provided. History shines a negative light on this era, but like anything else, there was both good and bad. While Danaher insiders credit the company's shrewd acquisitions and Lean manufacturing for its success today, most also say that junk bonds enabled the company to grow much faster than it otherwise would have at this crucial stage. In the late 1980s industrial assets were for sale on the cheap, but banks viewed these acquisitions as very risky. Even though junk bonds had high coupon debt levels, the returns on the deals were proportionally much higher. This new market fit Danaher's early needs perfectly.

In those early years, Danaher acquired businesses considered solid, yet poorly run and in need of very hands-on management support. Deal prices were low, partly due to the high interest rates at the time, but also because the age of conglomeration was passing and big companies were more likely to shed than acquire assets. Private equity was still in its infancy, and the concept of growth via acquisition was also still quite new. As a result, Danaher had few rival bidders, which made the deal math quite advantageous. From 1984 to 1990, Danaher bought 12 companies, mostly gritty B2B businesses such as Matco Tools, Qualitrol, and Veeder-Root. The returns on those deals were exceptional.

Just as importantly, Danaher passed on many other marginal transactions and didn't get overly carried away with debt, despite its availability. Insiders credit the finance chief Allender for keeping everyone grounded and bringing risk controls to the forefront as this young company was experiencing such rapid growth. He was quick to remind his bosses that one bad deal could unwind all their newfound credibility. Heightened risk management is a Danaher trait that lives on in today's culture.

EXPANDING THE DBS TOOLKIT

Though successful in its early days, it wasn't until the 1990s that the Danaher of today came into clearer focus. High debt levels, a cooling economy, and the notable stock market crash in the late 1980s had led to shareholder angst and prompted the Raleses to seek a more broadly experienced operator as CEO. The brothers lured George Sherman, who ran the tools business of Black & Decker, to become CEO of Danaher. (See Figure 4.1.)

Black & Decker was known for having exceptional sales and marketing teams with excellent customer relationships, something that Danaher was still developing. Once at Danaher, Sherman built the infrastructure needed to grow from the 1980s base and expanded the DBS toolkit to supplier- and customer-facing functions. Sherman didn't want to invite bureaucracy, but the rapidly growing company needed central staff for strategic planning, accounting, tax, human resources, investor relations, and acquisitions.

Danaher's mantra of "We compete for shareholders" came from both Sherman's and Allender's view that without a strong stock price and shareholder support, the entire growth model was at risk, particularly in a recession. (Danaher today remains one of the most focused investor communications companies on the planet.) Sherman didn't believe in just delivering the numbers and hoping that shareholders would show up. He left little to chance. He believed in actively courting and supporting shareholders and analysts. Over time Danaher built one of the most loyal shareholder bases ever compiled, allowing it to grow even more aggressively and to utilize equity capital (i.e., selling more shares) when needed.

All this, in turn, paid off for shareholders. During Sherman's 11-year tenure at Danaher that ended in 2001, the stock returned a 26 percent CAGR, more than double the still impressive 10 percent for the S&P 500. Revenues grew 350 percent from $845 million to $3.8 billion as higher-quality assets were added. Sustainable jobs were created as the employee count went from 7,000 to 23,000. Key acquisitions included Fluke, maker of electrical testing equipment, a major

Figure 4.1: **The early years and George Sherman era (1981–2001).**

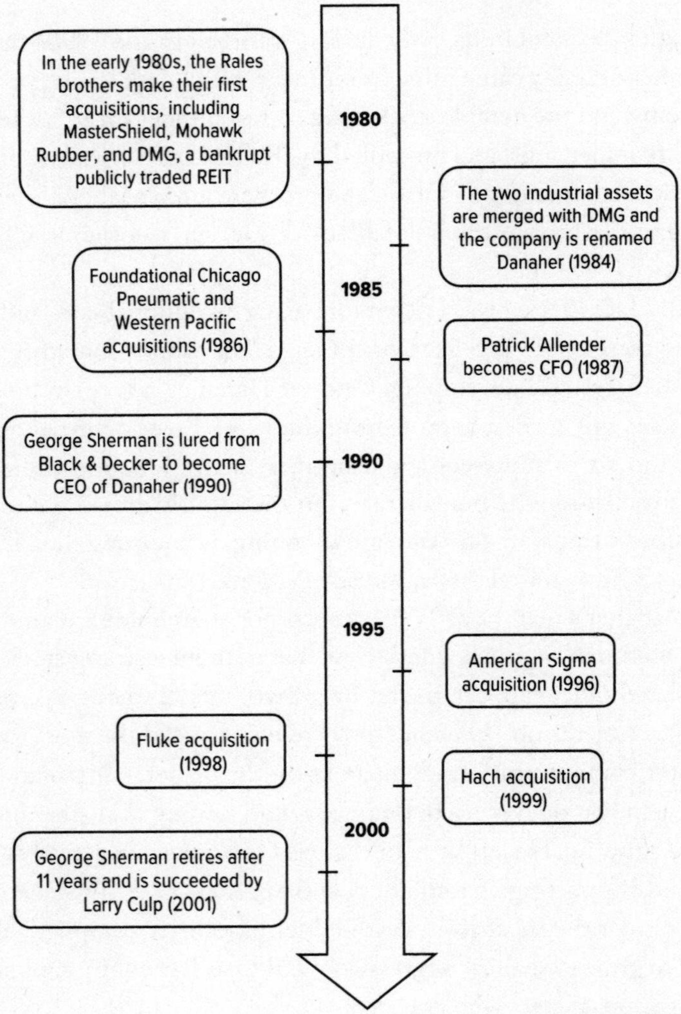

1980
In the early 1980s, the Rales brothers make their first acquisitions, including MasterShield, Mohawk Rubber, and DMG, a bankrupt publicly traded REIT
The two industrial assets are merged with DMG and the company is renamed Danaher (1984)
1985
Foundational Chicago Pneumatic and Western Pacific acquisitions (1986)
Patrick Allender becomes CFO (1987)
1990
George Sherman is lured from Black & Decker to become CEO of Danaher (1990)
1995
American Sigma acquisition (1996)
Fluke acquisition (1998)
Hach acquisition (1999)
2000
George Sherman retires after 11 years and is succeeded by Larry Culp (2001)

Source: Danaher filings, press reports

turnaround story, and the Hach and Lange water assets that remain high quality brands to this day.

Where Sherman turned the Raleses' batch of businesses into a strong holding company, his successor, Larry Culp, brought Danaher into the modern age. (See Figure 4.2.) Culp was hired right out of

Figure 4.2: **The Larry Culp (2001–2014) and Tom Joyce (2015–present) eras.**

Larry Culp becomes CEO (2001)
Videojet and Gilbarco acquisitions (2002)
2003
Radiometer and Gendex acquisitions (2004)
Pat Allender retires, succeeded by Dan Comas (2005)
Leica Microsystems acquisition (2005)
2007
Tektronix acquisition (2007)
Danaher forms Apex JV with Cooper for its legacy tools businesses (2010)
Beckman Coulter acquisition (2011)
2011
Larry Culp retires after 14 years and is succeeded by Tom Joyce (2014)
Pall acquisition, then the largest in the company's history at $14 billion (2015)
2015
Cepheid acquisition and spin-off of Fortive (2016)
Dan Comas retires, succeeded by Matt McGrew (2018)
Envista dental partial IPO (2019)
2019
GE Biopharma acquisition for $20 billion (2020)

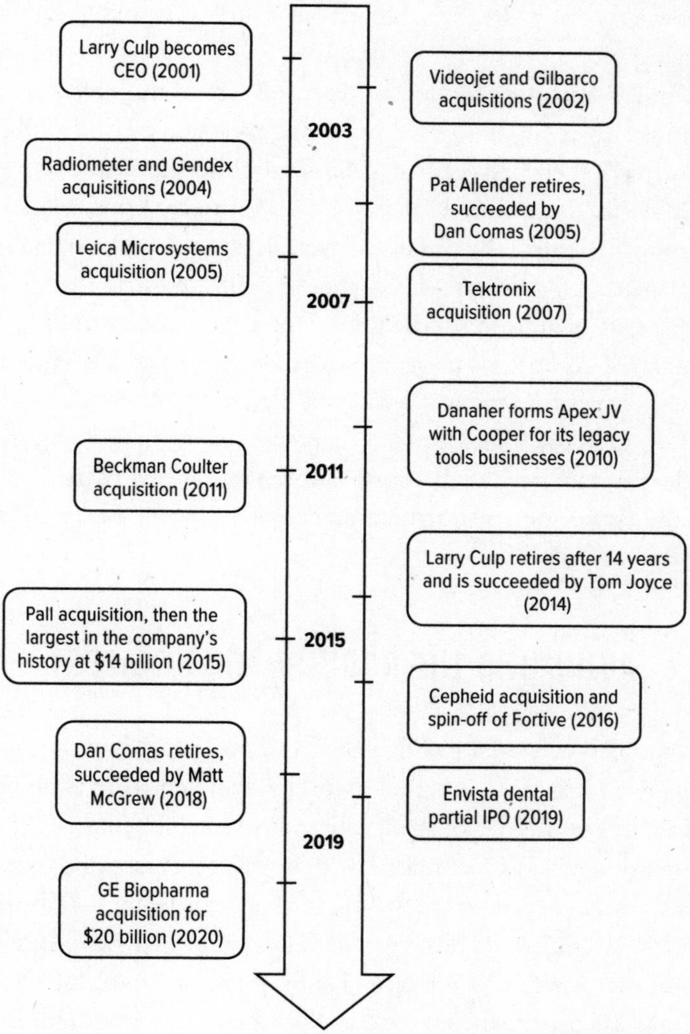

Source: Danaher filings, press reports

Harvard Business School, and insiders say he was groomed for the top job from day one. The brothers, then and today, are champions of humility, integrity, and transparency, and Culp embodied all those qualities. As they aggressively promoted continuous improvement, they sought capable people who saw flaws in themselves and in the organization enough to keep pushing to get better. Leaders inclined to believe they had already achieved great success would lack this bias for change.

Under Culp, their model faced greater tests than ever. His tenure was unusually volatile, with the humbling recession of 2001–2002, the high-growth recovery years of 2003–2007, and the severe downturn in 2008–2009. Extreme highs and lows in macro conditions made the company realize the pitfalls of cyclical businesses. Danaher's success also attracted imitators, many of which hired Danaher veterans to drive that agenda. With the growth of private equity funds, as well as industrial companies pressured to grow with peers, Danaher faced serious competition for acquisitions. Culp credits Allender for bridging the gap in the CEO transition and providing the continuity that was desperately needed in those formative first few years. But even with the established infrastructure, the odds were stacked against the 38-year-old Culp.

ADJUSTING THE ACQUISITION STRATEGY

Sherman had created amazing value, and now Culp had to grow the company on a larger base and in a world in which globalization threatened the very existence of American industrial companies. Folks were rightly asking, "Was Danaher just a product of farsighted entrepreneurs?" With competitors now fully awake to the benefits of Lean and the use of leverage to do deals, would Danaher now have to accept "normal" returns or worse? Culp faced hands-on bosses: most CEOs today also serve as board chair, but the Rales brothers wouldn't relinquish that title. They had entrusted him with their baby, as well as a big chunk of their assets. He also faced the high expectations of shareholders who wanted the already expensive share price (25x P/E versus an unusually high market P/E of 22x) to keep rising. The pressure was high.

Culp rose to the occasion and excelled. Danaher stock returned 485 percent in his tenure versus the S&P 500 return of 60 percent, even better than his predecessor. That performance is all the more impressive given how the technology world took over global stock markets and that Danaher's assets were plain vanilla industrial.

Much of Culp's success can be traced to three important initiatives: (1) He worked with the board on a portfolio of businesses that exploited all the powers of DBS. (2) Unlike leaders who prefer to hire those who aren't a threat, he increased the organization's focus on talent and surrounded himself with people who would keep up with his fast pace. (3) He pushed DBS deeper into the organization. He and his colleagues developed an expanded toolkit touching every facet of the company.

A NEW ACQUISITION STRATEGY: MID-GROWTH BUSINESSES

Within a few years of taking over, Culp became convinced of the need to change the portfolio with a revamped acquisition strategy. Not only was it getting harder to land the best deals, but shareholders preferred a steadier acquisition stream. The company found that Lean manufacturing, and productivity in general, worked best in companies with steady growth, neither high nor low. As Jack Welch at GE realized in his early days with Six Sigma, the ideal unit volume growth cadence for rising productivity is somewhere between 4 and 6 percent. A higher rate can work but requires putting a lot more capital in place, often at a lower return.

At its best, Lean and other productivity tools allow a company to add 2 to 3 percent of manufacturing capacity without adding equipment, people, or footprint—it's "free" capacity. With intensive, but not usually that expensive, up-front training to implement Lean, a growing manufacturer can therefore supply 2 to 3 percent more revenue with limited extra cost. The result is a higher ROI on the factory assets. With a little bit of capital to keep equipment up to date or enable the productivity that can come with software investments, the result is even more reasonable cost capacity. Taking the 2 to 3 percent "free" up to 4 to 6 percent in total.

Above that 4–6 percent growth range, you lose many of the benefits of Lean, as overtime wages are often required and supply chain partners struggle to keep pace. You make suboptimal decisions just to get goods out the door. Slow or negative growth that comes with a recession becomes even more problematic. If you resort to layoffs to offset the weaker demand, then you're dismissing people trained in Lean and immersed in your culture—which will mightily discourage remaining employees from adopting the best practices so needed to get there in the first place.

Under those conditions, with two otherwise identical businesses, buying the highly cyclical company is going to generate less value for Danaher than the steadier, less cyclical one. Nothing was more frustrating to Culp than getting a company fully ramped up on Lean, only to see a recession unwind so much of the hard work, so he pushed for a change in the type of assets that he wanted to acquire.

Culp's best solution was to focus on businesses with high aftermarket content—selling the installed base equipment that pulled through a steady stream of consumables required to keep the equipment running. For Danaher, the up-front hardware could be a tad cyclical as long as the aftermarket consumables were steady. The deals under Culp's tenure included Videojet (industrial printers that needed ink), Radiometer (imaging equipment), Vision Systems (medical instruments), ChemTreat (water treatment), AB Sciex (measurement equipment), and Beckman Coulter (testing equipment).

These assets were a bit more expensive than the traditional cyclical deal book, but Culp took on low-cost debt as an offset—not just from lower interest rates, but from the rating agencies' realization that Danaher was a cash flow machine. Another benefit from reducing cyclicality was that the market was willing to pay a premium for a Danaher stock with less variability. Culp saw that trend early—and got the Rales brothers and the board to agree to a strategy of paying more for the right kind of assets.

This shift in acquisition strategy generated enormous value, particularly since the new assets worked so well with Lean. Most corporate buyers fixate on either higher-growth game-changing transactions or deals that serve to consolidate their markets. But Culp went after solid assets—healthcare, dental, and testing equipment firms that often flew a bit under the radar—not high growth, and often very niche, which meant they didn't fit well with other strategic buyers. He also avoided low-growth businesses, however attractive the price, as the benefits of DBS would largely be wasted.

Separately Culp came to understand that DBS worked better with businesses with a high gross margin, especially those with a big spread between gross and operating margins. The wider the spread, the more opportunity for Danaher to take costs out with DBS. Culp had learned through operating experience that it was easier to improve the gross margin of a high-margin company versus a low-margin one. Low margins usually meant that customers saw the product as low value. Culp's judgment ran against the consensus view, as M&A bankers and business schools often presented low-margin businesses as opportunities, particularly for those good at taking out costs.

A RENEWED FOCUS ON TALENT

Under Culp's leadership, Danaher also worked more on attracting, retaining, and developing people. He realized early on that to succeed in a more competitive world, he needed more than a business system. He needed the type of people who worked well within that specific system, those committed to continuous improvement as a way of life.

DBS itself helped ordinary people execute at far higher levels. Culp was early in understanding that he wasn't going to have countless stars in his organization, so getting the average employee to perform a tad better than average had a big multiplier effect. But Culp also saw that many of the more critical roles did require very high-end talent—notably in the small corporate office where influence could be outsized, such as CFO, M&A, HR, investor relations, legal, and tax. These roles were rising in importance as the size and complexity of the company increased. In a world where capital was becoming easier to access, private equity was increasingly driving up deal valuations, which meant that execution levels needed to be higher than ever. The corporate folks involved in deal execution and integration needed to be exceptional, so Culp sought to build up that talent level to match the increasing needs of the organization.

PROCESS IN EVERYTHING

Culp knew that the DBS toolkit itself needed to be modernized, which largely meant adding tools that other organizations had developed and modifying them for Danaher's needs. These included funnel management in sales, value engineering, voice of the customer, value pricing, and procurement and logistics tools, which were adopted for nearly every Danaher function.

The commonality of those tools was not just in focusing staff and setting benchmarks to best in class, but in standardizing processes and adding predictability in a world that was becoming less predictable overall. A sales tool that helps a representative go from averaging three client visits per day to four client visits per day, for example, by cutting out waste and digitizing the sales process, has a huge impact on an organization with a large sales staff. Procurement managers who have a standardized approach to certifying suppliers will likely waste less time and bring more efficiency through the entire supply chain. R&D heads who start the new product development process around the explicit needs of the customer will likely waste less time in commercializing their innovations.

Culp wanted process in everything. He wanted no waste. Emails had to be to the point, with only the necessary folks cc'd. To prevent bureaucracy creep, he limited most meetings to 30 minutes, often done while standing. Simple visualization tools were encouraged, and daily management was emphasized.

It was no longer enough for Danaher to excel with Lean and smart M&A. Culp wanted every function and every employee living the culture of continuous improvement, and he put in the work to make it happen. He traveled constantly, immersing himself in the details of each business, helping to solve problems. He measured managers not just on results but on the how and why—sustainability over time, management of talent, and commitment to transparency. The result was a deeply rooted culture of pervasive improvement.

The company still made mistakes. In fact, the beauty of Danaher is how well it recognizes and accepts its mistakes. A dental franchise that never lived up to its potential, and the 2007 Tektronix deal that closed right before the economy fell off the cliff, are two examples. But with the prevailing discipline of the organization, those mistakes were never more than a blip. What could have sunk a less evolved organization became a learning experience for Danaher managers.

A larger challenge came, ironically, from the vast success the organization had achieved in its rapid growth. As the company grew to enormous size, Culp and his colleagues struggled to scale up their personalized "roll-up-your-sleeves" approach to fixing problems. A more global company required more long-distance travel through multiple time zones. Investors increasingly sought his time as Danaher's relevance in the S&P 500 grew. Larger meant more people to manage and recruit, and Culp's calendar filled up with interviews and people reviews. A bigger Danaher also meant more deals to vet, more complex assets to integrate, and just more to do, period. Culp was a deep-in-the-weeds, detail-oriented type of leader. He became quite good at delegating, but the workload was escalating.

It's not hard to imagine that working for the demanding Raleses and trying to run an aggressive M&A playbook would become overwhelming over time. It's impossible to know why top executives or elite athletes step aside while still in their prime. What makes them elite is often the ability to bring 100 percent effort every day. And that in itself is a grind that usually proves unsustainable. In any event, in 2014 the still relatively young Culp (then age 52) announced his retirement, the only CEO whom most shareholders and employees had known. Culp's answer to the "why now" question posed above is that he had accomplished even more than he had set out to do, had made more than enough money on his stock options to retire wealthy, and had a more-than-ready replacement in Tom Joyce waiting in the wings. Culp's accomplishments over 15 years place him among the most elite of CEOs. He was exceptional by any stakeholder measure. (See Figures 4.3–4.6.)

Figure 4.3: **Revenue change under Larry Culp.**

$20 billion
Up 425%
$4 billion
2001
2014

Source: Danaher filings

Figure 4.4: **Earnings per share change under Larry Culp.**

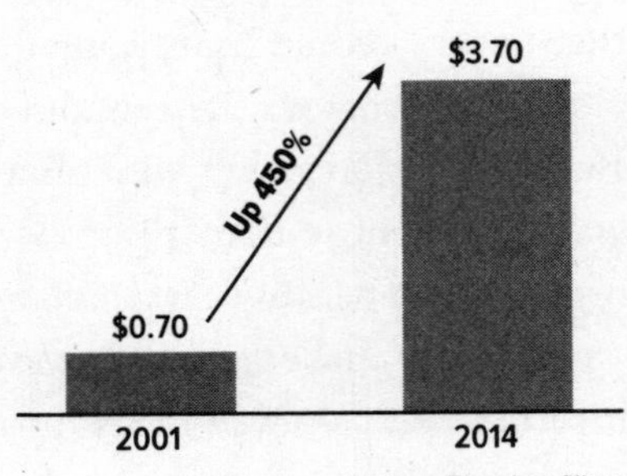

Source: Danaher filings

Figure 4.5: **Head-count change under Larry Culp.**

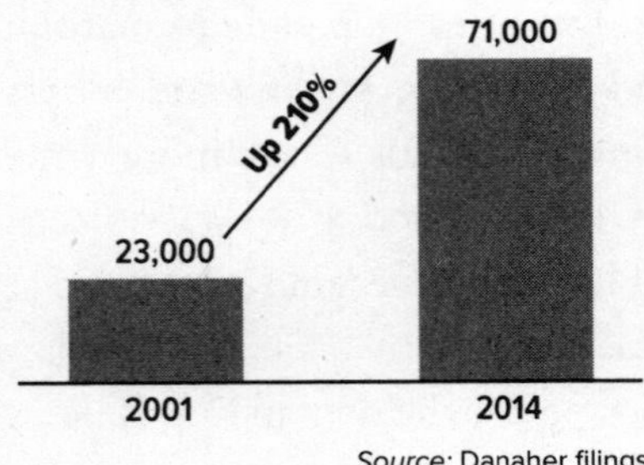

Source: Danaher filings

Figure 4.6: **Stock price change under Larry Culp.**

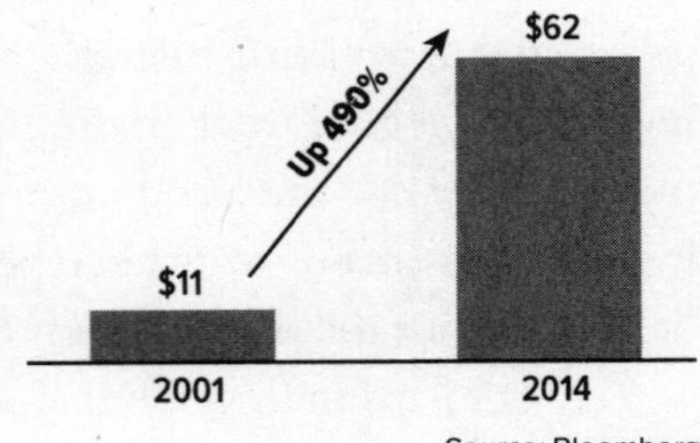

Source: Bloomberg

DANAHER AFTER CULP

By the time Culp retired, the economy was fully recovered from the financial crisis, banks were lending, and capital markets were functioning normally again—meaning Danaher faced an even more competitive M&A landscape. Increasingly, the company seemed to have a foot in two separate eras: its industrial past versus its healthcare future.

The portfolio suddenly seemed out of step with a market that was moving toward either very high-growth technology stories or more stable and focused pure plays.

To deal with the portfolio problem, the board and the new CEO decided to split the company into two. The vision was that Danaher proper kept the businesses that had razor/razorblade characteristics, those connected to healthcare, water, and product ID (printing). The other, more conventionally industrial assets were spun off into a new holding company, dubbed Fortive. Shareholders were surprised but quickly became comfortable with the move, or at least comfortable with the leadership and the cultures that defined these organizations.

The Rales brothers' top two management talents, Tom Joyce and Jim Lico, were already well-known rising stars, and if there ever was an ideal time to break up the company, 2015–2016 was it. A bull market combined with rising healthcare stock valuations made for compelling math. And the prevailing view was that with Joyce now tapped to run Danaher, if a bigger job wasn't created for Lico, the enterprise would risk losing him to an outside CEO offer. Lico had successfully run several of the businesses that were to be spun off, and he had run Danaher's DBS effort overall. He was perfect to take what was considered a less attractive set of businesses and capture investor interest through aggressive M&A efforts.

As for Danaher, the Rales brothers had tremendous confidence in Tom Joyce, who had joined the company many years earlier, in 1989, from Arthur Andersen. Joyce was similar to Culp in personality, intellect, and demeanor, but was more willing to make big acquisitions and be less hands-on with them afterward. And just as Culp had taken Danaher in a different direction from Sherman, Joyce was ready to remake it as a healthcare company with an intense focus on internal growth. M&A would still be critical, but only if it were additive to the growth rate of the existing organization. In the spirit of a company willing to completely reinvent itself, Danaher would now be a more traditional growth company. This was in sharp contrast to its more historic roots, first as a value buyer and then as a mid-growth cash flow machine. In that context, Joyce wanted more process and accountability around new products and closer customer connectivity to align product development with customer needs.

Joyce's résumé at Danaher is still in process, but over the more than five years since taking the role, he has proved to be the right choice. Besides managing the successful spin-off of Fortive and then later the spin-off of Danaher's dental assets, called Envista, he has aggressively grown the portfolio. His first big deal was the purchase of Pall Corporation, which makes filtration products for biotechnology companies, and at $14 billion was Danaher's largest transaction ever at the time. Joyce went on to buy high-flying Cepheid, a maker of molecular diagnostic equipment, for $4 billion. And in early 2020 he took on GE's Biopharma division, ironically from his former boss, Culp, who had gone on to run that conglomerate. That one had a whopping $20 billion price tag that takes Danaher deeper into the high-growth biotechnology space.

The debate about Joyce's ultimate success remains open for sure. But so far, the growth rate and execution of deals seem to support the higher acquisition prices he paid, all of which have been fueled by lower interest rates overall. In Danaher's junk bond days, it would commonly pay 10 percent to finance a deal on which it hoped to earn a minimum of 15 percent. In today's world, financing costs often fall below 3 percent, so to get the same investment impact, the return wouldn't have to be much more than 8 percent. On the GE Biopharma deal, Danaher was able to finance the debt at sub 1 percent—an unprecedented funding cost level. Simple math supports Joyce's more aggressive growth strategy. The deals are earning about the same net return spread as they did two decades ago but with less cyclical risk. An early look at the GE deal points to even higher than the historical average. In the Joyce era, growth on these higher-quality asset platforms is critical. And DBS and its metrics will ultimately adjust to support the new goals.

THE OUTSIZED VALUE CONTRIBUTION OF TWO STAR CFOS

We noted earlier the importance of Pat Allender, a CFO who played a huge role in Danaher's early to mid-growth stage. He was often credited by insiders for keeping the company's risk levels in check and focusing the entity on the highest-return opportunities, all while helping to advance DBS. These contributions cannot be understated. The Danaher that most know today, however, was more heavily influenced by Allender's replacement.

Dan Comas came to Danaher in 1991 in an M&A role and became CFO in 2005. He was well pedigreed with degrees, from Georgetown and Stanford, and had a reputation for intelligence and a rational thought process. Throughout his career at Danaher he closed more than 250 deals worth more than $45 billion, an astounding level of volume. His contributions to M&A alone could be considered his greatest achievement. Just as notably, he worked with Culp to take DBS from the factory floor into the corporate office. He was particularly impactful in simplifying the company's benchmarking and performance review efforts, which by the time he took over the CFO role, had become stifling.

In 1991 the company tracked just about everything it could, including at least 50 financial metrics that it used for performance appraisals and compensation. Comas found it overwhelming and unhelpful, and through many kaizen events and iterations, he narrowed down the focus to eight core metrics. Just four were financial: organic growth, margins, cash flow, and ROIC. Another two of the metrics related to the customer experience: on-time delivery and quality measured by defects/million. And the last two involved people: internal job fill rate and retention. Danaher still uses these eight simple metrics to measure manager performance and benchmarks across the organization and within specific regions, metrics we would consider a best practice overall. (See Figure 4.7.)

Figure 4.7: **Danaher's eight metrics.**

Financial	Customer	Talent
Organic revenue growth	Quality (external parts per million)*	Internal fill rate
Operating margin expansion	On-time delivery	Retention
Cash flow/working capital turns		
Return on invested capital		

* Refers to product defect rates.

Source: Danaher

Insiders also credit Comas with fine-tuning Danaher's M&A diligence and integration processes. When Danaher acquires a company, it usually replaces the CFO and immediately tracks the metrics that cross-compare with those of other Danaher businesses. Comas made a point of asking, "Now that the deal is closed, please tell us everything that you failed to tell us during diligence." He believed that things always go wrong in a deal; what distinguishes the good from the bad deals are the speed and permanence of the fixes. He put the people and processes in place to make sure the bad news traveled more quickly. Danaher also tracks the ROIC and other seven key metrics for the transaction each month for three years, and longer for the biggest deals.

Comas retired from the CFO role in 2018, well before his expiration date, and was succeeded by another talented young insider, Matt McGrew. We highlight the importance Danaher placed on its talent in the top finance job because it is a key differentiator in the outsized success of the company. In fact, most of our successful case studies had notable talent in the CFO seat. And just the opposite in our failure case studies. Failure often came down to lack of risk controls, lack of growth in free cash flow, and the inability to manage capital allocation overall. All issues heavily impacted at the CFO level. Danaher, with its star power in the finance ranks, freed up its high-performing operating heads to stay focused on the main core value drivers.

THE DANAHER BUSINESS SYSTEM IN CONTEXT

While effective leaders are essential, Danaher's success rests ultimately on the powerful system that guides everyone there each day. Although the basic commitment to Lean thinking and continuous improvement sounds easy, it is quite hard to execute. It's a journey, not a destination, and most cultures look for explicit goal lines. The result is that people focus on that goal line, rather than continuous improvement itself, and once that goal is achieved, the improvement stops. Most Lean-based companies have starts and stops and struggle to maintain focus, particularly through management changes and cyclical dynamics. Business gets hard, and Lean falls by the wayside. Business gets good again, and Lean is thrown out for risk of missing a customer order. There are always excuses. It is so much harder than it seems.

We've seen Danaher's approach up close and personal for many years, with tours of its factories around the world, countless meetings with management, and hundreds of hours analyzing financials. We kept looking for holes in the story. But over and over in our meetings with Danaher employees the consistency of answers to our questions is impressive. DBS is real. It focuses employees, it drives positive outcomes, and it facilitates a culture that encourages leaders to develop the next generation and leave before their effectiveness declines. It pragmatically embraces external hires and the tools they often bring from prior workplaces. Danaher says it is a shameless adopter of others' best practices, because DBS isn't good enough, never will be good enough, and will always have to change.

We just can't think of another company that exhibits that level of paranoia after such a track record of success or that shows such a willingness to experiment, tweak, and rapidly change. Of course, those experiments often fail, and that willingness to risk failure to change is the point. Truly exceptional people and cultures seem to understand that reinvention is critical in order to continue to thrive. At Danaher, DBS drives constant change and nurtures a culture that embraces such change.

THE DANAHER BUSINESS SYSTEM TODAY

DBS starts with productivity on the factory floor and works its way up the organization. Strong factory operations are table stakes in nearly every industry that has reached some level of maturity. For example, manufacturing excellence didn't matter in Apple's early days when it was completely dominant, but with rising global smartphone competition, it sure does now. It doesn't matter much when pharmaceuticals are under patent protection, but it sure matters when those patents expire and generics come into play. Elon Musk at Tesla knew early on that his vision would fall apart without exceptional manufacturing capabilities. When Tesla has struggled, problems with manufacturing were at the heart of the challenge. As simple as manufacturing excellence sounds, the reality is quite different—and that makes it all the more critical in differentiating a cost base.

DBS as a Lean-based system will likely always be a part of Danaher. In fact, as Danaher has sought higher growth and been willing to pay up for deals, factory floor exceptionalism becomes all the more a base-case minimum. The margin for error becomes smaller. When you pay high prices for a deal, the last thing in the world you can afford to do is inject even more capital into the asset. DBS frees up square footage in facilities and allows for free or low-cost capacity additions.

On the other hand, as Danaher has sought higher gross margin assets, the cost opportunity has increasingly been outside of manufacturing, and that's where the evolution of DBS has been most pronounced. Driving efficiency in sales and marketing then becomes crucial for the deal model overall—and Danaher has developed matching tools.

In Danaher's earlier days it would describe progress in driving DBS into an acquisition by talking about working capital turns, on-time delivery statistics, and safety. Now it's just as common for the company to comment on sales productivity with an emphasis on funnel management as Danaher converts its sales mentality from "farmer" to "hunter." It can take a while for that difference to sink in. "Hunter" implies greater focus on generating leads and working the sales funnel versus just servicing existing customers. Given the razor/razor blade nature of nearly all Danaher's businesses today, each new customer brings a very high present value calculation. The world at present is infatuated with the concept of customer acquisition cost, the tech world in particular. But how about holding on to that customer? If Danaher treats a customer well and makes it sticky, the company will be rewarded with years of high-margin consumables. As Joyce has pushed Danaher faster into growth mode, tools like digital marketing and the voice of the customer in new product development become all the more important.

Danaher's productivity tools are a collection of best practices, a collection that keeps growing and is divided by function. Some practices focus on costs, and others drive growth. And in any acquisition, there may be only one or two tools introduced to the new entity in the first year. The tools themselves are largely a function of aptitude, how far along the business has progressed with DBS.

There are notable commonalities in the tools, however, that make them easier to add once the basics are taught. Almost all incorporate some form of visual management. Danaher offices are plastered with Post-it notes, large worksheet paper is marked with different-color pens, and timelines typically resemble more of an eighth grade history project than a sophisticated company. Danaher believes that project management requires some form of visual aid, and that regular (but short) meetings should be held in front of the visual aid.

For example, every Danaher acquisition has a war room with timelines, maps, and checklists. Responsibilities are clearly noted, and if someone is falling behind, the red ink denotes that as an area of focus. Bad news travels fast, accountability is maximized, and the successful completion of tasks is noted. The feedback loop is nothing that email or Excel could accomplish. Visual management is a simple yet powerful tool.

Lean is based on identifying standard work and maximizing workflow. Repeatable functions are easily measured, and what's measured can usually be improved. All non–factory floor functions have some element of standard work, and DBS requires that each step be written down and that some level of value mapping needs to occur. A typical kaizen project will require doing some prework to identify standard work, and then getting a group together to brainstorm ideas on how to make it more efficient. Kaizen itself just seems like a superorganized, time-limited, low-expectation brainstorming session—with the goal of immediately implementing incremental yet permanent improvements.

Danaher insiders describe the process as kaizen/implement, and then rinse/repeat. Small increments of improvement, done in steps, become large increments of improvement over time. For example, value engineering kaizens may focus on reducing the number of parts of a product to simplify it, or standardizing parts with other SKUs. Kaizens in procurement could be for something as small as streamlining contract language, to full-blown efforts to improve some element of the supply chain, all done with little steps over time. Other companies have called it the power of 1 percent, which is another way to focus an entity on small incremental improvements that are easier to implement than more disruptive steps. The process is just more effective and sustainable.

PREFERRING PROCESS OVER CREATIVITY

From a hiring perspective, Danaher screens for character traits as much as talent. The company favors humility, as humble people are more likely to adopt the entire cultural concept of continuous improvement. Transparency is also critical to Danaher, as well as team-oriented players. The focus on character traits helps HR increase its hit rate of recruiting excellent prospects, filter talent successfully, and compensate high achievers to remain motivated and drive up retention. To find the traits it favors, Danaher uses an outside consultant to administer a personality test as well as something similar to an IQ test. The consultant is entrusted to give a thumbs-up or -down opinion.

Which begs the question, does Danaher just hire process-driven people with less interest in creativity? The answer on a historical basis is yes. Sometimes art is lost when you focus on process, and you create robots instead of leaders. Danaher is well aware of that shortcoming, and today's growth playbook tries to find balance. Having creative minds in R&D, for example, is now a higher priority. And DBS growth tools do require a more diverse, right brain–versus–left employee base. But for much of the rest of Danaher, process is too important for them to take the risk of swinging the pendulum too far away from the core process-driven culture.

HR at Danaher works on developing managers and pays just as much attention to the "how and why" as to outward performance. A manager who gets results but fails to develop a successor, for example, will be passed up for promotion. Talent development is mandatory, and a manager who scores poorly on employee engagement is on the way out. Danaher believes that people normally quit because of bad managers, not because of pay. If it sees unusually high turnover or some degradation in employee engagement, the manager is usually the root cause. In fact, Danaher sees high employee turnover as a lagging indicator, so the pressure to catch bad actors early is high. Performance reviews go beyond the core Danaher metrics to cover hard-to-measure aspects such as team building, leadership through DBS, and one's success in "charting the course."

Danaher is one of the more time-intensive HR organizations we've ever seen, all because it believes bad managers have a terrible impact that can last long after they are gone. On the positive side, the efforts and willingness to get rid of bad managers, even those with strong near-term results, will result in building culture. Employees see accountability at the highest levels, and that matters. All that accountability, though, requires time, with lots of on-site visits and discussions with all levels of staff.

Another HR differentiator is onboarding. Danaher's new hires (above a certain organizational level) go through a two to three-month immersion program during which they are not yet allowed to do their jobs. Instead they visit factories and facilities, sit in meetings unrelated to their role, and learn DBS and its tools. The company fully integrates them into the system without distraction.

This time investment is unique and tells recruits from day one that Danaher is interested in them for the long term. Furthermore, the immersion process itself has a filtering impact. Its intensity leads some to discover that "this company just isn't for me." For HR, exiting someone quickly who doesn't embrace DBS is a victory.

This unusually high investment in HR pays off in developing leaders who deliver exceptional results without the common breakdowns in integrity we often see in peers. Danaher is known for factory excellence, but having good people in place, with a strong culture to guide them, is what maintains this excellence over time.

THE OLD DANAHER IS THE NEW FORTIVE

For many long-time Danaher followers, Fortive looks far more familiar than today's largely healthcare-focused Danaher. And it should. Fortive was spun out in 2016 with many of the legacy Danaher industrial assets, such as Fluke, Tektronix, Gilbarco Veeder-Root, and Matco Tools. (See Figure 4.8.) These are solid, well-run businesses, but they largely lack the consumable aftermarket traits that Danaher had increasingly sought, and with the cyclicality that Danaher was increasingly trying to avoid. The revenue base was still large enough to scale out a legitimate company, and the market cap was big enough to garner investor attention. In any event, it was a divorce from Danaher. (See Figures 4.9 and 4.10.) When given a clean sheet of paper as a spun-out company, what part of the Danaher culture and the business system that defined that culture would Fortive keep, and what would it change?

The answer is that Fortive kept all the core tenets of DBS, but that's not the end of the story. The company is pushing even harder toward a more evolved version—in true Danaher form. This is not a total surprise, as the lion's share of the leadership at Fortive, including CEO Jim Lico, who as we noted above, came from Danaher.

Figure 4.8: **Fortive's businesses.**

Business	Year Acquired	Description
Matco Tools	1986	Mechanic tool distribution
Hennessy	1986	Wheel service equipment
Qualitrol	1986	Electric utility condition monitoring
Veeder-Root	1989	Retail fueling underground tank gauging
Fluke	1998	Handheld test and measurement equipment
Pacific Scientific EMC	1998	Energetic materials for aerospace/defense
Gems	1998	Pressure, level, and flow instrumentation
Invetech	2000	Healthcare/diagnostics product development
Setra	2001	Pressure, acceleration, and weight sensors
Gilbarco	2002	Retail fueling gas dispensers
Anderson-Negele	2004	Hygienic sensors for food and life sciences
Tektronix	2007	Oscilloscopes for testing/product development
Teletrac	2013	GPS tracking and fleet management software
Navman	2013	Fleet and asset management technology
Industrial Scientific	2017	Portable gas detection equipment
Landauer	2017	Radiation measurement and monitoring
Gordian	2018	Construction cost data and software
Accruent	2018	Facility and asset management software
Advanced Sterilization Products	2019	Sterilization/disinfection equipment for hospitals

Source: Fortive filings, press reports

Figure 4.9: **Change in revenue since spin-off.**

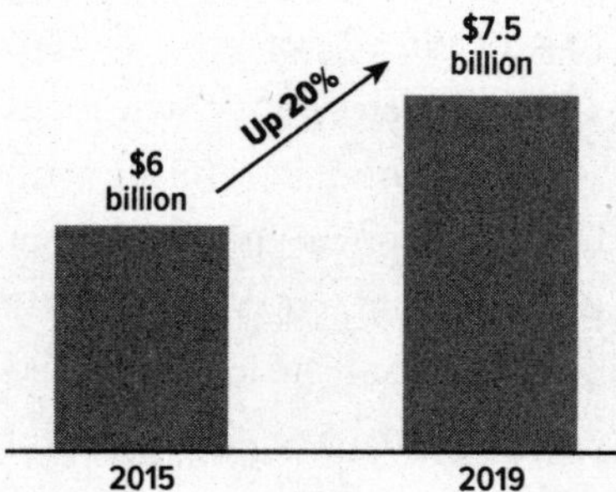

Note: Data is pro forma for JNJ Advanced Sterilization Products acquisition.

Source: Fortive filings

Figure 4.10: **Change in earnings per share since spin-off.**

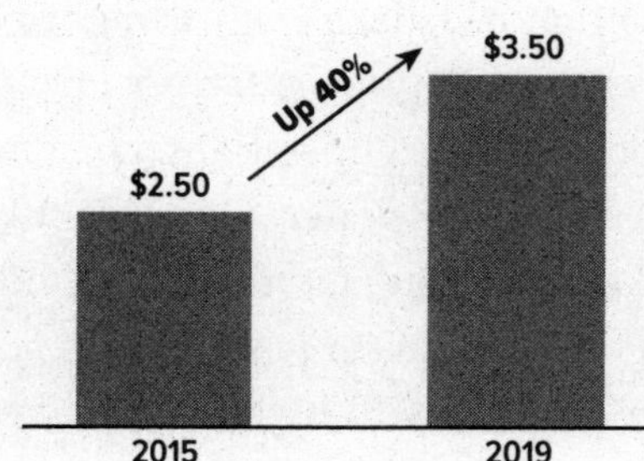

Source: Fortive filings

Lico, whom we mentioned earlier, joined Danaher in 1996 and rose through the ranks with a reputation as an exceptional operator and solid leader. Given that Fortive's portfolio includes most of Danaher's original industrial assets, it's no surprise that Lean is an essential part of Fortive's version of DBS—now called FBS. Fortive insiders describe their adherence to the process as more intense. It runs deeper and comes with different expectations, all driven by a deep-seated commitment to continuous improvement. Lico is quick to explain that the Fortive culture, like Danaher's, requires three key attributes: humility, transparency, and high expectations. And that part of the culture can never change.

Like Danaher, Fortive is changing its portfolio, utilizing cash flow to move it up the quality and growth curve by acquiring businesses that generally have higher gross margins and aftermarket revenues. This evolution is driving change in the FBS toolkit overall: tools for innovation and software development are being added and emphasized. The portfolio change itself is forcing changes in FBS.

Companies with higher gross margins typically have lower costs at the factory level and higher costs in other, nonfactory areas like sales, marketing, and even back office. For those companies, practicing Lean at the factory level still matters, but getting the nonfactory processes right matters even more. In a traditional industrial product offering with higher factory-level costs, for example, the distribution of kaizen events might be split so that 50 percent of them focus on improving factory operations and 50 percent of them focus on nonfactory operations. For a more advanced product offering with a higher gross margin product offering, that split might be closer to 25 percent factory related and 75 percent nonfactory related. As Fortive begins to reposition its portfolio away from the legacy industrial assets with high factory intensity and toward assets with lower factory intensity, the foundation of FBS itself will have to adapt to those changing realities.

These higher-margin products often come with higher R&D needs. Design, development, and delivery each require substantially different processes themselves. Design at Fortive, for example, is all about listening to the customer and creating only products that customers want, need, and are willing to pay for. The product development stage is all about milestones, and each design iteration is focused on simplicity. Using common parts and common processes with other existing products, for example, isn't always top of mind for scientists and engineers, but it is critical to keeping costs down. And last, the actual delivery of the product requires incredible hands-on efforts by the teams that get the purchase orders, namely sales/marketing. Where many companies will pass on responsibility for each step to different groups, FBS tools get all folks involved early in the process. There is codified collaboration among groups, which include early product developers, procurement, sales/marketing, and even digital partners, in war rooms teeming with visuals that keep all parties engaged and focused.

We'd be missing a key component of both the Danaher and Fortive stories if we weren't clear that both companies believe strongly in the autonomy of the individual operating companies. The corporate office will supply the tools and provide the common metrics on which folks are incentivized, but the business heads are empowered to deliver the results. It is a business model that has served the company very well over time.

POSTMORTEM

We tell the story of Danaher, including its big spin-off of Fortive, in a level of detail that may seem a tad dense, for several reasons. First, the story of Danaher itself has never been told before in any comprehensive way. There have been a few magazine articles here and there, but the Rales brothers are famously shy, burned many years ago by press that fixated on their wealth and use of junk bonds as opposed to the exceptional and sustainable businesses that were being created. Even though we go back with the company nearly 20 years and know many of the leaders quite well, it still took some convincing to get the company to cooperate. In true Danaher form, humility as a guiding principle implies a lack of willingness to talk about one's own successes.

We also focus on Lean manufacturing because it just works. At the minimum, it is a great foundational tool for any company that makes things: widgets, cell phones, airplanes . . . it doesn't matter. Lean works. And once Lean is fully adopted, then the real differentiation can occur. Continuous improvement can sustain those gains and build upon them, and additional focusing tools can be added to build a more complete system.

Next, we want to emphasize the power of compounding. At Danaher, it's multidimensional. Compounding via pure operations creates increments of productivity that add up over time: processes that can add low-cost capacity to factories just by making small process improvements and freeing up factory space, while helping employees get a little bit better at their jobs every day. Compounding via financial engineering is powerful as well—doing smart deals, bringing acquisitions into the culture successfully, improving the asset, and paying off the associated debt. This all creates a powerful flywheel effect. Compounding via DBS—making the business system itself better over time by incorporating tools learned from others, while constantly modernizing the core tenets, is foundational to Danaher's success.

Last, we focus on the leaders in the story—the Rales brothers, Sherman, Culp, Allender, Joyce, Comas, Lico—because they (and their staffs of increasingly diverse reports) are exceptional. Game changers, they are worth studying. Some of them continue to build their résumés: Culp may be in the middle of the biggest turnaround in American history, with GE. Joyce may end up building the largest biotech enabler. Lico is still in the early innings of a 10-year business plan (yes, we said "10 year") that might take us to places we couldn't even imagine. Make no mistake—each of these folks will hold a place in American business history.

We've recommended Danaher stock to our clients for about 15 years but not without some second thoughts at times. Successful companies that are willing to "blow it up" are rare, and there have been questionable moments: an industrial company that decides to become a healthcare company just when industrial companies are cheap and healthcare is not; a spun-off asset in Fortive that itself has announced a major spin-off of its transportation assets. And acquisitions that sometimes challenge even the most forward-thinking analyst. It all seems a bit too unorthodox. But perhaps that's one of the key lessons of this chapter: success often requires a wild ride, full of bold decisions and pivots, but transformational change anchored in a solid system. Change before you expect it is probably a good thing. In fact, a strong culture may drive that change. And the opposite of success through reinvention may just be failure through stagnation.

In the meantime, watch for Danaher and Fortive to operate with the mindset of "common sense vigorously applied." Because with all the complexity that the Danaher story seems to introduce, the truth is pretty basic: DBS is simple. At its core, it's just a set of tools that remind people what to do: To stay focused on what matters. To use visual tools. To keep meetings short and focused and email only what's necessary. To manage the little details. To measure what matters and improve on those measurements by doing a little every day versus taking big leaps in spurts. To benchmark to the best and be willing to accept the realities that others are getting better too. To hire humble and transparent folks. To develop internal talent so that when you get promoted, someone is ready to take your role. And to get rid of those who don't live those principles.

None of this is rocket science. There are no new paradigms. Danaher and Fortive employees aren't expected to reinvent the wheel. They're expected to make that wheel go a little faster and smoother every single day.

Lessons from Danaher

- Lean manufacturing works. It's the basis for every successful business system we know.
- Small improvements every day add up to massive change over time.
- Create process in everything—literally, everything.
- Business tools are focusing tools, and today focusing employees matters more than ever.
- Humility, transparency, and high expectations are three great cultural traits to develop.
- The CFO job matters more than most appreciate. Financial complexity is the new normal for global companies.
- Compounding is a financial theme, but the best make it an operating theme, too.
- Risk controls matter. A bad deal can unwind a lot of good work and goodwill.

CHAPTER

5

HONEYWELL

How Cultural Transformation Led One of the Greatest Turnarounds in History

BY SCOTT DAVIS

In early 2002, Honeywell was a company on the verge of complete failure yet was saved by a CEO and a team of mostly unknowns that few gave a chance of succeeding. It rebuilt its culture with Lean manufacturing on the factory floor, then rolled out a complete set of tools to the rest of the entity, the Honeywell Operating System (HOS). The turnaround was multidimensional and required time and patience: fix the factories, seed a culture of continuous improvement, creatively address a portfolio that was stale and well past its expiration date, aggressively manage liabilities, and play offense by rolling out cost-advantaged new products. Honeywell pivoted and reenergized around big themes: energy efficiency, productivity, and connectivity—more popularly known as the industrial internet of things (IIoT), with the high-margin software businesses that have accompanied the strategy. Today, it has become the envy of much of the industrial world.

The modern Honeywell story began on February 19, 2002, the start date of an unlikely corporate savior: CEO Dave Cote (pronounced "Cody"). He led a turnaround against tremendous odds—a broken company trying to survive an economic downturn with an unproven, unconventional CEO. Honeywell was challenged in almost every dimension: poor operations, lousy products, asbestos liabilities, a dysfunctional culture, and more. It needed cash to upgrade factories, invest in R&D, and expand into emerging markets, as well as satisfy debt holders by managing its potentially exploding set of liabilities. By the end of 2002, there had already been 78 companies bankrupted by overwhelming asbestos liabilities, including big Honeywell competitors like Federal Mogul and W. R. Grace. That alone brought the company into crisis mode, but it was hardly the only issue Cote inherited. Environmental liabilities were piling up as well, with the cities of Baltimore and Buffalo demanding massive water cleanups that could have escalated beyond his control. If Cote and his colleagues had failed, Honeywell could easily have spiraled into the abyss. Instead, they developed an organization with a market capitalization of $125 billion, one that supports 114,000 jobs, easily funds its shrinking liabilities, and has the reputation of a true technology leader.

From an operations perspective, Cote was an amazing tactician who balanced the long and short term perhaps better than any other leader in American corporate history. He "failed fast" before it became a familiar business concept, while driving deep change in the organization. All of that was possible because he gave employees strong direction and a set of practices and tools. The Honeywell Operating System greatly reduced costs in manufacturing, procurement, and logistics. It boosted margins and freed working capital to fund strategic investments and the turnaround that put Honeywell back on the offensive.

Though the turnaround took north of seven years from start to finish, progress was steady, and by the end of year two the company was clearly on the right path. But getting to that point was painful and teaches the lesson that there are no shortcuts. Once a company's reputation falters and morale plummets, climbing out takes time and incredible focus. Today's Honeywell shows how powerful a turnaround can be, particularly one driven by a culture transformation, with outsized rewards to all stakeholders.

THE RISE AND FALL OF HONEYWELL

Honeywell dates back to 1886, when Albert Butz commercialized an innovative thermostat for coal furnaces, founding the Butz Thermo-Electric Regulator Company in Chicago. (See Figure 5.1.) It took on the Honeywell name in 1927 after merging with a rival, and in the 1940s it expanded into high-tech military and aerospace products. It invented many of the controls used in autopilot systems, as well as periscopes for tanks and other hardware. Then in the 1970s it developed process controls for the petroleum and chemical industries. Through it all, the company had a track record of innovation and quality, but integrating these differing businesses proved challenging. And eventually its markets became mature with faster-moving competitors taking share.

Figure 5.1: **The creation of Honeywell, 1896–1986.**

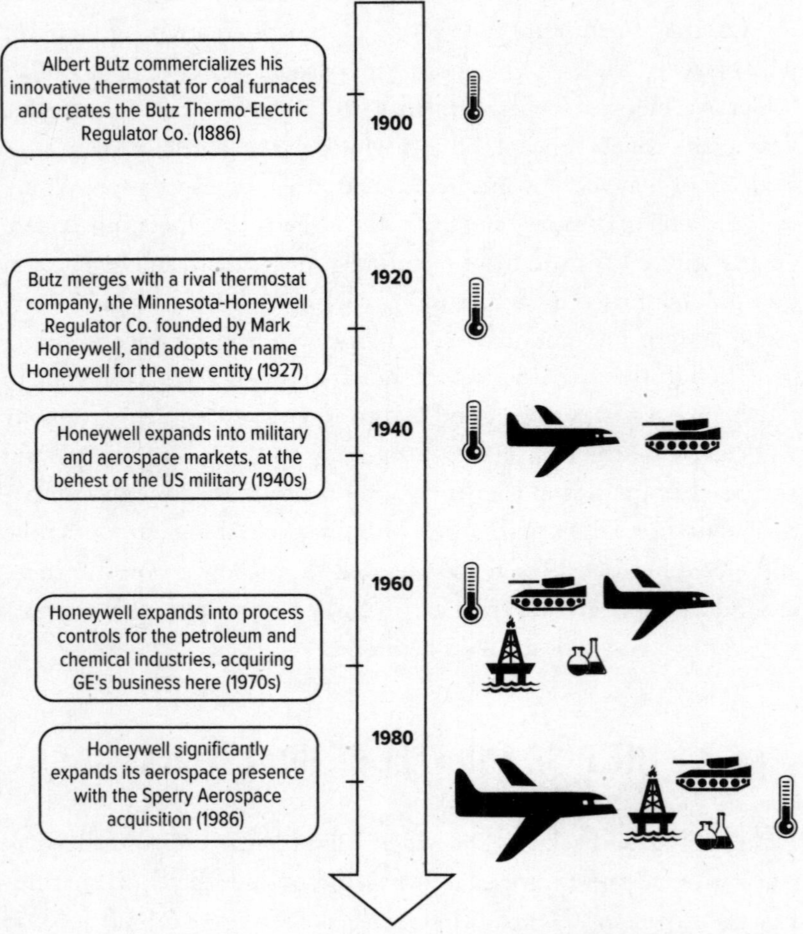

Source: Honeywell filings, press reports

By the late 1990s the company was a hodgepodge of legacy organizations and businesses struggling to stay relevant in a world moving away from slow-growth industrial assets. In 1999 it agreed to be acquired by AlliedSignal. (See Figure 5.2.) AlliedSignal itself was struggling to remain relevant but figured that a big M&A deal

Figure 5.2: **The creation of AlliedSignal, 1920–1985.**

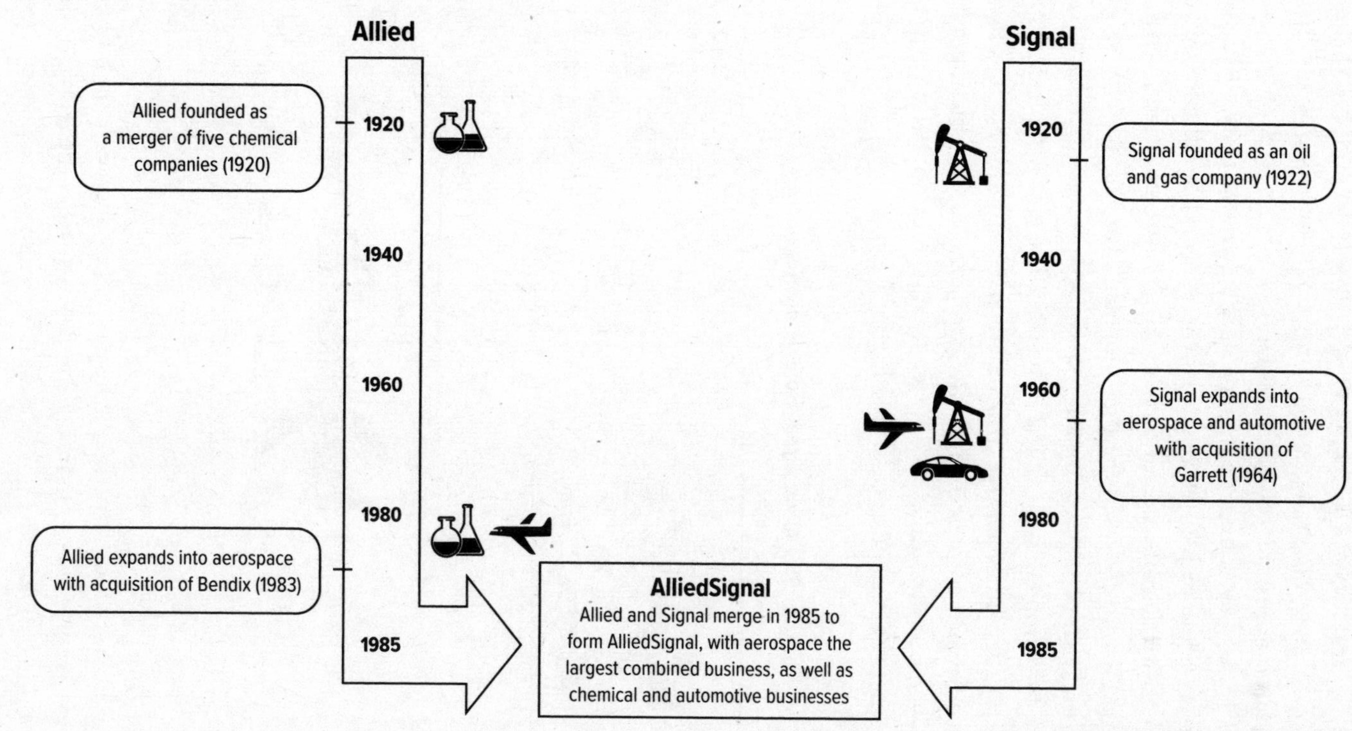
Allied
Allied founded as a merger of five chemical companies (1920)
1920
1940
1960
1980
Allied expands into aerospace with acquisition of Bendix (1983)
1985
Signal
1920
Signal founded as an oil and gas company (1922)
1940
1960
Signal expands into aerospace and automotive with acquisition of Garrett (1964)
1980
1985
AlliedSignal
Allied and Signal merge in 1985 to form AlliedSignal, with aerospace the largest combined business, as well as chemical and automotive businesses

Source: Honeywell filings, press reports

would create enough synergies to keep investors interested. Although AlliedSignal was the far larger company, it took on the Honeywell name because of its stronger brand.

In the 1990s, under celebrated CEO Larry Bossidy, a GE alumnus and one of Jack Welch's favorite executives, AlliedSignal had intensified its multigenerational build-out into a traditional conglomerate. Bossidy followed the then-popular advice of modern portfolio theory, that diversification allowed for solid returns while reducing risk for companies in cyclical industries. The reality typically proved quite different. In massive conglomerates, complexity and bureaucracy become the accepted default. The company just becomes larger and slower, and the weakest businesses at any given time often sap management's time and energy. (See Figure 5.3.)

Figure 5.3: **The 1999 AlliedSignal-Honeywell merger.**

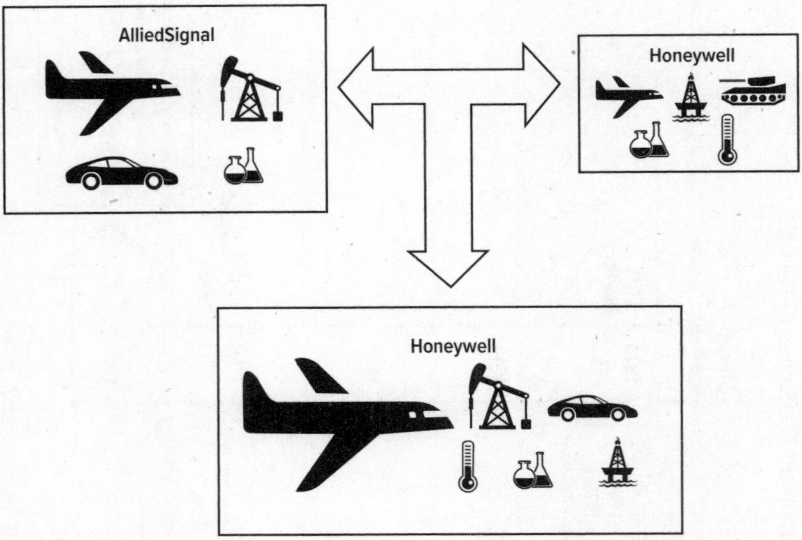

Source: Melius Research

Despite those strategic failings, Bossidy succeeded in building a strong senior team, and he benefited greatly from the tailwinds of the booming 1990s. Buying Honeywell was supposed to be his crowning achievement before retirement. Instead, it exposed underlying weaknesses: both companies were seeing sharply greater global competition and product commoditization.

The merger of AlliedSignal and Honeywell is a useful lesson in the limitations of traditional deal analysis. These were two solid companies with substantial aerospace operations and little direct overlap. Yet the organizations had very different cultures: Honeywell favored creativity, while AlliedSignal pushed for strict engineering discipline. Michael Bonsignore, a 30-year veteran of Honeywell, succeeded Bossidy and tried to integrate the two organizations, but he made little headway. People considered themselves either Honeywell or Allied employees, and they strongly disliked each other. Honeywell viewed AlliedSignal as arrogant, while AlliedSignal saw Honeywell folks as soft and lazy. AlliedSignal incentivized the organization on profits; Honeywell focused on market share. The two companies could not have been more different.

Viewed as a wounded duck but with good assets, the combined company soon attracted outside interest, and it was effectively put up for sale. Two giants showed up to the party, with United Technologies taking an early lead, but GE coming in later with the promise of a bidding war. The much larger GE easily won with a cash and stock deal totaling $45 billion.

As soon as the Honeywell board accepted the offer in October 2000—but before gaining regulatory approval—GE managers moved in and began running the company as if the deal had already closed. They made it clear to key Honeywell executives that their days were numbered. Honeywell's more talented leaders raced out the door as competitors swooped in and took as much engineering and research talent as they could get.

Then suddenly in July 2001, after a protracted review process, the European Union blocked the deal for antitrust reasons. It argued that GE's aircraft engine and airplane leasing businesses, combined with Honeywell's cockpit controls and braking systems, would constitute too much power in the marketplace.

GE pulled out, leaving a managerially depleted company already showing signs of falling apart. The board fired Bonsignore and brought back Bossidy as interim CEO. Bonsignore's quick exit crushed the morale of employees from the legacy Honeywell side, but the AlliedSignal people were not much better off. Then the recession of 2001–2002 brought the company to its knees.

By 2002 Honeywell was in disarray, and Bossidy was struggling to hold it together. It had employees at war with each other, unhappy customers, inefficient factories, little innovation, and a burden of liabilities that would sink most companies. Its accounting was aggressive by any definition, and cash flow was falling. All this was happening as orders were still barely recovering from the 2001 recession, and the big aerospace division suffered the added hit of the post-9/11 travel slowdown. It was a perfect storm for Honeywell, and the board quickly needed to find a new leadership team.

There were so few executives left at Honeywell that the board considered no internal candidates for the CEO seat. Instead the board aimed at prominent outsiders, such as GE alumnus Jim McNerney (then running 3M before moving on to run Boeing) and GE executive Dave Calhoun (who later ran Nielsen before moving to his current position as CEO of Boeing). Neither was interested, and the stock continued to slide.

Eventually the job went to David Cote, a far less noteworthy GE alumnus who gained little attention running GE's appliance business, after which he had a brief and unremarkable tenure running another conglomerate, TRW. He was reportedly the board's fifth choice, and word that the board was forced to settle for a "second-tier" leader quickly leaked out. Wall Street saw Cote as such a weak selection that a CNBC commentator proclaimed: "Honeywell is probably not fixable, and if it is, it's probably not fixable by Dave Cote."

THE OUTSIDER WITH A MISSION

Cote didn't fit the CEO mold. A degree from the University of New Hampshire matched poorly with the Ivy League pedigree of most prominent leaders at that time. His father had owned a small gas station, and Dave's youth showed little evidence that he had aspirations much beyond his humble roots. He found little inspiration in college, even dropping out for a spell to try his hand at becoming a commercial fisherman. By the time he graduated, he was already married with a young child to support.

He wore cheap suits that never seemed to fit his unusually large body, and he spoke with a New Hampshire accent that offended the financial elite. He pronounced China "Chiner" and called cash "cabbage," as in, "That's a lot of cabbage." Jack Welch had liked him as a hardworking, thick-skinned, honest leader, but his colleagues had found him boisterous and unpolished. Senior GE leaders were quick to dismiss Cote, including GE's new CEO Jeff Immelt, who viewed him as a lightweight and most certainly not a peer.

That reputation permeated Wall Street. Only five analysts covered Honeywell at the time, and all reacted to Cote's hiring with either a sell or a tepid neutral rating. GE had valued Honeywell at $55 per share; when Cote took over 16 months later in February 2002, it had fallen to $35, finally bottoming in late 2002 near $18. Beyond a failing stock price, employees continued to rush for the exits, customers noticed a sharp falloff in product quality, and bondholders began to get nervous. Honeywell was spiraling downward.

Cote walked into a seemingly impossible situation. The prior team had pulled every lever possible to show stable earnings even as the underlying fundamentals eroded. The desperately needed cash flow was sinking, leaving the company vulnerable to mounting liabilities from legacy asbestos and environmental damages. Most of the remaining operating managers either had been too lazy to quit when GE took over or, worse, had so little talent that no one else wanted them. Cote had only one thing going for him: the board had no alternative CEO in the wings, and activists believed the company too broken to touch, so he had time to right the ship.

We're now used to CEOs operating as crisis managers to carry out a turnaround, but Cote did it before it was popular. He moved quickly and decisively, with a fail-fast approach that pushed people to perform immediately. He recruited outside managers and supplemented with younger talent that had been overlooked. He overhauled incentives to focus people on stabilizing existing operations and generating cash flow. He also managed to hire back some talent that had left in the GE debacle, key people in technology and R&D.

Most important to the longer-term turnaround, he introduced Lean manufacturing and began to measure and pay for progress, incentivizing continuous improvement. The Honeywell Operating System started within the four walls of the factory floor well before it spread to the wider organization. The beginning targets were basic and centered on inventory turnover, defect rates, and on-time delivery. He combined that system with the vision of a renewed Honeywell with new products, modernized factories, and expansion into emerging markets.

He told the organization that Honeywell was not for sale and that loyal employees would be treated well. He said the company would rise again if it controlled costs and built a backlog of exceptional new products. And he preached a wider stakeholder vision: he wanted everyone who touched Honeywell to be successful—customers, suppliers, employees, and shareholders. In 2002, this was not a common CEO message. But it resonated at Honeywell, and his plan began to gain traction.

With Wall Street, he had less success. He was too busy internally to focus on building analyst relationships, so his iffy GE reputation, whether fair or not, was slow to improve. One of his first public appearances was in May 2002 at the Electrical Products Group (EPG) Conference. As mentioned in Chapter 2, EPG is the three-day annual get-together in Florida of roughly 150 Wall Street analysts and executives from 25 of the largest industrial companies in the United States and Europe. Regular attendees include GE, 3M, United Technologies, Danaher, Ingersoll-Rand, Siemens, Emerson, and Honeywell. I have attended this conference nearly every year since 2002, including this notorious one.

Florida is often hot in May, but that year was particularly harsh. At the first night's dinner, Cote showed up in a standard wool suit and white shirt with no undershirt, while veteran attendees were wearing freshly pressed, summer-weight dress slacks and golf shirts. Within

10 minutes Cote had drenched his clothes with sweat, and his stocky frame with a wet white shirt left little to the imagination. I overheard one of the top-ranked industrial analysts at that time say, "This guy isn't going to cut it," before walking away to chat with more important people. Other CEOs looked over at Cote and snickered.

Particularly in those days, most Wall Street analysts were snooty and opinionated. Nearly all of them were white men educated at elite universities. Those who worked at big banks came from wealthy places like Greenwich, Connecticut, while those who managed mutual funds hailed from the leafy suburbs of Boston. They favored leaders who played the game and looked the part: tall, athletic build, CEO hair, a good golf game, and custom suits. This was long before CEOs outside of Silicon Valley wore blue jeans and T-shirts and hosted TED Talks.

Cote favored hunting and fishing over golf. He drank diet soda and beer from a can and ate fast food, Kentucky Fried Chicken I recall being his favorite. He liked to ride his motorcycle on weekends and smoke cigars. Years later, he visited my home for an event I was hosting and introduced himself to my wife by saying, "Hi, I'm Dave. I run Honeywell." She walked over to me and said, "I think he picked up his jeans from the floor, where he left them the night before." He hardly looked the part of the game-changing leader of a critical American company.

If you could get past his appearance and the wilted look, however, Cote's speech at EPG showed a clear strategy. He was working an early turnaround playbook, which meant stabilizing existing operations, bringing in outside talent where needed, making long-term investments, and taking the inevitable short-term criticism. He was playing defense, buying time for the turnaround. The stock kept lagging that of peers for the better part of his first year as investors continued to view the odds as heavily stacked against him. What began as a 2003 forward-earnings forecast of $2.00 per share by the Street was on its way to a low-quality $1.54, even as peers were showing better numbers and higher-quality results in a stabilizing economy.

I had just been promoted to run Morgan Stanley's industrial research group. Perhaps naïvely, I liked what he said and how he said it, and I especially liked that no one else liked it. Cote spoke my language, as I was a Wall Street outsider myself. I had grown up in numerous factory towns and didn't have an Ivy League résumé. My only asset was my willingness to work hard and tolerate the pain that goes along with long hours and intense work pressures.

In college, Cote worked the night shift at a GE aircraft engine factory to cover tuition and support his new family. By the time he graduated and had his first salaried job, he took nothing for granted and worked maniacally, struggling through two marriages in the process. Cote was focused on success and was confident in his abilities. Just as important, though, he never wanted to go back to the life of struggling paycheck to paycheck. His time as a fisherman in the cold waters off the coast of Maine and his dreary night-shift factory work solidified that view. He wasn't about to squander the opportunity. In those days, few on Wall Street understood how motivating that experience could be. I definitely did. In today's world, being an outsider can be considered an asset; in those days, outsiders were just . . . outsiders.

I put a buy rating on Honeywell stock in October 2002 and published a detailed 80-page report to support it. I thought Cote's plan had an honest shot and believed the company would get earnings up to $3 per share in a few years. At $20 the stock didn't seem to discount much of that earnings potential. It was the only buy rating I had on any stock in industrials at that time. In fact, I still have a buy rating on the stock today, a recommendation I have made since that day in 2002. My boss said it was foolish, and if I were wrong, it would be the end of my time on Wall Street—especially as I was not positive on two Wall Street darlings, General Electric and Emerson Electric. Having a neutral rating on GE in those days was considered blasphemous. Back then, neutral was Wall Street code for sell. And recommending a company run by one of GE's least favorite alumni could be career suicide. A buy on Honeywell and a neutral on GE was equivalent to saying today, "Sell your Google stock and go buy General Motors."

The pushback I received on this recommendation was mountainous, much of it bordering on harassment. I got it especially from the large mutual fund shops, which favored polished CEOs like George

David at United Technologies, Jeff Immelt at GE, and Jim McNerney at 3M. Emails called me incompetent, and I got countless "I told you so's" every time Cote had a hiccup. Turnarounds take time and patience, and Cote hadn't yet built up the team capable of executing on his plan.

The first year was rough, but Cote stuck with the playbook, and in the second and third years results began to show progress. Earnings perked up, employees received long overdue raises, jobs were being created, and suppliers and customers saw sharp improvements in their Honeywell experience. The stock price found solid footing and began to capture more attention from longer-term, larger funds. (See Figure 5.4.)

Figure 5.4: **HON stock outperformed the S&P by nearly 3x from trough during Dave Cote's 15-year tenure.**

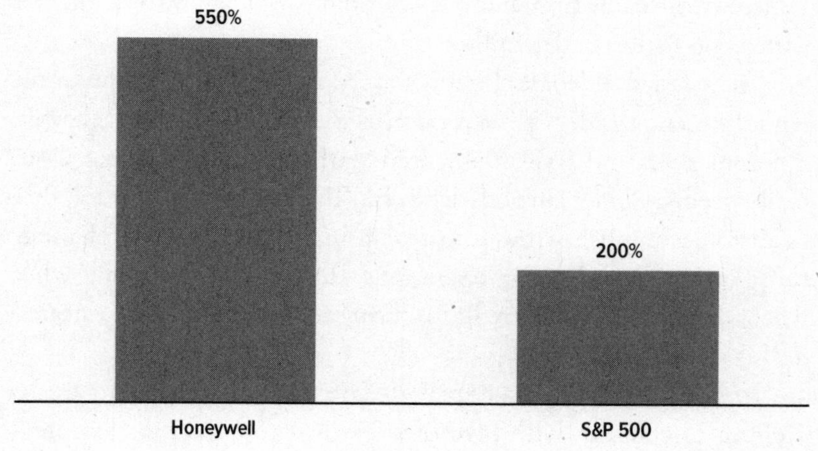

Source: Bloomberg

ENTER A WORLD-CLASS CFO AND A TEAM THAT BEGINS TO GEL

As the world recovered from the 2001–2002 recession, Honeywell's improved operations and revived morale started to translate into higher margins and greater cash flow. Wall Street's reluctance to accept Cote began to turn, but only slightly, as the company's liabilities remained: an underfunded pension, asbestos liabilities, and a big environmental cleanup bill. All were sins of the past, mostly decades prior, but had to be fixed. Cote needed a credible finance chief who could manage the mess.

Enter Dave Anderson, who became CFO in June 2003. Anderson is the polar opposite of Cote: a polished, well-dressed executive who favors healthy food and fine wine and is more likely to have sparkling water than a can of Coke or Mountain Dew that Cote preferred. A fitness enthusiast who runs six miles before most people hit the snooze button, with an MBA from the University of Chicago, he was liked by Wall Street. He had proved himself as a shareholder-friendly CFO at ITT during the later years of its deconglomeration phase in the 1990s. And though polished, Anderson had the work ethic of someone who came from humble beginnings: a small town in Indiana with a population under 7,000.

There is active debate about who accomplished what in the Cote/Anderson era. Insiders viewed them as the odd couple, with sharply different skills and styles that often clashed. My take is that Cote badly needed Anderson and vice versa. The turnaround was too difficult to accomplish without a strong finance head to complement those on the front lines in operations. Regardless of who did what when, Cote deserves the credit for hiring someone who compensated for his weaknesses.

In addition, Cote had struggled to connect, or even care to attempt to connect, with investors. He had too much to fix internally to spend an ounce of energy otherwise. Anderson knew how to speak the language that investors trusted. Just as important, he could deliver and present the reliable financial numbers that investors favored: straightforward results with limited surprises quarter to quarter. Beyond that, Anderson helped Cote to execute on a mile-long to-do list internally. There was no shortage of work.

The CFO job is underappreciated by a country mile in almost every great corporate story. Fifty years ago, the job was more bookkeeper than strategist, but today it's about as complex as anything out there. Globalization means countless tax codes to navigate, debt and cash exist in many new forms around the world, acquisitions require thoughtful and consistent diligence, and Wall Street itself is full of pitfalls. We find CFOs heavily influencing strategic direction, offering eyes and ears on disruption risks and competitive context that operating executives often miss. Some CFOs are very qualified operators; many have run rather large businesses or have had a front-row seat otherwise. In a world where company guidance still gyrates stock prices, a good CFO can earn his or her keep with conservative, yet accurate, forecasting. Forecasting at a high level builds credibility and often translates into a higher stock price, often higher and stickier than deserved.

Anderson started by cleaning up the company's accounting, especially in aerospace. The accounting in this industry borders on questionable even in normal times, as companies spread costs across the life of a product rather than when incurred. The allocation of expenses among discretionary buckets invites all kinds of abuse, and Anderson's predecessors had pushed the envelope to the limit. He mandated simpler, clean accounting methods, which sent the message that ethics mattered and that everyone would be assessed on a comparable set of metrics.

Anderson's strong stance on earnings quality wasn't popular, and he had to replace most of his 70+ reports. In a company where being average had been accepted for some time, setting a high bar was important.

After getting the books in order, Anderson moved on to the liabilities. He took the cash freed up by HOS and its Lean foundation, used it to pay down debt, and got back to minimum funding levels for the pension plan, all while reaching quick settlements on much of the asbestos and environmental damages. Wall Street eventually noticed the sharply falling risk profile.

A portfolio revamp via asset sales and M&A was next, and the new senior leadership team got Honeywell out of some lousy businesses at decent prices. Gone were the worst of the commodity chemical assets, a large consumer auto business, and a subscale alarm monitoring service. At businesses the company couldn't sell, costs were cut and customer contracts restructured. The company also bought some new businesses that proved a good fit and entered new markets with attractive characteristics—all while avoiding expensive targets where Honeywell couldn't add much value.

Honeywell's turnaround had many elements, but underappreciated was how Cote, Anderson, and the team used the company's expanding free cash flow to cut risk while also compounding returns. The liabilities were impossible to get rid of easily, but they did their best to keep them from growing, so that greater cash flow would make them an afterthought. The goal was to double the cash flow over its current level, so the company could go after acquisitions, raise the dividend, and buy back stock in slow times—all while paying off legacy liabilities.

Most CFOs back then focused on boosting cash flow through higher earnings, but Anderson saw multipliers on that opportunity. He was astounded by the cash tied up in working capital: billions of dollars in inventory, accounts receivable, and other areas. He saw overlapping office space in major cities, often overseen by different business units that seemingly had no way to know where other local Honeywell operations existed. The company had also mishandled basic matters such as the timing of capital spending and the structures of debt. Anderson introduced a commercial paper program to add flexibility and lower interest payments. He helped hedge overseas activities by issuing foreign debt. He also hedged currencies to help deliver the more predictable results that investors care about.

Prior to the Cote/Anderson era, the company converted less than 80 percent of its net income to cash flow, was starving its operations of investment, and was underfunding its pension. Once the asbestos and environmental liabilities were stabilized, the pension began to get greater attention. Like most corporate pension plans at that time, it assumed an unrealistic long-term rate of return and discount rate, making it look better on paper than in economic reality. These assumptions were quickly adjusted downward by the more conservative Anderson accounting team.

FILLING OUT THE TEAM

By the time Cote took over, the company had already alienated two of its most important customers, Boeing and Embraer, with shipments that were late and were beset with quality issues. R&D investment had fallen behind that of competitors, and the factories were starved of investment.

After customer complaints intensified and cultural friction rose, Cote fired the senior aerospace team that he had inherited. The bench was thin, and the only manager Cote saw fit to take over the most senior aerospace role was one who had run the company's much smaller turbocharger business, Rob Gillette. This promotion created even more problems. More than most industries, aerospace was an old boys' club that shunned outsiders. Bringing in an auto guy to run an aerospace business was viewed as a statement that Honeywell just didn't get it or didn't care. Customers continued to fade as fast as possible, which fortunately in aerospace is pretty slowly. New products and programs are often decades apart, which bought Cote time to fix the underlying problems. Gillette struggled to get traction, but eventually he was able to stabilize the business before he departed in 2009 for a CEO job elsewhere. The stabilization that Gillette established enabled Cote to develop and filter internal talent. Cote already had his eyes on an aerospace leader with a more traditional aerospace background, Tim Mahoney, who went on to run the business during its greatest decade, 2009–2019.

In the early days, Cote had only a few proven executives with legitimate operating experience. A couple came from one thing the company had done right between 1999 and 2002: acquire Pittway, a leading maker of fire and security alarm systems. Roger Fradin was the CEO of Pittway and Andreas Kramvis a top lieutenant. Both were critical to the operating turnaround. Alex Ismail was a rising star, and Cote's faith in him paid off over time. Anne Madden was critical as head of M&A. And we'll talk later about the importance of hiring Shane Tedjarati, who turned Honeywell China around. This group of people constituted a thin bench of grown-ups. Only a couple of them had been at Honeywell for more than a few years, and none were known at all in aerospace, arguably the company's most important business.

For the first few years, Cote and his team played whack-a-mole, replacing failing leaders, often with poorly trained successors. That's why turnarounds can take a while—you need new leadership, and those leaders need to fit culturally and be process driven, but it takes time to really know if your new appointments are up to the job. Cote's challenges here played into Wall Street's "not fixable" narrative, but he kept at it and eventually found people good enough to get Honeywell humming again.

Despite the mountain of skepticism if not outright contempt, Cote held to his bold ambitions. In my first meeting with him, in spring 2002, I was struck by the clarity of his vision and how broadly he defined success. He wanted to make money for all his stakeholders, not just stockholders. He wanted to treat suppliers well so that they could in turn develop better products for Honeywell. It would be a virtuous circle. He wanted customers to love Honeywell through an exceptional user experience and products that in turn helped the customer to be more successful. Employees, he said, should be paid for performance and even those at the lowest level should be treated with respect.

He believed in paying top performers not just for the job they do today, but for the job they will be offered tomorrow. Retention was as big a focus for Cote as recruiting, and he believed in paying executives in stock, so they have the same incentives as owners. He asked his board to pay him in stock options versus just stock; it was a risky bet that could have sunk his compensation if he had failed but instead made him a fortune. Note that in Cote's early years most executives favored RSUs (restricted stock units) over options because of the downside protection. After the tech bubble burst in 2001, so many stock options became worthless that compensation programs moved sharply away from using them. While some have viewed Cote's option-heavy pay package as greedy, at the time most viewed it as gutsy, even dumb.

Cote also believed in developing leaders, perhaps because of his GE training and how he himself had benefited from development as a young manager. He expected to hire externally for only the first year or two; then the company would have to sustain itself from within. Two Cote quotes I remember from that meeting: "I want to make money on the stock 10 years after I retire" and "I want people to say, 'If I want a good leader, I hire a Honeywell guy'—except they can't get our guys because Honeywell is such a great place to have a career." Not only were these grand ambitions for a company on the ropes, but we rarely hear new CEOs at even healthy companies express such long-term visions. Think about it: in the early days of a 15+-year career at Honeywell, Cote was already thinking about his legacy and the stock value after his retirement. In hindsight, it seems Cote wanted to replicate the GE that he grew up with, but in a more collaborative and caring way. He wanted everyone to win.

One thing Cote didn't dwell on in that first meeting was culture. I don't recall him even using the word. If it was up to Honeywell's current culture to save the company, Cote knew he didn't have a chance. Nor was he interested in mandating the culture directly or by waging a war against it. He couldn't force it; the company was still too fragile. The change had to be sincere and lasting. So instead he focused on reassuring and reorienting the organization with his vision, and the system he wanted to implement would have far more influence over time. HOS would play a very big role in defining the Honeywell employee experience. He seeded a continuous improvement culture, one with high expectations and humility. But he did it indirectly. This is a key lesson we have seen in all other winning cases: culture as an output of incentives and the actions and direction of leadership, not an input.

THE FIVE COMPONENTS OF THE TURNAROUND

The turnaround consisted of five components: (1) taking out costs, (2) developing new products, (3) fixing the portfolio, (4) expanding in emerging markets, and (5) doing a financial overhaul. These were about equal in importance, and Honeywell addressed them all as quickly as it could—not exactly an easy exercise.

Step 1: Cutting Costs

On the cost side, the key was boosting productivity, rather than just firing people or closing factories. The Honeywell that Dave Cote walked into had $22 billion in revenues and an operating profit margin of 11 percent. A good industrial company at the time had a margin close to 15 percent, while best-in-class folks approached 20 percent. Honeywell's 11 percent margin wasn't even sustainable, maybe not even real; its leaders had cut corners by underinvesting in everything from R&D and engineering to sales and marketing. The aggressive accounting inflated profits. And the 11 percent excluded the lion's share of liabilities (asbestos, environmental, and pension) that threatened the solvency of the company. A generous estimate put the real margin at 7 percent, and you could have argued it was closer to 5 percent. Today's Honeywell has operating margins around 20 percent and rising while they will undoubtedly be impacted by the pandemic, the longer term trajectory remains positive.

In one of our early meetings in 2003, Cote emphasized that the key to his operating plan was boosting revenue while holding the line on fixed costs, especially employment at headquarters. He talked about how hiring people leads them to hire other people, who then need people to support them, and everyone needs IT systems, employee benefits, and office space. He wanted to raise the head count only in areas of aggressive expansion, such as emerging markets or products with outsized growth potential: business jets, environmental products, and turbochargers, for example.

On this promise, Cote delivered. In his 15 years at the helm, 400 basis points of the margin improvement (about half the total) came from flat corporate expense while revenues grew. He accomplished that without the usual distracting restructuring and layoffs. Head-count reductions over time came largely from attrition. (See Figures 5.5 and 5.6.)

Figure 5.5: **Revenue and profits grew far faster . . .**

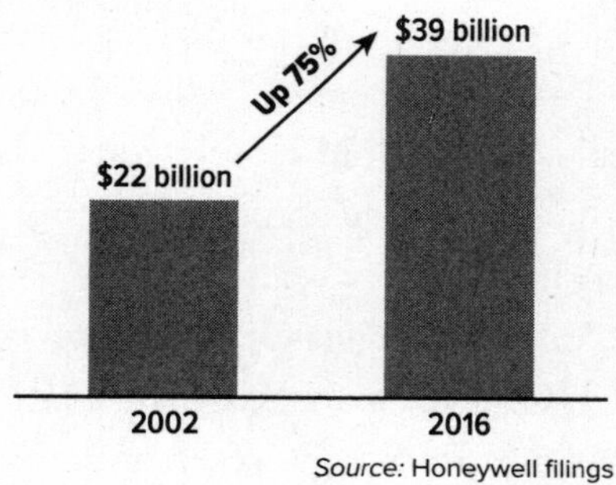

Source: Honeywell filings

Figure 5.6: **. . . than head count during Cote's tenure.**

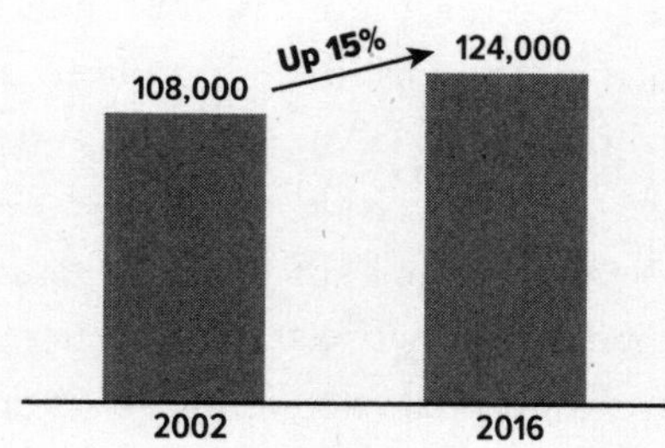

Note: Data is pro forma for the 2015 Elster deal, which added 6,800 employees.

Source: Honeywell filings

Importantly, the jobs that remained at Honeywell became more permanent and sustainable, often with high and rising salaries. Cote invested in and saved factories that likely would have been closed by others. He funded research positions, added sales and marketing, and built up a software capability that continues to expand today.

Manufacturing offered an even more interesting savings opportunity than corporate overhead, and the company succeeded here, too—and not by offshoring production, the option preferred by most American companies. Cote wanted to localize manufacturing: products sold in the United States were to be made in the United States, and products for China were to be made in China. To compensate for higher-cost labor in the United States and Europe, he needed a sharp boost in factory productivity. Once he had somewhat capable leaders in place by 2005, he introduced Lean manufacturing and components of Six Sigma quality control, combined into HOS. In hindsight, treating his factory workers well and not exporting jobs to China likely helped Cote get the support from workers, including unionized employees, to drive the changes necessary to implement HOS. Implementing Lean is hard: it's disruptive in the early days and requires a completely changed mindset at the factory level.

In practice, HOS was a set of common metrics on which each factory could be judged: quality (defects per million units), on-time delivery, safety, and working capital (i.e., inventory turnover). A factory could achieve HOS bronze, silver, or gold levels, so the leaders had clear goals. Bronze showed minimum competence, while those who reached silver and gold were celebrated. Gold closely equated with world-class levels achieved by the top factory managers around the world. And since world class gets better every year, the requirements rose each year. HOS generated tangible targets for each factory and a rationale for capital allocation. HOS kept managers focused. It drove compensation and was competitive. Rankings were regularly distributed. Leaders who succeeded had better odds of advancing. At the beginning of Cote's tenure, his cost base was bloated and noncompetitive, with barely a profit margin to show for it. By the end, the asset base was excellent, with margins near best in class among peers. This put Honeywell back in a position to play offense.

Step 2: Developing New Products

The cost-cutting was essential, but Honeywell also needed new products to reach its goals. Cote often said in folksy language, "The cupboard was bare," as the company had starved its R&D for years. Instead of investing 3 percent of revenue in R&D when he arrived, he aimed for 6 percent, which meant cash he didn't have. As with GE under Welch, the cost-cutting had to work in order to fund the new products—another reason why the Honeywell fix was more complex than most. The funding needs were many, but the resources were scarce.

Cote didn't believe in R&D centralization. The giant R&D labs at enterprises like GE and IBM he found ill-suited to the changing global realities, especially given that most of the growth in the world was now coming from outside the United States. In that spirit, he wanted scientists and engineers located in the countries aligned and responsive to the local market. It also meant that more collaborative R&D was now around the clock. Scientists going to bed in America could hand off a project to those just waking up in China or India. The need for 24/7 development had become more acute, as technological advances were getting more complex and the pace was faster, in aerospace in particular.

As Jack Welch did with jet travel and gas-fueled electric power, Cote put R&D funds to work in areas with a high growth potential. Products aimed at reducing environmental impacts were a big focus: software to boost airplane efficiency, business jet cockpits that catered to sophisticated airplane designs and faster flights, and chemicals, notably air-conditioning gases, that did less harm to the environment. He also had scientists working on biofuels and automation for buildings. Separately, he put R&D into military projects that got little attention but that generated substantial and countercyclical profits. Much of that military R&D was paid for by the US government, help that Honeywell certainly needed. Cote needed as much of the R&D paid for by others as he could get, including from suppliers and, in some cases, customers.

Cote always described himself as "New Hampshire cheap." His R&D spend needed to double, and that doubling had to yield much more than double the new products. He required at least four times the products to reach the market position he wanted, and those new products had to be relevant. R&D was highly focused and on a shoestring budget.

New product development takes patience and focus. Anyone can throw money at an R&D department and hope for a result, but Cote's emphasis on local design paid off. Honeywell is one of the rare American companies that not only gained market share in China, but continues to grow that share today, even amid strained government relations.

Beyond the vision, Cote added structures and hard goals that would help with the cash shortfall. He introduced two initiatives for R&D: velocity product development (VPD) and the Honeywell User Experience (HUE). VPD was a set of practices to simplify and thereby accelerate the new product launch cycle. New products needed to be designed for factory floor efficiency—more common parts, fewer total parts overall—which doesn't require massive factory investment to make. HUE focused engineers on products that users found simple and effective to use.

Success in R&D is often measured in market share terms, but we find pricing power and resulting higher margins to be equally important. Honeywell's growth above its peers, plus sharp margin improvements, is proof that Cote's efforts yielded the results he sought. (See Figure 5.7.) We talk about the flywheel effect in most of our case studies. Enabling R&D to deliver new product flow, in the relevant regions where the investment is being made, is critical to getting and staying on the flywheel. Rising sales, margins, and cash reinvested properly widen the competitive moat versus peers.

Figure 5.7: **Honeywell's profit margins nearly doubled under Dave Cote.**

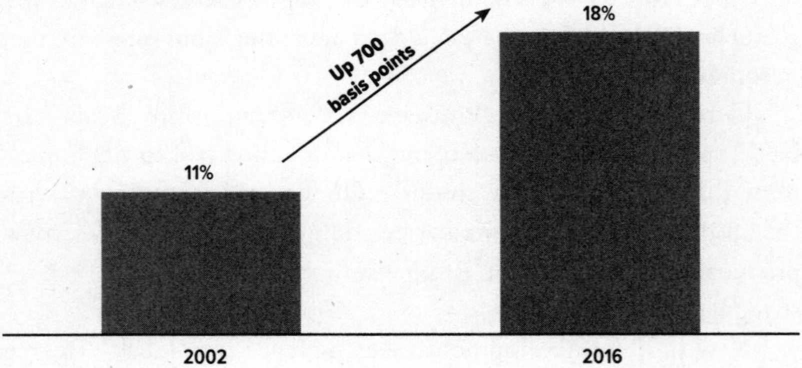

Source: Honeywell filings

Step 3: Fixing the Portfolio

Anne Madden, whom Cote promoted to run M&A, took the lead here. Her first decision was to commission a study of all past deals at AlliedSignal and Honeywell to figure out what worked, what didn't, and why. The results were astonishing. The average return on invested capital for deals in the preceding decade (1991–2001) was 0 percent—and that was a time when deal prices were not especially high.

As it turns out, most of the deals had projected generous benefits from revenue synergies that never played out. Most of the deals also involved assets with rising product commoditization, where the seller had underinvested and customers were unhappy, but neither AlliedSignal nor Honeywell factored in those problems. Perhaps they didn't even know about them.

In response, Madden overhauled the acquisition process by installing new people, instituting much tougher due diligence, and introducing a rule against revenue synergies in the deal model. Cote added the requirement that all deals involve "great businesses in good industries." That meant, for example, no deals in the traditional auto-supply industry or commodity chemicals, which were too competitive to achieve differentiation and high margins.

Honeywell was admittedly starting from a low base, but the results were excellent. We estimate at least a 15 percent ROIC throughout the Cote/Anderson/Madden tenure. By comparison, from 2002 to 2017, Honeywell's closest rivals had deal returns meaningfully lower; we estimate in the mid-single digits. At GE the results were closer to zero or worse.

Honeywell's first big acquisition under Cote came in 2005 when it bought Novar, a building automation company. It also bought the 50 percent share it didn't own in UOP, an oil and gas processing business, from Dow Chemical. Both deals resulted in some of the best deal returns in industrials in those years—yet Wall Street was initially skeptical. UOP was cyclical, and Honeywell bought it while numbers were still falling, while Novar was itself a conglomerate with noncore businesses that Honeywell needed to exit. Cote managed to sell the "junk," including a check printing business and an aluminum extrusion business, at levels that were much better than expected: the net purchase price was below 6x EBITDA (earnings before interest, taxes, depreciation, and amortization) for the part of Novar that Honeywell wanted to keep and viewed so favorably. In comparison, most deals today are done at 12x EBITDA or higher. Six times for a good-growth, high-margin business is unusually cheap, and returns from that deal are well over 20 percent.

Other notable transactions were Norcross Safety Products and Metrologic, both in 2008. Not only was Metrologic a great acquisition for Honeywell, but Darius Adamczyk, Honeywell's current CEO, came over with that deal. In 2015, Honeywell bought Elster (gas metering), followed by Intelligrated (warehouse automation) in 2016. (See Figure 5.8.) It also kept up a steady pace of smaller deals that boosted revenue in the slower periods. When prospective deals were too expensive, Cote put the spare cash into buying back stock. Honeywell's share count fell 10 percent from 2002 to 2017, all while revenues and profits compounded.

Figure 5.8: **Honeywell's M&A history under Dave Cote.**

Asset	Year Acquired	Description
Novar	2005	Building systems, aluminum extruding, printing
UOP (remaining 50% stake)	2005	Gas processing equipment
First Technology	2006	Gas detection
Hand Held Products	2007	ID/data collection
Safety Products Holding (Norcross)	2008	Personal protective equipment
Metrologic Instruments	2008	Data capture hardware/software
RMG	2009	Gas measurement
Sperian	2010	Personal protective equipment
King's Safetywear	2011	Safety footwear
EMS Technologies	2011	Rugged mobile computers
Thomas Russell (70% stake)	2012	Natural gas processing/treating
Intermec	2013	Mobile computing, RFID, printers
RAE	2013	Gas/radiation detection
Elster	2015	Gas metering
COMDEV	2016	Satellite/space components
Xtralis	2016	Smoke detection/perimeter security
Intelligrated	2016	Warehouse automation

Source: Honeywell filings, press reports

Asset sales were just as important as acquisitions for improving the portfolio. Honeywell had some mediocre businesses that Cote couldn't immediately sell without taking a bath, however desperate he was for cash, so he waited patiently. In automotive, for example, it took eight years to finally get out of businesses including brake pads, spark plugs, and antifreeze, along with other lower-quality businesses like security monitoring, aerospace parts consulting, and commodity chemicals. But Honeywell got respectable prices for these assets, selling them for about the same valuation as the higher-quality businesses it bought.

Some have asked why Honeywell wasn't more aggressive with M&A, and maybe Cote should have done more. But it may also just speak to the challenge of orchestrating a turnaround. Turnarounds of this magnitude require a delicate balancing act, both culturally and operationally. In those years Cote likely lacked the management talent deep in the organization to pull off large-scale integrations.

Step 4: Expanding in Emerging Markets

In 2003 I took a group of investors to visit companies in China, when US companies were still small in the region. Some had interesting stories to tell. Caterpillar was lined up to sell into a construction boom, GE was going to help China generate cleaner electric power, and Emerson was set to build out telecom and internet infrastructure. As for Honeywell, it was lined up to sell not much of anything.

The company had a promising turbocharger business, but the product was overengineered and built to last far longer than the somewhat disposable cars made in China at the time. It was selling some process automation products, but it was losing share to everyone, including ABB, Emerson, and Yokogawa.

Honeywell executives were glad to receive us at their Shanghai office and take us through the main turbocharger factory. In those days they had few visitors. It was a relatively junior workforce of almost all US and European expats, with little seniority. Few local Chinese seemed to be on the payroll other than on the assembly line. There was little to showcase in the factory. In short, Honeywell's effort in China was nothing short of embarrassing. Of the dozen or more companies I visited that week in 2003, it was by far the weakest.

The good news was that China was just starting to open to outsiders, so Cote still had time to catch up to his rivals there.

There was just one problem. Not only did he want to design, produce, and sell in the region; he wanted locals to run the operations. Expats were too costly, but local managers were hard to come by. China was still a giant, unknown country for most foreign companies, and it was nearly impossible to navigate through a web of government rules and controls. While there were plenty of workers, even some engineers with factory experience, they rarely came from well-run factories. Excellence was just not part of the narrative in China at the time.

Enter Shane Tedjarati in September 2004, one of Cote's most impactful hires and arguably the best emerging markets leader in industrials. Prior to joining Honeywell, he headed Deloitte's consulting business in China, working with state-owned enterprises just beginning to think about running their businesses efficiently. He had learned the local rules and customs and had built relationships with key government leaders.

Cote gave Tedjarati a directive—"Get Honeywell China in a winning position"—and he gave Tedjarati every resource he needed. Tedjarati decided that the company needed to start over. The only way to sustain the turbocharger business was to fight its local rivals at their own game—by becoming the low-cost Chinese supplier. He wanted a product and a price point that customers could afford and the scale to deliver it at lower cost. That meant not only making products in local factories but also buying from local suppliers. Hardly any US companies were working that way, not back in 2003 at least. The strategy worked perfectly.

Tedjarati then extended the strategy to other businesses: automation and controls—check; fire and security—check; safety products—check. In just two years, Honeywell went from nowhere in China to having a legitimate story to tell. Within five years, it was best in class, while the other big US industrials were struggling to keep pace. It remains such today. And the China playbook has been deployed around the world, fueling Honeywell's growth in emerging markets more broadly.

Step 5: Undertaking a Financial Overhaul

All these fixes depended on Honeywell shoring up its financial position, notably generating far greater cash flow. Early on, Anderson as CFO had committed to investors that Honeywell would raise its cash/net income ratio to 95 percent, up from the historical 80 percent level. Actual results were closer to 100 percent. That cash came from the benefits that accrued from introducing Lean manufacturing, using better pricing strategies, having more value-added products, and holding the line on fixed costs. All of these drove sustainable changes.

To accelerate a decline in liabilities, Cote and Anderson got creative. They believed the company's stock was deeply undervalued, so they issued new shares and put them in the underfunded pension plan. Investors hated the move because it diluted their ownership stake, but it went a long way to solving the immediate liability crisis. As usual, Cote took the heat and stayed focused. As the stock firmed up over time, the pension did as well. The strategy worked, and the pension has been fully funded for some time now.

On asbestos liabilities, the company had exposure from two separate legacy businesses: Narco and Bendix. Combined, the two exposures scared people; separately they seemed manageable. So Cote and Anderson ring-fenced Narco by getting the claimants' permission to set up a trust with all liability and associated insurance coverage. The trust freed Honeywell from Narco exposure even if the claim forecasts proved inaccurate. Getting that freedom proved expensive, and Cote received fresh criticism for the hit. But he needed certainty from at least one of the asbestos battles. As for the environmental liabilities, Cote and Anderson likewise created some certainty by settling claims and ring-fencing what they could, all with a high level of transparency and integrity.

The company needed a capital structure for its debt that didn't make investors nervous. Until cash flow improved a lot, Honeywell had to stay conservative. It had to self-fund all investments, keep fixed costs flat, and sell off weak assets at decent prices. Over time, growth in cash flow was so high that liabilities became an afterthought. In fact, by 2008, investors pushed for greater risk taking, not less.

PLAYING OFFENSE AFTER 2008

From 2002 to 2007 Cote had to balance playing defense with opportunistic offense. Once the company proved itself, particularly in boosting margins and stabilizing the portfolio, it could show the growth and sustainability of the "new Honeywell."

But then came the financial crisis of 2008, which was tough on all industrials. Cote took the downturn harder than most, feeling he had let shareholders down. He cut executive bonus payouts to near zero but felt empathy for the factory workers and other lower-level employees. Rather than resort to full-scale layoffs, like most industrials, he offered workers the option of keeping their job at reduced hours and pay, but with full healthcare and other benefits. He believed he could cut enough to survive the downturn while treating people humanely—and once business conditions improved, he'd have a trained and loyal workforce to go full-time.

When business did come back in 2010, Honeywell had the people already lined up to add hours to their workweek. It could fill orders that others struggled to ramp up for. His customers were happier, the company achieved higher margins, and the stage was set for several years of prosperity—the fruits of all those tough decisions made earlier.

From 2010 onward Honeywell was clearly on the flywheel. Growth was steady at higher levels, margins expanded far more than expected, and cash flow grew with profits. The Cote turnaround was complete, and stakeholders rode a steady, predictable, and impressive company upward.

POSTMORTEM

Cote's final act at Honeywell, on the eve of his retirement in 2017, was to convince the board to promote Darius Adamczyk as his successor. Rather than a Cote clone, Adamczyk is a far different breed.

Where Cote had less interest in (or time for) advanced technology, the kind usually reserved for West Coast high-flyers, the new CEO has invested heavily in the industrial internet of things. It's an important pivot for the company. Adamczyk's vision of software, digital connectivity, and emerging technologies like quantum computing is edgier than that of his predecessor, but it's better suited to Honeywell's strong current position. The company can afford to play offense now.

That's how a company sustains growth over time: Combine a clear vision with systems to keep people focused on delivering value every day. Always look to the future and be willing to completely reinvent as needed—or better yet, before it's needed. Adamczyk's early success is a tribute to Cote. The pivot is the natural evolution of a company truly on the flywheel.

In the end, this turnaround was a battle far harder than words can do justice. For most of the early days, Cote was isolated. He had to build his senior team one person at a time, somehow convincing each to join a struggling organization. He needed strong leaders in all major regions, a superior finance staff, and engineers and scientists focused on solving customer problems. These take time, years in fact. Of the many lessons from the Honeywell turnaround, the time factor is perhaps most critical. Cultures don't develop and become sustainable overnight. That is a key lesson for the less patient tech world to consider. Patient reinforcement is needed. Honeywell's results in 2002 versus 2017 show a remarkable improvement, but the progress was steady, requiring daily management and the baby-step gains that are typical of a good Lean manufacturing, process-centric rollout.

Despite his lack of a pedigree and the fancy suits that help define success in a shallow world, Cote focused on the basics: having financial discipline in M&A, holding the line on fixed costs, and treating employees with compassion; and he did so with integrity. Cote used to say, "What you think, what you say, and what you do shouldn't be three separate decisions. They should be the same." That summarizes the Cote era perfectly. He delivered on his promises with a level of humility and transparency that builds the foundation for a great corporate culture and engenders a loyal following. It's easy to forget about that in the good times, but in the tough times, it matters.

My time with Dave Cote always came with a lot of laughing, joking, and the occasional prank. He never seemed to take himself too seriously. It was a far different experience from time spent with leaders at other industrial companies. I would take him on trips to visit investors, and the smallest things made him happy. He got excited if he was allowed to wear blue jeans to dinner and seemed like he would have been just as happy at a Motel 6 as at the Four Seasons. And maybe, just maybe, that's why people performed for him. He worked hard, he led by example, he pushed folks to get a little bit better every day, and his message translated at all levels. He kept it simple. He rewarded substance over style. He was a rare CEO, unconventional for sure, but one well worthy of emulation.

Lessons from Honeywell

- In massive conglomerates, complexity and bureaucracy become the accepted default.
- Turnarounds take time, patience, and persistence.
- Make the difficult and unpopular decisions as soon as possible.
- Cost structure and liabilities need to be addressed before growth can become the focus.
- Hold the line on fixed costs—people hire people who hire people—often unproductively.
- Pay top talent not just for the job they do today, but for the job they will be offered tomorrow.
- Localized strategies often yield better results than global strategies.
- Favorite "Cote-ism": "What you think, what you say, and what you do shouldn't be three separate decisions."

CHAPTER 6

UNITED TECHNOLOGIES

The Dangers of Fixed Incentives

BY CARTER COPELAND

"People do what you pay them to do" is a guiding principle of management. How much and toward what end an organization incentivizes its employees has a profound impact on how the business performs. The history of United Technologies (UTC) is a story of amazing success and failure with an incentive structure built around a simple goal, "Grow earnings 10 percent per year," at the center of the company's rise and fall.

UTC is one of the great industrial mega-conglomerates. For much of the 1900s, the company was known as United Aircraft and focused on the aviation market. However, in the 1970s, a new CEO named Harry Gray sought to diversify the company's interests away from aerospace, changing the name to United Technologies. In the years that followed, he acquired several iconic companies including Carrier Air Conditioning, founded by Willis Carrier, the inventor of modern air conditioning, and Otis Elevator, started by Elisha Otis, designer of the world's first elevator. These businesses operated in industries outside of United Technologies' legacy businesses, which included Pratt & Whitney Aircraft Engines and Sikorsky Helicopter, founded by Igor Sikorsky, the inventor of the first mass-produced helicopter. Taken together, this was a collection of some of the strongest brands in the world. After building this portfolio of high-quality and enviable businesses, the company shifted its focus in the 1980s to reducing bureaucracy and improving financial performance.

By the time George David, a Harvard-educated consultant, took the reins from Gray's successor, Robert Daniell, in 1994, UTC's efforts to optimize the financial performance of its various businesses hadn't fully captured Wall Street's imagination. This was especially true when compared with the rock star status bestowed upon Jack Welch and General Electric. In fact, late in Welch's tenure at GE, during a famous investor event, the distance between GE and UTC was on full display.

Both UTC and GE had long been regular attendees of the Electrical Products Group Conference in Florida. During GE's presentation, Welch was answering a question about well-managed and poorly managed companies. In his response, he called out UTC as one of the more poorly managed companies in the sector, suggesting it was permanently relegated to mediocrity. George David was sitting in the back of the room, something that Welch didn't realize until David got up and walked out.

A few years later, David was giving a motivational speech to UTC's senior-most leaders (200 or so out of more than 100,000 employees). He stated, "A couple of years ago, I met with Jack Welch, and he looked at me wistfully and said, 'I wish my businesses had the margin runway that yours do.'" At least some of the people who were there at the time think these two events were connected, with Welch's "margin runway" comments being a mea culpa of sorts. However, what's important isn't whether Welch apologized to David for embarrassing him in Florida, but rather how these interactions defined the next 20+ years at UTC. Over that time, margin expansion and strong management became inextricably linked via the company's long-term compensation program that paid managers for delivering 10 percent earnings growth. Through his tenure as CEO, George David reoriented United Technologies and its fabled brands to drive outsized earnings growth by consistently pushing margins higher. UTC became a Wall Street darling and David a legendary CEO, one who would be mentioned in the same breath as Jack Welch by the time he handed the company off to his successor.

Sadly, the United Technologies story doesn't end there. Future CEOs struggled to re-create the margin magic that defined David's tenure, and a once powerful incentive compensation scheme with margin improvement at its center proved too rigid. It drove suboptimal decisions around investment that weakened the company's competitive positioning. As a result, 10 percent growth targets became 6 percent, and 6 percent targets later became 4.5 percent. Years of underperformance culminated in the entrance of activist investors and the breakup of the once mighty conglomerate.

Incentives drive outcomes in an organization. At UTC, corporate incentives and a focus on improving margins led to many years of success, followed by several years of failure. The rise and fall of United Technologies highlights that the best incentive systems are not static or myopically focused; they should exhibit the same dynamism as an organization's ever-evolving set of opportunities and risks.

BUILDING THE RIGHT TEAM WITH THE RIGHT INCENTIVES

George David was an intellectual. The son of a Rhodes scholar and professor, David made his way to UTC via Harvard, the University of Virginia's Darden School, and the Boston Consulting Group. He came to UTC from the company's hostile takeover of Otis Elevator in 1976. He was promoted to president of Otis in 1986, where he oversaw six strong years of steady performance improvement before becoming president of UTC in 1992.

By the time David ascended to the CEO role in 1994, UTC was a massive company composed of six major business units. Pratt & Whitney, Hamilton Standard, and Sikorsky were the firm's aerospace businesses, while Otis, Carrier, and an automotive segment served more traditionally commercial markets. At the time, the combined sales of the company totaled more than $20 billion, making it one of the 20 largest companies in the United States.

In the mid-1990s, UTC was a large company in revenue terms, but its profit margins were far from stellar. A consolidated operating margin of ~7 percent at the time of David's promotion was nothing to brag about, as peers such as GE enjoyed margins that were more than double that. (See Figure 6.1.) This gap represented UTC's historical mediocrity as well as the "margin runway" that became the source of its future success. In his first four years as CEO, David attacked margins aggressively and oversaw their expansion to 9 percent, a laudable improvement, but still a level that didn't command full respect from investors and peers. David realized that he needed to source top-level talent both internally and externally in order to bring his strategic vision to reality.

Figure 6.1: **UTC margins were well below those of industrial peers when George David took over in 1994.**

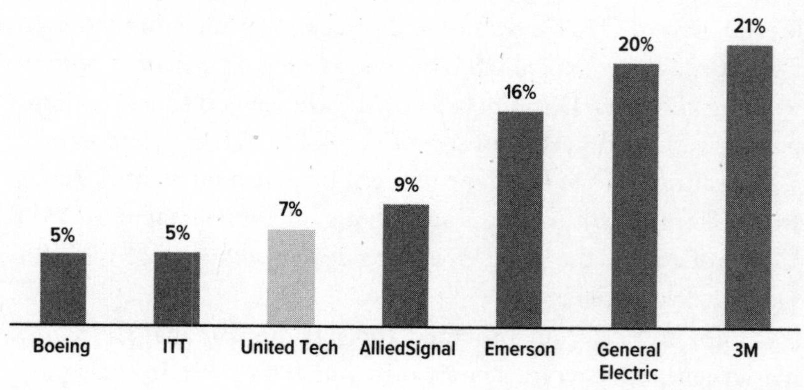

Source: Company filings

In order to attract top talent, UTC employees needed to be well compensated. Choosing a career at United Technologies meant forgoing a career as a high-paid investment banker, consultant, or private equity director. Other conglomerates like GE had stepped up pay rates, and UTC needed to as well. Consequently, long-term compensation incentives were increased and directly aligned with the company's principal opportunity—margin expansion and, by extension, growth in earnings per share (EPS).

By the early 2000s, annual EPS growth in excess of 10 percent on a compounded three-year basis became a central pillar of long-term incentive compensation at UTC. Stock/option payouts were sized accordingly to drive buy-in from employees across the enterprise. If the company delivered on its financial goals, business unit presidents, corporate executives, and numerous other senior managers stood to make a lot of money.

GOING LEAN

Beyond talent, David also saw the need to make bigger moves with regard to manufacturing. During his time at Otis, David came to appreciate the power of Lean manufacturing and the Toyota Production System (TPS) after Otis had a falling out with its Japanese joint venture partner, Matsushita. Matsushita uncovered flaws in Otis's quality control systems that were leading to frequent breakdowns of Otis elevators installed at Matsushita's headquarters. The Japanese were appalled. Otis was an elevator company without working elevators. David flew to Japan, where his Japanese counterparts gave him a crash course on Lean/TPS. When David eventually became CEO of UTC, he brought his Japanese mentor, Yuzuru Itō, to Connecticut to help implement a TPS-like system. In 1998, UTC rolled out the ACE operating system (short for Achieving Competitive Excellence).

The ACE system provided tools to help managers benchmark their performance against other units and best-in-class peers. Achievements were marked by recognizing individual work sites as gold, silver, or bronze. These classifications were based on a comprehensive set of criteria, going beyond productivity, quality, and financial performance to include employee engagement and customer satisfaction. ACE was incredibly successful at driving sustainable performance improvements across multiple facets of the enterprise.

Under David's watch, UTC closed hundreds of factories and dramatically restructured others, often moving the manufacturing footprint to Mexico or China. These closures were essential, as international competitors were emerging, and supply chains were increasingly being relocated overseas. At the time, David liked to say that a "typical" UTC factory restructuring doubled capacity and halved cost. As a result, massive gains fell to the bottom line in nearly every instance, fueling margin expansion and capital efficiency.

In the late 1990s and early 2000s, everything at UTC was focused on driving higher returns in one form or another: greater efficiency and productivity in factories, lower capital committed to new projects, and less waste at the corporate headquarters. During this time, UTC's operating margins expanded to 15 percent, more than double what they were when David took over. Toward the end of this period, it was not uncommon to see senior executives and sector presidents with $10 million to $25 million in accumulated but not-yet-exercised stock options as the incentive compensation program and rising stock price paid out. (See Figures 6.2 and 6.3.)

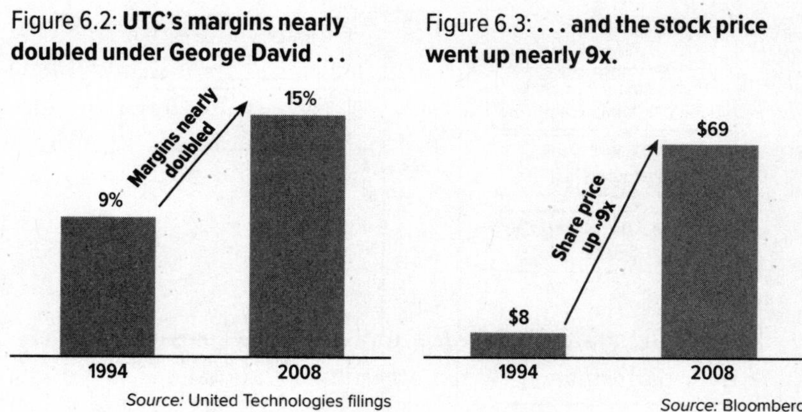

Figure 6.2: **UTC's margins nearly doubled under George David . . .**

Source: United Technologies filings

Figure 6.3: **. . . and the stock price went up nearly 9x.**

Source: Bloomberg

ACQUIRING MORE MARGIN EXPANSION

Fully appreciating how far they'd come, by the early 2000s UTC leadership concluded that if the company was going to keep things going, it required more substantial investment through M&A. By buying companies in which UTC's refined operating principles could be applied, acquisitions created margin expansion opportunities similar to those already achieved at the legacy franchises.

The first big portfolio move happened earlier in the George David era. In 1999, UTC acquired aerospace parts maker Sundstrand and sold its automotive business. (See Figure 6.4.) The automotive segment had the lowest margins in the corporation and didn't enjoy the same upside potential, or "runway," as the other operating units. On the other hand, Sundstrand was an aerospace supplier that enjoyed double-digit profitability, with room for further improvement. For many years, these actions were referred to internally as the "aero for auto" trade, the earliest evidence that portfolio moves and M&A could significantly enhance earnings growth prospects and strategic positioning.

Figure 6.4: **History of United Technologies (1972–2018).**

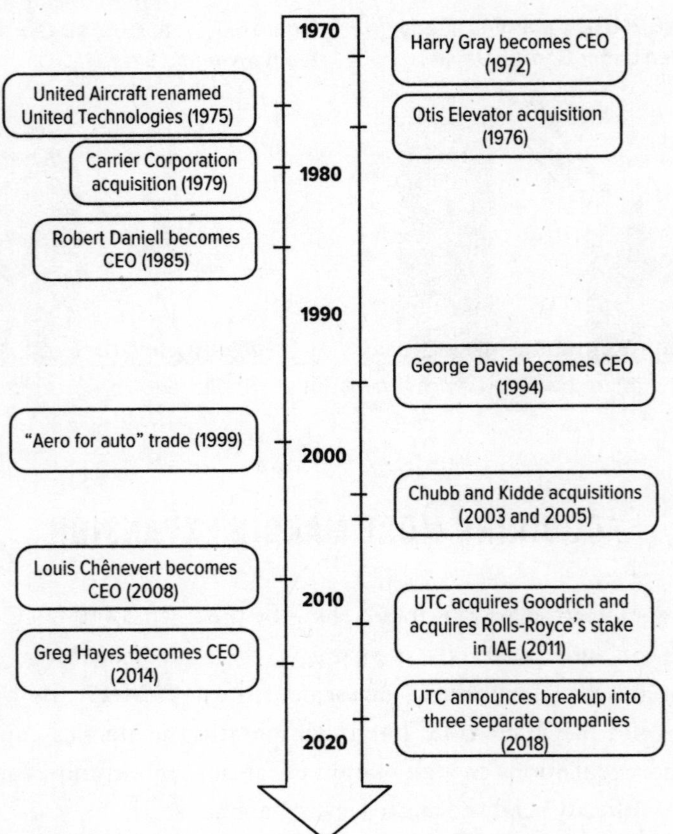

Source: United Technologies filings, press reports

UTC's expansion kicked into high gear with the acquisition of Chubb Fire & Security in 2003 and then Kidde, a British fire safety company, in 2005. The combined investment of $4 billion was a purposeful move to create an entirely new Fire & Security segment to operate alongside Otis, Carrier, and the aerospace businesses. The strategic rationale for these transactions was that since Otis and Carrier were global leaders in building systems (elevators and air conditioners), fire safety and security products and services were natural adjacencies. Furthermore, given UTC's success in rationalizing costs and improving margins in its own businesses, the company believed it could apply those same principles to the newly formed Fire & Security unit. Extending this line of thinking, UTC followed the Chubb and Kidde deals with acquisitions of everything from fluidless fire sprinkler systems to a wide array of home security products. UTC Fire & Security went on a major buying spree.

Unfortunately, many of these businesses didn't have the same competitive advantages, scale, or longstanding market positions of the existing UTC franchises. George David liked to say that UTC was in the business of "gravity, weather, and war, and these things aren't going away any time soon." This was a witty reference to the company's role in helping humans defy the laws of gravity in elevators and on airplanes, make life more livable with heating and cooling products, and support national security ambitions by supplying military helicopters and aircraft engines. The Fire & Security unit was different. The markets the business served were more fragmented and competitive. As a result, the UTC value creation formula didn't work as well at Fire & Security. The company had moved a bit out of its comfort zone. While the segment undoubtedly enjoyed some success in the years that followed, its creation felt like the first time that UTC was reaching for returns.

THE FIRST CRACKS EMERGE

Roughly a decade into David's tenure, it wasn't yet evident to external observers that things in the organization were beginning to change for the worse. However, on the inside, there were growing questions around the sustainability of the efforts being taken to push margins higher. Principal among these concerns was underinvestment in new products and technologies, as R&D projects were being shelved in favor of maintaining or expanding shorter-term profits.

In David's first five years as CEO, company spending on R&D totaled ~5 percent of revenue on average. However, this spending fell to roughly 3 percent by the time he retired. (See Figure 6.5.) Across several of the business segments, the next generation of R&D projects was delayed or abandoned entirely. After Otis successfully introduced the Gen2 elevator in 2000, new product introductions fell dramatically. And at Pratt, a decision to pull out of the engine competition for the 787 Dreamliner due to the longer-dated nature of the program's returns and the heavy up-front investment resulted in the business missing out on a new aircraft program that would be around for 30+ years.

Figure 6.5: **R&D spending fell consistently.**

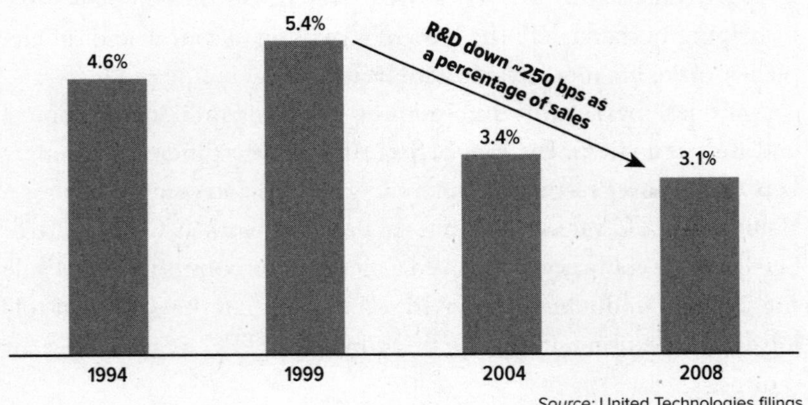

Source: United Technologies filings

Many inside the company later argued that this golden era of profitability and growth was the perfect time to be reinvesting in the next generation of products that could set the company up for long-term success. However, the organization and its leaders were largely oriented around a 10 percent earnings growth target that was only feasible if margins continued to move higher. Margin expansion was core to the company's success and its managers' paychecks. It had become culturally ingrained deep in the bowels of the organization via ACE, and it manifested itself as a perpetual war on costs, even good ones.

The pursuit of cost minimization and profit maximization is great in principle. Efficiency isn't a bad thing, but taken too far it comes with consequences. Lower costs applied to well-understood, preexisting businesses are pretty straightforward, as they fall straight to the bottom line. However, if new business opportunities are judged versus legacy margin rates, investments in projects that offer growth potential, attractive returns on capital, or even more loosely defined "strategic value" may never materialize.

What happened at UTC toward the end of the David era was a textbook example of margin focus taken too far. Otis eclipsed the 20 percent margin mark in 2009 and spent the end of David's tenure eight margin points ahead of its closest competitor. Some of this margin differential was understandable, as the company possessed the largest collection of installed and serviceable elevators on the planet. Since service sales feature the highest margins, this pointed to a margin premium of a few percentage points. The rest of the difference came from lower spending on new products and a focus on selling high-end elevators rather than lower-margin, entry-level products. This focus kept margins high but resulted in the company ceding significant market share to competitors in the world's fastest-growing new elevator market, China.

Carrier similarly doubled reported margin rates under David's watch, but near the end of his tenure and following his retirement it needed to sell off lower-margin distribution assets to do so. Air conditioners aren't sold direct from the factory. They get to the end customer through a two-step distribution system. The profits from the distribution part of the sales process aren't particularly high, so pulling the distribution assets out of Carrier pushed margins higher simply by improving the mix. Better yet, if Carrier sold only a portion of those assets (anything more than 50 percent), the remaining share of the profits from the distribution assets would be treated as an "unconsolidated joint venture." This quirky accounting recognition resulted in the counting of profits without the associated revenue and pushed reported margins even higher. Finally, at the aerospace units, Pratt's more than doubling of margins was helped by skipping the investment in the next generation of aircraft engines.

At the latter stages of the David era, finding ways to continue to expand margins became more difficult, and yet the company stuck to its 10 percent EPS growth target. In order to keep getting paid, this once highly successful incentive compensation scheme began to drive decisions that skewed in favor of short-term profits versus long-term business health. By the time Louis Chênevert was named COO, marking him as David's successor, UTC was on a challenging path.

STICKING TO THE PLAN

Louis Chênevert came to the CEO role from the Pratt & Whitney engine business. The Montreal native began his career as a factory floor guy, working for General Motors in Canada, where he rose to become general manager of a large production site before leaving to join Pratt & Whitney Canada in 1993. His rise through the Pratt organization coincided with the early years of the George David era, and his promotion to the role of president at Pratt happened just after the adoption of ACE.

The internal race to succeed David was won unexpectedly by Chênevert. Most assumed that Ari Bousbib, who ran Otis Elevator, was best suited to carry on after David. Yet David and the board chose Chênevert, in part because of his devotion to the people-focused values of the company. The chief example of that devotion was Chênevert's steadfast commitment to an initiative known as the Employee Scholars Program. Started by David in 1996, the program offered to pay all tuition-related expenses for employees in any field of their choice. During Chênevert's tenure leading Pratt, no business unit was as successful at helping employees advance their skills through the program. Among other factors, David and the UTC board saw Chênevert's understanding of the importance of investing in people as a key strength.

Chênevert's thinking on the future of UTC's end markets was influenced by the power of "megatrends"—the expansion of the global middle class, the urbanization of global populations, and secular growth in air travel demand. This was similar to David's "gravity, weather, and war" characterization, as both pointed to long-term growth. Together with investments in talent, Chênevert believed these trends formed the backbone of the UTC investment story.

Just after Chênevert was promoted to CEO, and while David was still chairman of the board, UTC ran into the Great Recession and experienced significant financial challenges. UTC managed through the crisis with some tough actions, including a nearly 10 percent reduction in the company's global workforce. These actions helped preserve overall margin levels and also provided some headroom for modest increases in development spending on new products.

Despite the challenges brought on by the broader economy, the 10 percent earnings growth target remained essentially unchanged. Some modest tweaks to how the measure was calculated helped make up for the "missing" year of performance caused by the recession. However, the fundamental philosophy remained the same. The margin magic needed to be recaptured in order for executives to receive their full bonuses. As a result, Chênevert emerged from the crisis by setting bigger, bolder long-term targets for each business segment at UTC. They were all consistent with the 10 percent growth framework and the megatrends that defined the company's longer-term outlook.

It's difficult to know how much of the "same playbook" storyline is directly attributable to Chênevert. During the first two years of his tenure, George David remained at the company as chairman. It can be very challenging for a new CEO to chart a different path from one's predecessor, especially when that predecessor retains control of the board. This dynamic may have hamstrung Chênevert's ability to plot a truly differentiated course for the company. Regardless of the contributing factors, Chênevert did not attempt to dramatically alter the company's existing strategic priorities or direction.

ENDGAME

At the turn of the decade in 2010, the internal cracks in confidence that were formed during the tail end of the David era became more pronounced. More executives were taking notice of the increasingly tenuous situation that several of the business units found themselves in. At the same time, the company conducted its first-ever 10-year business review, an exercise dubbed "UTC 2020."

In one UTC 2020 review, a Pratt & Whitney executive delivered a sobering presentation on Pratt's outlook. By skipping a generation of new engine development on the 787, Pratt was approaching a point where the profits on engines sold in prior decades risked material declines. Profit growth was set to slow dramatically before heading into negative territory. Investments to refill the tank with new products were under way, but they needed to be bigger and faster than currently envisioned to pay off in time to offset the pressures, and further cost-reduction actions wouldn't make up the looming shortfall either. Chênevert didn't want to hear it. He wanted his leaders to find solutions and deliver results. The executive was gone from Pratt by year-end. This meeting established the future rules of engagement: If you couldn't hit the earnings growth targets, keep it to yourself. In the years that followed, revelations on similar growth challenges spiraled across the enterprise, but the business unit presidents put their heads down and attempted to march toward the longer-term targets, cobbling together a series of shorter-term wins along the way.

The best example was at Otis, where an effort to draw a hard line on maintaining margins during a period of slower revenue growth created disastrous consequences. Geographically, Europe was the most profitable region in the world for Otis, as the company had lucrative service contracts on nearly one million elevators across the continent. When new construction activity ground to a halt in Europe in the wake of the financial crisis, Otis aimed to maintain margin rates by holding firm on service contract pricing. What Otis leaders failed to realize was that the weak economy had created a glut of new elevator installers with nothing to do. These technicians were happy to service Otis's elevators at much lower prices. When contract renewals came up and Otis held firm on price, customers began to defect. This resulted in UTC's single largest profit pool shrinking by more than half.

Cost reduction and productivity enhancement as drivers of margin expansion were also significantly more difficult to manifest during the Chênevert era. The low-hanging fruit had been captured years ago by David and his team. The segments were forced to defy the laws of supply and demand, ignore investments required to maintain competitiveness, and use accounting quirks to maintain or boost margins. The company was getting stuck.

With the traditional UTC playbook running out of steam, the focus shifted to changes that could be made to the overall portfolio of businesses in order to deliver the necessary levels of growth. The pressure was on the leadership team to find gigantic acquisitions in UTC's fastest-growing end market, commercial aerospace.

The big deals came in late 2011. UTC announced the acquisition of aerospace supplier Goodrich for $18.4 billion, in what, at the time, was the largest aerospace transaction on record. Then, not even a month later, UTC bought out JV partner Rolls-Royce's stake in the International Aero Engines (IAE) Alliance for a $1.5 billion payment upon closure and billions more in promised royalty payments over the next 15 years. The IAE deal consolidated the economic interests in the popular V2500 aircraft engine under the UTC umbrella, bolstering the commercial franchise at Pratt.

Both deals helped earnings in the short to medium term, as UTC planned to generate $350 million in cost synergies from the Goodrich deal that would drop directly to the bottom line (it ultimately achieved nearly double this amount). The IAE transaction was structured in a way that pulled Rolls-Royce's share of earnings onto UTC's financial statements, while deferring royalty payments into future years. This boosted short-term EPS at the expense of future cash flow.

Following the closure of the Goodrich and IAE transactions, earnings continued to grow, from $5.49 in 2011 to $6.82 in 2014, a ~7 percent annualized rate, still shy of the 10 percent target. However, the company's cash flows grew approximately half as fast (see Figures 6.6 and 6.7), suggesting that the reported earnings were being overstated. This proved to be the case, as some benefits that had been counted as earnings didn't have cash flow to go along with them. Chênevert continued to publicly promote the achievability of UTC's longer-term targets, but it all came crashing down in 2015. He wasn't around to witness the collapse, as he was abruptly pushed out of the CEO seat just before Thanksgiving weekend in late 2014. The UTC board had grown frustrated with the extent of Chênevert's time out of the office, including his frequent trips to Asia to oversee the construction of his 110-foot yacht.

Figure 6.6: **UTC cash flows grew at . . .**

Figure 6.7: **. . . about half the pace of earnings.**

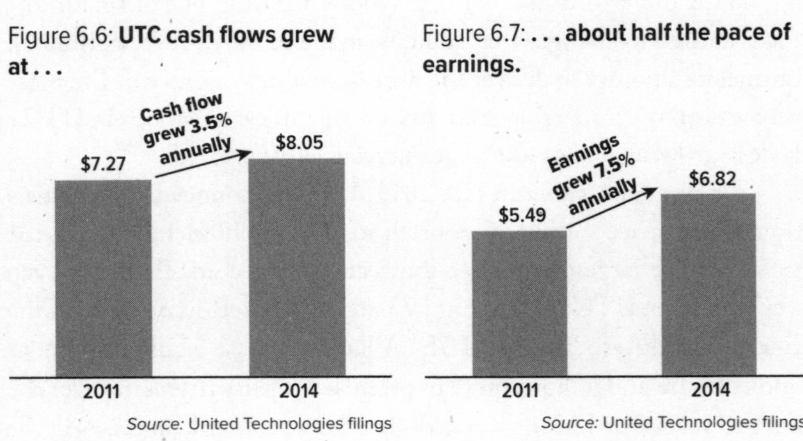

Source: United Technologies filings

Source: United Technologies filings

WHEN THE MUSIC STOPPED

UTC's board began to appreciate the lack of relevance of the old double-digit framework just as Chênevert was ousted, as long-term incentive targets were reduced to 6 percent in 2015. It was evident that prior levels of growth could no longer be delivered. This was again reduced to 4.5 percent a year later, a level below what UTC was projecting for sales growth. This implied a contraction in profit margins after years of promising endless expansion.

Replacing Chênevert was Gregory Hayes, UTC's CFO, widely regarded by Wall Street as more cognizant of and willing to face the company's challenges. By the time he took the reins from Chênevert, however, UTC's course was already plotted, and in 2015 the financials began to unravel. UTC's EPS stagnated in the mid-$6 range for effectively five years following the big M&A deals that were completed in 2012. (See Figure 6.8.) Hayes was left to refill the earnings tank in multiple segments by accelerating reinvestment in new product development and breaking the margin mindset that had dominated UTC's culture for so long.

Figure 6.8: **UTC's EPS stagnated for five years.**

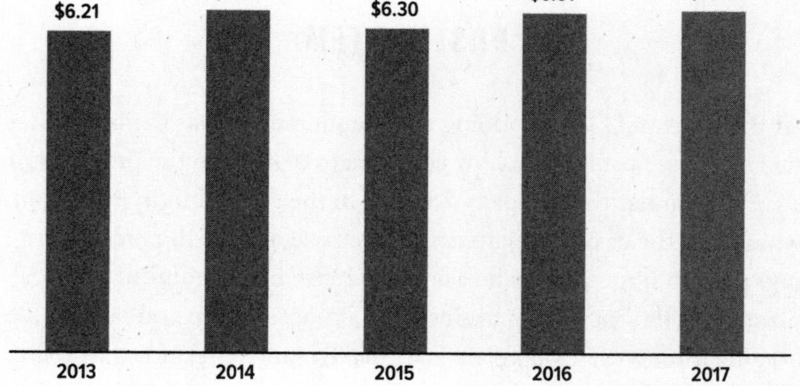

Source: United Technologies filings
Note: EPS adjusted for company-defined extraordinary items

This reversal of fortunes was painful. Otis's margins had already begun falling before Hayes took over, but within four years they stood nearly eight percentage points below their peak. Otis required investment to help regain lost market share, and the high-margin service business had shrunk materially for reasons already discussed. Similarly, on the back of a build-out in Pratt's newest commercial engine, the Geared Turbofan (GTF), margins bottomed out at 8 percent, nearly half of the peak realized when Chênevert was CEO. UTC's combined aerospace parts business, United Technologies

Aerospace Systems (UTAS), saw the synergies from the Goodrich transaction spent in later years, as investments required for future aircraft platforms emerged.

Hayes took a lot of heat from Wall Street during this time. Ultimately, he and the board agreed that the best course of action for UTC's longer-term health was to break up the company into three smaller pieces: Otis, Carrier, and an aerospace conglomerate. Shortly after the break up was announced, the remaining aerospace conglomerate announced that it would merge with defense contractor Raytheon, creating a giant aerospace and defense enterprise that in many ways resembled United Aircraft, the company Harry Gray fought hard to diversify a half century before.

POSTMORTEM

At the heart of UTC's undoing as a conglomerate was the belief that the enterprise could somehow continue to deliver on the promises of a CEO who ran the company 25 years in the past. Margin expansion, which was the easiest way to drive success against a 10 percent earnings growth target, is much easier to achieve in a suboptimized organization with 7 percent margins than a more mature and productive organization with 15 percent margins. In hindsight, it is surprising that a company that had gone through such a great level of transformation didn't think it was necessary to reassess the incentive structure at the center of its success, especially when performance began to fall short of targets. Cultural convictions were very firmly entrenched and never questioned loudly enough until it was too late.

Today's new economy firms may be especially vulnerable to simple, rigid incentive plans, as they tend to favor highly ambitious and narrowly focused or even singular goals earlier on in a company's life cycle. UTC's experience shows that a single overarching goal can help drive transformation in the short term, but the organization needs new goals after that transformation.

For organizations large and small, it's nearly impossible to find singular metrics that appropriately drive the needed behavior across organizations, especially over extended periods of time. Business conditions, competitive dynamics, product/technology cycles, and talent availability are all dynamic variables. Compensation and incentives for executives and managers should be as well. Few companies do this well. It requires a thorough examination of the particular opportunities and constraints that an organization faces over both the short and long term and the courage to shift course when internal and external conditions change.

Lessons from United Technologies

- Incentives drive organizational behavior.
- Sustainable success requires changing incentives on a semi-regular basis.
- The best incentives are dynamic and fuel long-term, systematic improvements.
- CEO transitions are opportunities to apply fresh thinking across the business.
- Underinvestment trades short-term gains for longer-term pain.
- Don't fire the bearers of bad news. Feedback is essential.

CHAPTER

7

CATERPILLAR

Avoiding the Forecasting Trap

BY ROB WERTHEIMER

Caterpillar is one of the industrial world's best-known brands, with its yellow bulldozers and excavators visible on construction projects around the world. As of 2019 more than a hundred thousand people worked at CAT, and the stock market valued the company at $80 billion—but those numbers could have been much higher. The company just recently came out of a two-decade-long stretch with painful periods of poor performance and destructive acquisitions.

Great industrials have endured through continuous improvement—a slow, iterative process with increasingly huge benefits as time goes by—the benefits of which are locked in as competence becomes ingrained across the employee base. Caterpillar's experience illustrates the depth of the problems that can arise when a systematic culture and operating system *isn't* present in a large organization. Without that, a company is forced to try to manage by feel, using forecasting and intuition to guess demand. In a cyclical industry, staying true to Lean is even harder, but also more important. There are some booms and busts in the end markets in this case study, but they aren't the focus. Rather, it's how CAT dealt with them and how that accentuated the volatility.

CAT lost out on billions in potential revenues and earnings by having inadequate management systems. Competitors took advantage, using their own Lean and flexible production to enter markets that had been CAT strongholds. CAT then made the mistake of overcorrecting, losing billions more in potential earnings. Instead of large profits compounding in fruitful acquisitions, CAT reinvested its *lower* earnings base poorly, with billions spent on acquisitions that deliver negligible sales today. Skittish investors now value its current earnings below those of its industrial peers, making for another missing pool of billions of dollars. This was a spiral of great proportions.

CAT's strengths have always been in its products: high-quality, durable equipment that worked harder and outlasted the competition, by years in many cases. Its dealers are also second to none, the result of decades of careful growth and cultivation, market share gains, and leadership. No one can match CAT for service, and customer loyalty grows with each new generation. But it still lost market share, let competitors gain footholds in markets where CAT had been dominant, and suffered poor margins for nearly two decades.

What went wrong at CAT couldn't be fixed by dramatic, brute-force decisions; yet the company's leaders, acting with a sense of urgency and frustration with past problems, made such choices anyway. CAT's end markets are very cyclical: sales move up and down 20 to 30 percent, not the 2 to 3 percent common in noncyclical markets. That's just the nature of the business. Excellence in production systems can dampen the swings by controlling everything else *other* than demand: quality, on-time delivery, safety, and many other metrics that are independent of volume. Robust and disciplined business systems help ensure that. In CAT's case, the absence of a robust operating system *heightened* the cyclical swings instead of dampening them—by a material amount, an additional 20 percent volatility stacked onto the already swinging markets. Mistakes made in one direction were ultimately countered with hard pushes in the other, driving increasing pain across the enterprise.

An analogy: Years ago I served in the Peace Corps in West Africa. My job involved visiting very remote villages by motorcycle. One village I visited occasionally was at the end of a three-mile-long stretch of road made of loose sand, with foot-deep ruts all along it from trucks taking villagers to market. There was only one way to go: full speed, to push through the sand, keeping RPMs up, while riding in the high spot between the curving, deeply rutted tracks. As long as I stayed smoothly in the middle, all was fine, but a little swerve to one side would bring me close to falling into one tire track, and a correction to that, closer to the other. Small corrections led to bigger ones, and eventually the front wheel would dig in, the bike would go haywire, and I'd end up buried headfirst in sand and an hour late. Riders who lived there made tiny, micro adjustments smoothly throughout the ride, never overcorrecting and never falling.

CAT: MORE THAN DIRT MOVING

Caterpillar is a heavy equipment manufacturer, founded in 1925. The company makes a wide array of products, including the broadest line of construction equipment in the industry: excavators, graders, scrapers for moving dirt around. It produces large equipment for roadwork, and smaller machines for landscaping and residential construction. Notably, it also has the largest mining equipment division in the world, with massive machines: a CAT 797 mining truck can carry 400 tons of dirt and ore, using a 3,800-horsepower engine that could light up more than a thousand homes.

Aside from machines, CAT makes engines and turbines for heavy jobs around the world. Its diesel and natural gas engines power all kinds of marine vessels, drilling rigs, fracking pumps, and locomotives. They compress natural gas for transmission in pipelines. CAT engines are often the backup power in generator sets for data centers and office buildings. But demand in all these markets can be quite cyclical.

Those cycles got worse starting in the 1980s. A long downturn followed the bursting of a commodities bubble in the 1970s, and there were few reasons to think recovery was anywhere on the horizon. CAT also went through periods of debilitating strikes, which only added to the pressure resulting from weak demand. Coming out of the 1990s, CAT had spent too little on capacity in the face of these challenges. In fact, annual capital expenditures from 1993 to 2003 averaged just about in line with depreciation, meaning spending on factories and equipment was only enough to replace what was wearing out.

Experience has taught many manufacturers that it is hard to foresee the swings up and down in demand, especially in highly cyclical markets. Making cars in the 1950s involved making annual forecasts, estimating demand, and then setting production to meet that expected demand. That meant the factory was going to produce a certain number of cars, no matter what, this day, this month, maybe even this quarter or year. The factory could then plan accordingly so that everything was smooth, with no unpredictable swings up or down in volume. At first glance this makes sense.

The problem is, planning rarely works well. Not with cars, and certainly not with mining trucks. When demand is lower than expected, you've just built too many cars, and they are out there sitting in lots somewhere. Eventually production has to be cut, and cut deeper than the level of current demand, to get rid of all the extra unsold inventory. Workers feel the disruption in both boom and bust directions, with disruptive calls for overtime and extra shifts and then hours cut or layoffs, and it hurts. CAT has end markets that swing wider than the market for autos and has experienced this problem repeatedly. Furthermore, the amount of equipment needed to extract desired materials from a mine, or to power huge jobs in remote parts of the world, can vary dramatically over time, further complicating any forecasting.

Take for example the CAT 777 mining truck. In 1990, a truck carrying 100 tons of dirt and rock would have had about 20 ounces of gold ore mixed in. By 2015, that same load might have had only five ounces of gold because of lower ore grades. The good mines were drying up, and the new ones had lower-quality resources. For CAT's customers, that meant four times as many trucks to get the same gold output. This was also true of copper. And the situation in oil and gas extraction is even more dramatic. A drilling rig that might have used 500 to 1,000 horsepower from the 1950s into the 1990s now needs 5,000 horsepower, with 50,000 more for fracking the well. That's hundreds of times the CAT power needed to get a barrel of oil out of the ground. The combined change in these factors was far more abrupt than forecasts based on historical ordering levels and fleet replacement could have ever predicted.

Forecasting feels like a science, but it isn't. To be fair, CAT hasn't just blindly guessed what the world would look like at any given time. The company has typically used a detailed combination of historical fleet sales, replacement demand estimates, and forward-looking customer demand. As analysts, we do the same thing, and we have been just as wrong as CAT over the years. There are just too many variables and external factors that swing demand, often to extremes.

Another problem is that customers sometimes lie or spin the truth to suit their own needs. During the upturn in commodities, one of CAT's mining customers infamously told the company it could buy every truck CAT could make for several years. This customer was probably only 10 to 20 percent of CAT's business; if all the other miners had the same demand, capacity needed to quintuple. As it turned out, it just wasn't true. The customer was probably ticked off that the trucks it had ordered in prior years hadn't come fast enough.

Similar bad data came from customers on how many mining trucks were running every day. In 2011 CAT's mining customers were saying that they ran trucks 24/7, close to 8,000 hours a year. Turns out a lot of them weren't, and many of those hours that the trucks *were* running weren't needed. The trucks were just idling or engaged in some other inefficiency. These challenges contributed to violent swings in an already cyclical business.

THE JIM OWENS ERA: PROTECTING DOWNSIDE WITH A HIGH OPPORTUNITY COST

In 2004 Jim Owens took over as CAT's CEO. An economist by training, Owens was a bespectacled gray-haired man. He'd spent decades with the company, pushing through supply chain improvements, running successively larger businesses, and eventually serving as CFO. This type of career success is common at CAT, but it can be problematic. The company's culture is exceptionally insular, and CAT could have used some fresh ideas on production systems back then.

Owens's message to investors focused on ensuring that CAT could weather the next cyclical downturn, whenever it came. This meant making money instead of losing it when times were tough, an aspiration seeded in the hard-learned lessons of the 1980s. Recessions, poor management, and inflexible labor had driven International Harvester, the largest machinery company in the world, into bankruptcy in that decade. CAT lost $1 million a day for two years in the 1980s.

CAT's leaders, almost all of whom had 20 to 30 years with the company, still felt the pain from that time. Owens believed that the stock market still paid too much attention to it, and that CAT got too little credit for the company's hard work making its cost structure more flexible, so subsequent downturns inflicted less damage. That improved flexibility, however, wasn't exactly due to the systematic improvements we emphasize throughout this book. It came from lower investment and hard-won concessions from the unions via strikebreaking.

By 2004, 15 years of underinvestment had weakened the company. Unlike some companies, CAT did generate enough cash to have invested more, but not enough money flowed to the factories to secure future growth. At that point CAT may have eventually gotten some credit for managing well through recessions, but the leadership team's cautious approach had missed the fat pitches thrown in many of CAT's end markets. Market share losses hurt equipment sales in one year, and then they hurt parts and aftermarket sales for the next 15 years that CAT's machine would have been running. On top of that, without a strong production system to bring discipline, the company mis-executed on the lower volumes it did produce. Quality issues that should have been fixed permanently on the spot were not, which led to delays in deliveries. In the end, while Owens invested more in factory capacity than prior leaders had, it would prove too conservative a response to how the world was developing.

The world was on the cusp of a boom in both commodity and construction markets. CAT excels in mining and oil and gas, delivering big, durable engines to power the work. Drilling rigs can cost tens to hundreds of thousands of dollars a day to run, and the folks running them want tough, reliable equipment. Mining is similar home turf—no one can keep trucks running better than CAT. When copper booms, customers want to fix up every truck they have and buy more to maximize the amount of resources they can take out of the mine. A mining truck carrying 300 tons of dirt and copper is moving $40,000 worth of copper every hour, maybe a million dollars in a day. A $4 million mining truck looks like a small investment when profits are high. On the other hand, it also looks like a high-cost anchor on profits when copper prices are low.

In the early 2000s China was at the inflection point of an amazing run of growth, and its need for iron, coal, and copper to fuel its infrastructure and factory surge was straining the global base of mine production. Copper prices that had been flat for 20 years reached new highs, then doubled, and rose 50 percent again after that. Gold prices reached prior highs as well. The price of metallurgical coal, used to make steel, rose more than five times. These are precisely the sorts of unpredictable compounding factors that can make demand for equipment explode.

The surge in mining demand came alongside not only a rise in oil prices but also a structural shift in how oil was extracted. Hydraulic fracturing, or "fracking," of wells was becoming far more important than drilling holes. Wells had been fracked for many decades, sometimes with dynamite and once with a 43-kiloton nuclear bomb (1969, in Rulison, Colorado), but widespread horizontal drilling and fracking of wells as a primary strategy was new. Fracking has mostly been confined to North America, but it has provided most of the world's incremental oil and gas for the past decade, and very quickly it started to displace investments elsewhere.

The power required was massive. By 2008, engines for fracking were roughly as numerous as all the engines in US drilling rigs combined. By 2012, fracking engine horsepower was greater than the collective power used globally in drilling rigs, pipelines, and gas storage and processing, both onshore and offshore.

An official at Aramco, Saudi Arabia's national oil company, once mentioned to me that a good well drilled in the Ghawar oilfield today might flow 50,000 barrels a day, and a bad one, 10,000 barrels. These simple vertical wells take a 3,000-horsepower drilling rig, make a hole, and oil comes out. A frack site uses dozens of trucks carrying water and sand, and dozens of big diesel engines totaling 50,000 horsepower to force that water and sand down the well hole to fracture the rock containing oil. With all that effort, a typical well might flow 500,000 barrels, maybe a million, across its entire life, which is about what a good well in Saudi Arabia might flow in a couple of weeks.

While fracking requires much more power input to get a barrel of oil out, the cost is partially offset by the relative certainty that oil will flow once fracked. There aren't many dry holes in well-established fracking regions. Fracking remains the source of most growth in global oil and gas today.

Just as global commodities started to boom under pressure from China in the 2000s, the US construction economy was also seeing a burst of demand. Following the recession of 2001, the US stimulated construction demand with lower interest rates. That fueled a record bubble that would ultimately pop, precipitating the plunge into the Great Recession we're all familiar with, but not until after a period of significant growth.

At the end of the day, CAT simply hadn't invested in the capacity to come anywhere near meeting this simultaneous growth in demand in its end markets. Fracking customers bought engines from Cummins instead. CAT's capacity shortage thus let a competitor into a business where CAT had been the primary, most trusted supplier. More important, CAT hadn't gained control over the aspects of the business that *were* within its power, making the situation much worse. Otherwise loyal customers went elsewhere, not just to Cummins in fracking but also to Cummins in power generation sets and to Komatsu in mining.

FAILURE SHOWS ON THE FACTORY FLOOR

I've toured countless factories on five continents, over many years, as a part of covering machinery companies. Usually I get to talk to line operators and learn about products, production schedules, and culture. In the Owens era, Caterpillar factories shocked me with their disorganization.

Employee engagement is a key metric of a well-run company. The essence of continuous improvement is collaboration: workers identify hiccups to be smoothed out; engineers consult on how to redesign a part or a process. In modern production, quality is critical, and problems need to be identified, showered with resources, and corrected on the spot so they don't recur. That's why any worker can call a stop to the entire production line in auto factories—unthinkable in the 1950s but standard nowadays. CAT's problems in 2006–2008 included the fact that a great many quality issues were not fixed on the spot: demand was surging, capacity was inadequate to meet it, and the company didn't want to slow down production to fix problems. Some of the issues were supply chain shortages, where it seemed to make no sense to hold up a bulldozer line while waiting for a hydraulic hose to arrive. Whether because bad blood between management and workers hindered continuous improvement (bitter labor disputes in the 1990s had ended with the union gaining almost nothing) or because CAT was pushing too hard to get product out the door, quality control was broken.

In 2007, I arrived in Peoria, Illinois, for a factory visit that showed just how disorganized production can get when a sharp rise in demand meets a poorly running system. I saw a crowded, inefficient space that, even to an inexpert eye, looked like a problem. Machines were pulled off to the side of the line, waiting for hoses or a touch-up on paint. There were piles of extra inventory at workstations along the production line. And most memorably, there were bins filled with components that should have been on newly made bulldozers and other machines, but instead were labeled "re-work." At one point those bins were stacked more than head high and obscured the first aid station. The money spent on all this waste limited the funds available to invest in process improvement.

"First-pass quality" is a simple measure of the percentage of time that a product comes out correctly. Most factories have percentages in the high 90s, and 98–99 percent is common (dirty work like casting and forging often scores lower). The first-pass quality numbers on this tour were in the low 80s. CAT was spending huge amounts to fix and rework what should have been done right the first time. Any nonstandard process in a factory, or a company for that matter, is expensive, and doing things a second time is not standard. This and the visual evidence were clear signals: the production process was broken.

With simultaneous surges in construction, oil and gas, powergen, and mining, CAT should have been printing money. But due to these inefficiencies, the demand they did satisfy came at low margins.

Some costs in manufacturing are fixed, so when sales go up, margins should rise materially. "Incremental" margins of 20 to 35 percent on the extra revenue are typical for the construction and mining equipment businesses. Between 2004 and 2006 CAT's construction and mining equipment sales rose by almost 40 percent, but its margin on selling that equipment went from around 9 percent to only 12 percent, meaning its incremental margin on those extra sales was only about 15 percent. It also likely burned out more than its fair share of employees, with line managers under extreme stress to produce more and faster and overtime hours pushing the limits. This type of imbalance often creates cultural breakdowns. It rewards people who muscle through bad processes to get the job done, not people who stop and fix, as proper Lean management demands. CAT got all that fresh tension in the system for barely any incremental profit. CAT's response to this was to raise prices to capture some extra margin, risking its long-term competitiveness and market share, because its production system wasn't working well.

By 2007 the US housing bubble was popping, but CAT machine sales were still growing, up about 10 percent in 2007 and again in 2008. But now profit margins actually went *down*, with the 2007 margin falling back to 10 percent. Despite extra pricing taken, 2008 margins were worse still, even before the financial collapse—all setting up for a fourth quarter that was nothing short of a disaster.

The failure to profit from surging demand was just one of the consequences of CAT's underinvestment in a robust production system.

Sizable losses in market share constituted another. Just as Caterpillar was struggling with deliveries, Komatsu, the company's major rival in construction and mining, was smoothly churning out more trucks in its factories. CAT customers faced longer and longer delays, and the desire to get equipment was so strong that even loyal CAT operators switched to Komatsu. They just did not have a choice.

Ironically, Komatsu makes its mining trucks in Peoria, right down the street from what was the global headquarters of Caterpillar. In 2006, CAT was the largest surface mining equipment maker in the world. Its market share has never been officially disclosed, but it was probably about twice as big as Komatsu's. By 2018, Komatsu's mining business was bigger than CAT's.

Komatsu didn't gain significant share by simply pouring investment dollars into its factory, at least not at first. When we visited its plant in the booming years leading up to 2008, the manager there joked that his nephew started at a junior position with CAT a few streets away, and the kid's capital budget to fit out his cubicle was higher than the budget he himself had to upgrade the mining truck factory that was beating out CAT. The comment was made in jest, but reality wasn't much different. Komatsu spent just tens of millions of dollars upgrading equipment in the early part of this boom, not hundreds of millions or billions. Instead, Komatsu used the basics of Lean production: implementing continuous improvement, finding the slowdowns in production, and fixing them. This was two decades after US automakers had a similar moment of panic, with competitors from Japan beating them on quality and production steadiness by using Lean. Komatsu was doing the same to CAT 20 years later.

Finally, as if sagging margins and waning market share weren't enough, CAT's conservative posture bled into the strategic realm. The company passed on complementary acquisitions that could have helped meet demand.

Back in Peoria in 2007, I was presenting to a group of Caterpillar employees, who were local Morgan Stanley brokerage clients, when CAT CFO Dave Burritt wandered into the room. I don't know if he had heard about the event and wanted to see what I was saying to his managers and employees or if he was simply curious. We had a brief chat about press rumors on M&A at the time and potential strategic holes CAT might fill by acquisition. CAT's mining business had a broad product lineup, but it was too weighted toward mining trucks and bulldozers. Komatsu and other mining equipment manufacturers had shovels as well as trucks, a pretty obvious synergy. The shovel scoops up dirt and dumps it into a truck. Mines are often found in remote places, so there's a natural advantage to selling parts if you are the largest provider with the most local scale. Designing products together has benefits, too. The shovels that scoop up ore from the ground can be designed to match up efficiently with trucks: four scoops to load a truck is good; four-and-a-half scoops, not so much.

CAT didn't have a shovel and could have used one at the time. It had developed one internally but had given up on it in the early 2000s, just before the mining boom started up again, not believing the cost was worth it in a mining market that never seemed to recover. Various assets from another machinery company, Terex, were then up for sale, including mining shovels. The strategic fit was quite attractive; yet Burritt's only comment on my presentation was that assets don't come cheap, and CAT had no desire to overpay. Instead, CAT rival Bucyrus bought the Terex assets for $1.3 billion in 2009.

The lesson from the Owens era is that the economist's approach failed. Forecasting supply and demand levels didn't work; expecting a continuation of weak demand, CAT lost market share, margin, and strategic position. Its factories were overburdened as it fought to keep up with demand, and quality suffered as a result. The only upside was that the company weathered the 2009 recession fairly well. It gave away a lot of the cycle's upside, but its downside planning paid off. Coming out of it, Owens, nearing 65, turned over the reins to the next CEO. (See Figure 7.1.)

Figure 7.1: **Caterpillar's volatile history.**

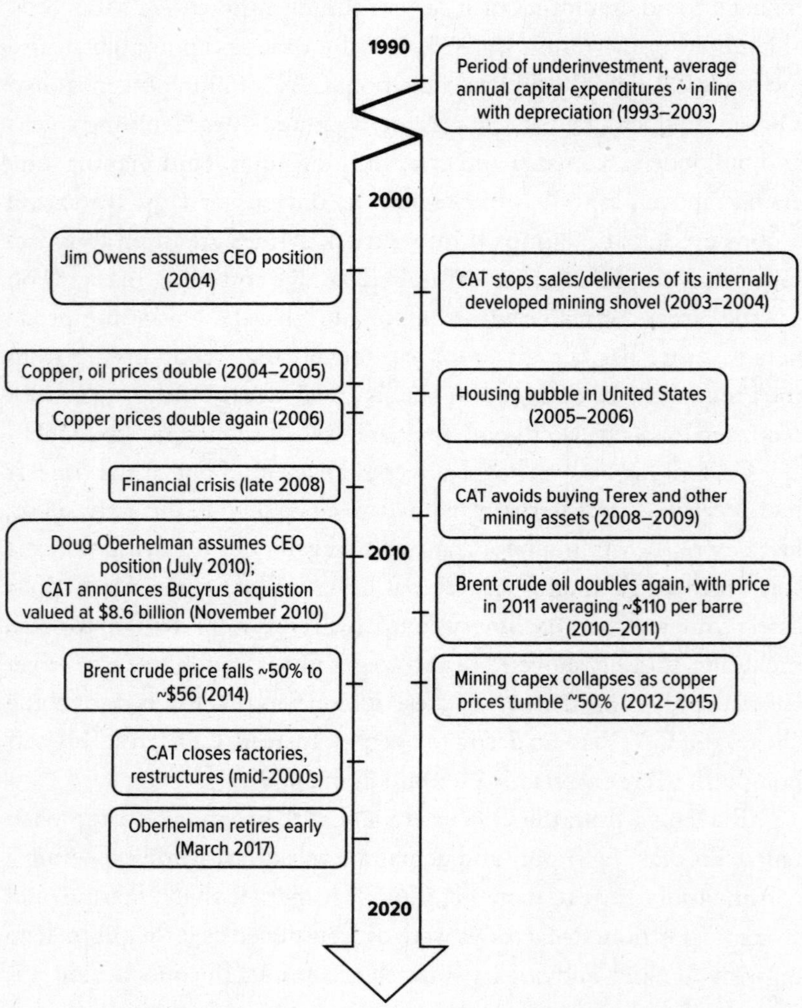

Source: Caterpillar filings, Bloomberg, press reports

NEW LEADERSHIP OVERCORRECTS

Doug Oberhelman took over in July 2010. China was still booming, and mining was booming along with it. Oil prices had corrected sharply down for a short while, falling from a peak of almost $140 per barrel down to $40, but by 2010 they were back up over $100. CAT's sales were rising again, up a remarkable 35 percent in 2010 and then another 44 percent in 2011 to an all-time high, about 20 percent above the pre-crisis record in 2008. However, CAT still hadn't had time to invest enough in its factories, and it still didn't have a production system that would allow it to crank out product without more capital.

It had also missed the remarkable rise in the need for construction equipment in China. The country had bought about 30,000 excavators in 2005, over 60,000 in 2006, and more than 160,000 in 2010. In five years, it had gone from a middling market to comprising *half* the world's sales, and CAT was nowhere to be seen. Its 8 percent market share in 2006 fell to just 6 percent in 2010. CAT was losing its position as world leader.

Oberhelman had spent the middle 2000s privately fuming as the company ceded market share to competitors. CAT makes decent money selling machines, but selling repair parts for those machines for the next 15 to 20 years is more profitable. Giving up market share hurt long-term as well as near-term profits, and that drove Oberhelman nuts. He had previously run CAT's engine business, which performed far better than the rest of the company during the ramp-up in the mid-2000s when CAT was struggling to make construction and mining equipment. Parts of the engines business had made the transition to Lean operations, good employee relations, employee engagement, and continuous improvement. Oberhelman had good reason to think the whole company could operate at a higher level.

Right from the start Oberhelman invested in growth. If CAT had captured more of the 2000s boom, perhaps he wouldn't have pushed so hard to add capacity. If CAT's production systems had been more well developed, perhaps he wouldn't have needed to. In hindsight it looks like an overcorrection for sins of the past.

My first meeting with Oberhelman was dramatically different from those with other CAT leaders. He had strong opinions and shared them forcefully, and he didn't do anything halfway. I arrived with plenty of time to spare that morning (traffic in downtown Peoria is seldom a risk), but my meeting was delayed. There had been storms in the area the night before, and large parts of the town had lost power. While waiting in a conference room, I wondered out loud if Oberhelman had lost power too and was late as a result. The CAT folks around the table chuckled at that idea, and when he came in looking fresh, he commented that his backup power had worked just fine; he was late because he had stopped to help a neighbor with some storm-related issue on the way in. CAT makes diesel engines for backup power, generally a lot bigger than what a house would use. The backup at the Oberhelman house was high quality and could've lit up half the neighborhood. Maybe it did. Oberhelman was well prepared, and he loved CAT engines, though he did look sheepish when he mentioned how big his diesel was.

Oberhelman answered questions clearly and passionately, with good reasoning and clear direction. He was a bold and decisive leader, confident and inspiring, and upon taking over as CEO, he tried to fix a lot of things, all at once. He called it being "on a roll and in a hurry." He made some immediate, important, and lasting improvements in how the company was managed. CAT had long used a structure of group presidents. When we first started following the company, we couldn't figure out who did what. CAT had group presidents who might oversee global production of bulldozers, for example, but also sales of all equipment in Asia. The org chart crisscrossed all over itself.

Oberhelman reorganized reporting lines to give the group presidents clear responsibilities for the first time. And with these positions came compensation of more than $5 million a year, meant to drive results; many industrial segment heads at other companies made half that. Oberhelman felt that the previous process of managing the company by committee was a criminal waste of talent. He implemented a level of accountability not seen before in a culture that had too little of it—overlapping responsibilities had previously made it hard to find the right throat to choke. One group president told me in 2011 that in 30 years at CAT, he'd never seen a vice president let go. In the first years Oberhelman was in charge, 6 out of about 25 left. With the group presidents having "real jobs" for the first time—clear profit and loss responsibilities—compensation could now be tied to results. That included profit and the cost of the assets used to generate it.

Unfortunately, even with this strong push, CAT's culture made it hard to refresh the production system sufficiently. There were lots of experts in Lean and supply chain in other industries, but CAT tended to promote from within. Under Oberhelman the company saw an influx of talent from the outside. Small, but unprecedented for CAT.

While those implementing these well-intentioned efforts tried to gain traction, it was clear that Oberhelman didn't want to miss another boom and lose further market share. The company needed to figure out a way to participate in the up cycle while waiting on systematic improvement. Normal capital budgeting at CAT and other heavy manufacturers operates more on the scale of two years than two months, but Oberhelman accelerated everything. In 2011, just a few months after he took over, Caterpillar's capital expenditure rose by $1 billion (up 60 percent from the year before and about double the average of the prior 10 years), and another $1 billion in 2012. He sharply increased capacity in China and broader Asia. Some of that capex paid off: CAT's market share in China, which had fallen steadily in a booming market, improved. And by 2018 its market share in China for excavators had doubled.

Along with organic investments in capacity, Oberhelman took an aggressive stance on acquisitions. He saw it as a mistake that CAT had passed on buying the Terex mining trucks and shovels. CAT's dealers were clamoring for a broader mining product line, so within four months of taking over, Oberhelman approved a nearly $9 billion purchase of Bucyrus. That was more than six times higher than what Bucyrus paid for the Terex trucks and shovels just a year prior. Bucyrus had other products, to be sure, but they were less strategically attractive, being more specific to coal, and in a few cases in declining markets and product types.

A year after that, CAT bought a Chinese coal mining machinery supplier for about $700 million. Buying a company that made low-value products was an aggressive attempt to get into the huge underground coal mining market in China. As it turned out, the company's accounting was highly questionable, and the business effectively evaporated after CAT purchased it. That was a spectacular failure, one born of speed rather than prudence and careful diligence. Wasting a few hundred million dollars isn't the end of the world for a company CAT's size, but leaders who make serial mistakes can lose the confidence of their employees and shareholders.

Even if CAT had done better due diligence, it was still focused on anticipating demand, rather than on its ability to improve internally. An ideal acquisition process starts with a wide funnel of many opportunities, and the urgency to invest isn't confined to any one of them. Great companies can see which acquisitions fit best and add value through their unique operations. The reality for CAT isn't much different, though the opportunity set is less diverse.

Managing the decision to acquire is just as much a systematic process as managing a factory floor, and CAT's was distorted by its previous failures. The pressure from having underperformed the last mining cycle was strong. CAT's independent dealers might not have been calling so hard for more product if they had had more wins in the years prior. But they were calling, and in a dramatic pivot from the prior era of caution, Oberhelman answered, short-circuiting the normal process.

If a poorly executed acquisition strategy wasn't enough, maybe the worst decision Oberhelman made was on inventory. He was intent on getting CAT back into a position of gaining market share, not losing it. Lost sales from inadequate capacity were painful and expensive, and neither the capex surge nor the production improvements being put through could have an immediate result. CAT did the opposite of every lesson of modern manufacturing: it decided to build inventory rather than reduce it. CAT created regional "Product Distribution Centers," which were basically warehouses for extra inventory, ready to be shipped to dealers and on to customers quickly. To be fair, an increase wasn't the intent, but it turned out to be the reality.

The inability to fill orders from 2005 to 2008 had made dealers mistrust CAT and its production promises. That had a terrible consequence. It led to double ordering: a dealership might want two machines to sell to its customers, but historically it had only gotten one in a timely manner. So now the dealer orders four, figuring it will get two and will cancel the other orders later if equipment isn't moving.

In the preceding decades, CAT had widened out its construction product lines materially, adding new machines and model variants, which enhanced the company's position as the biggest and broadest manufacturer. Without a true Lean manufacturing system, that bigger product line was guaranteed to produce extra inventory or longer waits for machines ordered. So CAT tried to streamline its product line, prioritizing standardized models that would ship quickly, often from the newly established warehouses.

CAT's warehouses were a Band-Aid fix attempting to address all these issues at once. Dealers could look at the inventory sitting in the regional distribution center and know that if they needed to get a machine, they could. In theory, not only would they stop double ordering; they would reduce their own inventory, relying on the distribution center for quick shipment. Product complexity would be reduced by standard models, and planning for custom orders could be slower and more deliberate.

It takes years (at least five, maybe more) to fix production, and Oberhelman didn't want to wait. Continuous improvement and employee engagement mean exactly that: little ideas need to be found, implemented, improved, and improved again. That improvement uncovers other processes that can then be optimized. There is no shortcutting the process.

Oberhelman made a bet that demand would be strong with capacity, acquisitions, and inventory build. He then ran into the longest stretch of depressed revenues CAT has ever experienced, including the Great Depression. With too much capacity and too much inventory on top of that, CAT's bubble imploded.

Mining equipment sales that had grown at a blistering pace from 2008 to 2012 suddenly stopped growing and then collapsed alongside commodities. CAT and its dealers had far too much inventory in a market that fell 80 percent from 2012 to 2015. Mines that had been spending aggressively when copper, gold, and coal prices were high suddenly found they weren't using their equipment prudently. They had lower cash flows, and instead of buying more or replacing old equipment, they began using the trucks they had more efficiently. And fracking, which in just five years had doubled all the engine power in global oil and gas, also collapsed. Oil prices came down, and frackers figured out how to drill multiple oil and gas wells from the same drilling pad, using a quarter of the equipment.

To top it all off, the recovery in the United States after the 2008–2009 collapse continued to be weak, and construction equipment sales faltered. CAT found itself with too many factories, excess inventory, and busted acquisitions, all made to chase growth that no longer existed. The company under Oberhelman's leadership reacted a little late, but aggressively, to these developments, closing factories and consolidating production.

After the bubbles had all burst, the last of which was oil and gas in 2014–2016, Oberhelman was forced out early. He had implemented many positive changes, some of which will benefit CAT for decades: instituting greater accountability, welcoming outside expertise, adding new capacity and shuttering old, and reforming compensation systems. One board member, when asked for a postmortem on the former CEO's tenure, said Oberhelman didn't know Lean manufacturing from a hole in the wall. He said it with some force and bitterness, and maybe the statement was a little unfair. Oberhelman *did* know Lean and was putting it in as a part of a production system, along with other positive structural changes. He knew it would take time to gain traction, though, so he decided to make some very large bets on growth in the meantime. CAT's culture had long rewarded leaders for heroics, not process discipline—these are two very different traits. Oberhelman's heroic bets failed, and it ended his career.

POSTMORTEM

Caterpillar is thriving today. Its CEO and senior leaders are committed to data-driven, properly incentivized, Lean operations. Results in the mild upturn years of 2017–2019 were among the best of its peers. Safety is dramatically better over the past decade; injury rates that fell 75 percent in the Oberhelman years are down another 50 percent, or a full 90 percent better than the Owens years, when I saw firsthand the chaos in the factories. It took time, but after years of work, the operating system is finally functioning well, thanks in part to some progress in the Owens era and more under Oberhelman. We expect that future volatility will be successfully dampened by the improved operations.

There's no simple way for Caterpillar to have avoided all this pain, and suggesting so is not the point of this chapter. The company operates in a cyclical industry. Moreover, it was hit with explosive growth when China spurred the global commodities markets early in the 2000s, then a collapse in 2009 nearly as severe as the Great Depression, followed by explosive growth in mining and oil and gas, and then the popping of those two bubbles—all within a 15-year period. That's a wild ride. As analysts our job is to forecast end markets and earnings, and we got only one of the three huge moves solidly right (the 2008 downturn) and got one terribly wrong—missing the fact that the 2012–2013 peak in mining and oil and gas was actually a bubble. That is the point, though. Forecasting is bound to be wrong and should be done as little as possible. The better path is flexible, rapidly responding, Lean operations.

The problem is that companies are just too tempted to shortcut the process. The hard part about business systems isn't getting started, nor is it doing kaizens or talking about Lean; the hard part is staying committed. It's all too easy for a management team to see its time filled with planning, forecasting, and budgeting and then to set systems aside to chase growth when given the chance.

Operational excellence takes tremendous discipline and patience. Either missing out on sales or overproducing or underproducing is unavoidable. It takes a lot of discipline to let that improvement process play out knowing what's being given up. Most new CEOs we see, particularly in struggling companies, feel pressure to make quick, bold, and impactful changes. It might work, but then again, it might turn ugly.

Much like the sandy road I failed to master in West Africa, learning not to overreact takes a long time, lots of experience, and a system. But it's the only way to skillfully and consistently handle the booms and busts inherent in cyclical markets.

Lessons from Caterpillar

- Volatility is inherent in all markets and is difficult to predict. Forecasting with any accuracy over time is almost impossible.
- New leaders face pressure to fix difficult situations quickly, but tackling everything all at once rarely works.
- There are no shortcuts to building a continuous improvement culture. "Band-Aid" fixes are inevitably inadequate in the long run.
- Cultural change is hard to achieve in an insular organization. Bringing in outside perspectives is often necessary to navigate new challenges.
- Employee relations matter. Getting buy-in at all levels of the organization is critical to success.
- Accountability and compensation systems are vital. It can take years to correct bad habits.

CHAPTER

8

ROPER

The Amazing Untold Story of Brian Jellison and His Timeless Lessons on Compounding

BY SCOTT DAVIS

Roper's success stems from the power of compounding, investing cash into higher- and then . . . even higher-returning assets. For all the value that was created over time at Roper, it all came from a simple acquisition model, a singular management philosophy, and a one-variable compensation scheme. That touches on something we may fail to highlight enough in this book. In all the ways that smart people can complicate all forms of business, the best of the best just seem to focus on a few basic drivers of value. Roper is perhaps the best illustration of this dynamic.

Roper's unconventional CEO, Brian Jellison, saw the market for M&A stuck in an old paradigm—one that undervalued true cash flow, misunderstood the future capital needs of asset-intensive businesses, and overlooked hidden potential liabilities like healthcare, environmental, and pension costs. Jellison's vision itself was basic—focus on generating cash flow, invest that cash flow opportunistically, and employ capable leaders to run newly acquired assets. He articulated a framework for success and then got out of their way. Sound familiar? It's perhaps closest to the strategy employed by Warren Buffett. Not exactly a new model, but shockingly underutilized.

From a shareholder return perspective, the 17 years of Jellison's leadership, from 2001 to 2018, were outstanding, making even amazing companies like Berkshire Hathaway look pretty darn average. The stock during the Jellison tenure returned 1,300 percent, rising from $20 to $300. That 1,300 percent quadruples Berkshire's return of 330 percent. The overall S&P had a fantastic two-decade run, up 160 percent in that time period, but achieved only a tenth of Roper's return. (See Figure 8.1.) A wide set of stakeholders went along for the ride: debt holders were rewarded with high and consistent cash flow, employees gained career opportunities and wealth that go along with a winning organization, and customers benefited from a supplier committed to investing in its value-added products.

Figure 8.1: **Roper stock massively outperformed during Brian Jellison's 17-year tenure.**

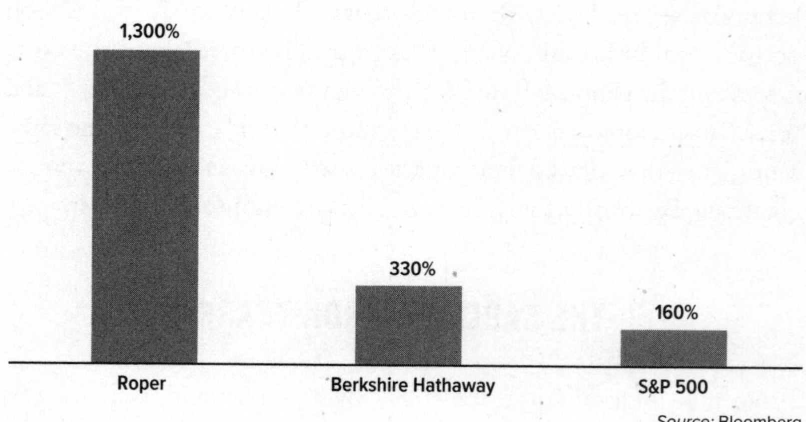

Source: Bloomberg

Few companies in American history have treated stakeholders so well and with so little drama. There were no near-death experiences or huge market gyrations like we've seen so commonly with others. It's a company that we have never once had an incoming press call on, even after the death of its visionary. Roper found comfort in remaining off the radar, focusing on the day-to-day power of compounding returns and letting the results speak for themselves. No advertising budget or PR campaign. Just a quiet and steady focus on the power of investing cash flow in higher-return assets and using those cash flows to reinvent its portfolio from its cyclical industrial roots to a higher-return, more predictable software future. By 2001, American businesses had lost focus on cash flow, just when that cash was so valuable. Jellison exploited this market inefficiency over and over in a remarkable 17-year run.

Unfortunately, Jellison isn't alive to tell his own story. He passed away in the fall of 2018, shortly after he had stepped down from the CEO role. The nuances of his success may never be known, and we are left to piece it all together from personal interactions with him and those who worked alongside him. At times grumpy, he viewed Wall Street with disdain. He once dressed me down in front of a dozen of my best clients for asking a question he deemed stupid. He was dismissive of critics. He worked his staff hard and worked himself even harder. He was at times a tough, seemingly distant man. All the brilliant ones are restless, with notable flaws. Deep down, he was a good person, loyal to his family and friends, and he cared about the businesses and the people within. We interviewed a number of current and prior Roper employees for this project, and they all expressed the same sentiments: they viewed their experience with him as valuable, even life changing. Personally, I miss him, and it's an honor to share his story.

THE EARLY JELLISON YEARS

Brian Jellison grew up in the small town of Portland, Indiana. His father was the owner of the local hardware store, where he taught his son traditional Midwest values and the importance of education. In his youth, Jellison worked six days a week for his dad, who expected him to put in a full shift when the school day was done. Jellison had to learn how to be fully independent early in his life, as both parents had passed away by the time he was 18. He earned an economics degree at Indiana University and an advanced degree from Columbia University.

After graduating from Columbia, Jellison went through GE's management training program but spent most of the early to middle part of his career at Ingersoll-Rand, where he was viewed as a smart, very capable leader. While he was considered a bit harsh on his underlings, his financial IQ caught the attention of senior leaders, and by the time Jellison left Ingersoll-Rand in 2001, he had risen to become an EVP and was a candidate for CEO.

Although a high-ranking executive, Jellison was frustrated with Ingersoll-Rand. At that time, the company was intensely bureaucratic. His days were filled with endless meetings, budget planning, and business reviews, and he was surrounded with leaders that always seemed satisfied with mediocrity. Corporate initiatives changed with the wind and were largely ineffective. Time and value were destroyed, and complexity built. Jellison despised these structures common to the industrial world. Even in his final days, Jellison criticized companies such as GE and 3M for their layers of bureaucracy and overly centralized business models. Furthermore, Ingersoll-Rand began shifting its portfolio into more asset-intensive businesses, which Jellison strongly believed to be a mistake.

In those days, large capital equipment was all the rage in industrials. Most were trying to model themselves on GE with big-ticket items like compressors, turbines, and engines—the belief was that the spare parts and service made up for a lower-margin install price and high capital costs. Business schools and management programs focused on concepts like "Porter's Five Forces" analysis. Big pieces of capital equipment seemed to offer amazing barriers to entry and power over suppliers, and the power in the sales channel grew with each install, even if it meant sacrificing cash terms in order to close an order. At Ingersoll-Rand, Jellison saw firsthand the obsession that leaders had with this business model. GE's success was so well established at that point that few questioned any of the basic assumptions. Razor/razorblade was the business model everyone wanted to copy, no matter the cost.

By contrast, Jellison saw far higher margin and cash flow characteristics in basic businesses, notably the instrumentation and controls that often sat on top of these pieces of capital equipment. Flying under the radar often meant margins twice what the main suppliers earned, and the overall investment needs were limited and easier to cut back on in recession periods. The factories were smaller, closer to the customer overall, and focused on final assembly. Jellison also saw the big players increasingly interested in larger, splashy M&A deals. Smaller, niche assets (sub-$500 million and even sub-$100 million) garnered more attractive prices. In addition, he saw that smaller company managers were usually more intimate with their businesses overall and respected within their organizations but had not been incentivized appropriately.

Critical to Jellison's contrarian view was the mathematical reality that stock market P/E ratios directly correlate to returns on the underlying asset base of the entity, meaning that P/E ratios usually rise as the returns on the underlying assets grow. The very highest P/E multiples are at companies whose business models have few physical assets to maintain and high margins on that low asset base. Companies with low asset intensity and high margins typically generate lots of cash. And companies with these characteristics that also grow are particularly attractive, as each incremental dollar of growth drives returns even higher. This is a concept Jellison called CRI—cash return on investment—and its correlation with valuation was central to his vision. The best example of a high-CRI sector would be software. The best example of a low-CRI sector would be automotive. (See Figure 8.2.)

Figure 8.2: **Roper's CRI metric.**

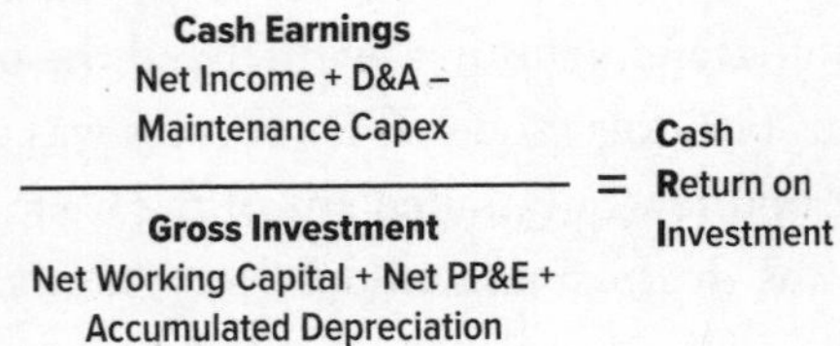

Source: Roper

Jellison vowed that if he ever got a chance to be a CEO, he would do it all very differently. He would squash the bureaucracy, simplify the business model, and focus on compounding the company's cash flow. But Ingersoll-Rand had become intolerable for Jellison by the time he was 55, and his career overall was at risk of coming to an end—until he got a phone call from a company desperate to fill a job that seemingly few wanted anything to do with. That company was Roper Industries, a small and largely irrelevant, underperforming manufacturer.

THE JELLISON PLAYBOOK

In 2001, the world was all about the internet, the rise of consumer technology, and the visionary leaders from Silicon Valley. Roper was about as far away from that as you could get. It was largely a niche oil and gas supplier with a product line of pumps and test and measurement equipment. Its business was deeply cyclical with near-death experiences every time oil prices went into a down cycle. Jellison ran the pumps business at Ingersoll-Rand, so he was well suited for the job. But Roper was a small company, sub-$600 million in revenues, a big step back in most regards for an executive with a GE and Ingersoll-Rand résumé. Jellison had few other options and viewed Roper as the perfect vessel to build the type of company that he had always wanted, a company virtually the opposite of the two at which he had spent his entire career up to then.

Roper was small, but its niche products delivered high margins overall. Jellison saw promise in the high cash flow characteristics of the business and reinvestment levels that were not overly demanding, but the cyclicality was a problem. Jellison knew that a small company with deeply cyclical assets would struggle to survive the increasingly deeper cycles he worried about (his concerns became a reality when the 2008–2009 financial crisis hit). Even during the smaller but still painful 2001–2002 recession, he saw the risks playing out in real time. He needed to build a more solid foundation for Roper. The company also needed to grow faster than what his inherited portfolio could deliver. The portfolio needed a drastic makeover, and the only way to get there was to do M&A far away from its core. Jellison wanted to focus explicitly on high-margin, high cash flow assets as far away from the oil and gas industry as possible. He wanted asset-light businesses with cash flow that increased over time. This involved substantially higher levels of debt leverage in the process, all of which required approval from Roper's risk-averse board.

Convincing the board to be aggressive was no easy task. Roper's legacy board was conservative, and Jellison had not yet been named chairman. His plan was compelling and simple but required a level of change the board struggled with. Many board members flat-out rejected the notion that anything other than smaller bolt-on acquisitions were needed. Several other board members wanted Roper to stick to its core and roll up other pump assets. Beyond the unconventional M&A strategy that Jellison was pitching, he wanted to drive change within the organization itself. He wanted to upgrade management more broadly, run a more decentralized playbook, and change compensation schemes, all of which made the conservative board uncomfortable.

With the high volume of potential M&A targets in the $100 million–$500 million range, Jellison could afford to be picky with his deals. He had three requirements: (1) lower asset intensity than ROP's existing portfolio, (2) good businesses within niche industries, and (3) excellent management. He would walk away from any deal that lacked all three.

The first asset that made it through this unique diligence filter was Neptune, a well-regarded water meter company. The timing of the deal in 2003 was perfect. Coming out of a deep recession, other potential buyers were hindered by high debt levels and were still licking their wounds from tech-bubble excesses. Jellison loved the asset and saw it as an immediate upgrade from the Roper legacy core. Neptune had a relatively noncyclical water utility customer base and had secular growth from the adoption of automated meter-reading technologies. Margins were high, and customers paid on time if not early; and while factories were needed, it was mostly an assembly-type business with limited heavy equipment or tooling.

Growth had stalled at Neptune, which was the key risk to Roper at the time. Did Roper buy a dud, or would utilities begin to invest again after the recession? The answer came quickly. The growth did materialize, and to this day, water companies continue to change out old meters that require in-person reading with wireless ones that are run off radio frequency identification (RFID). Neptune was a big bet. Its cash flow was three times larger in size than the cash flow Roper was producing—and far larger than what most board members were comfortable with. Had that first deal not been a success from day one, there likely would not have been a second. For Jellison, Neptune was the most important bet of his career. And though he was always comfortable with the math, it paid off well more than anyone had expected.

Just a year later in 2004, and encouraged by the success of Neptune, Jellison closed another game-changing acquisition called TransCore. Better known as the backbone behind much of the US highway electronic tolling system, it uses RFID to read vehicle tags and charge a toll accordingly. It was another high-margin, noncyclical, high-cash-generating asset. At the time, tolling was a limited-growth industry, as the US federal and state gas taxes were more than sufficient to pay for road maintenance. But those funds have become deficient, driving much of the growth in tolling. The deal was another amazing success.

By the end of 2004, less than 2½ years into the job, Jellison had already done $1.5 billion in deals, taking a sub-$600 million revenue company that he inherited in 2001 to one that did $1.5 billion in 2005. He accomplished this while maintaining a minimum 50 percent gross margin threshold with operating margins in the high teens, nearly tripling cash flow from $100 million to $250 million—all while decreasing the asset intensity and volatility of the company overall. (See Figure 8.3.)

The 2004 TransCore deal was Jellison's first major foray into software, and the success of that deal would influence M&A priorities from then on. At Ingersoll-Rand he ran businesses that required as much as 20 percent working capital as a percentage of sales in order to operate. Those industrial assets required capital investment on top of the daily cash needs: new factories, replacement of old equipment, etc., often adding another 2 to 4 percent of sales, not including what needed to be spent on R&D (3 percent of sales or more) to keep the product cycles moving. That doesn't even account for hidden expenses that often weigh on traditional manufacturers, including legacy environmental and pension liabilities. Jellison was astounded that those risks were never even considered by most companies when they bought assets. M&A deals were largely valued the same. The val-

Figure 8.3: **History of Roper's major deals.**

Asset	Year Acquired	Description	Deal Price ($ M)
Neptune	2003	Water meter technology	$475
TransCore	2004	Electronic tolling equipment and software	$600
CBORD	2008	Radio frequency card and security solutions	$367
Verathon	2009	Bladder volume measurement, intubation imaging	$356
iTrade Networks	2010	Trading network software for food industry	$525
Sunquest	2012	Hospital lab automation software	$1,415
Managed Health Care Associates	2013	Long-term care pharmacy group purchasing organization	$1,000
Aderant	2015	ERP software for legal industry	$675
ConstructConnect	2016	Commercial construction data/collaboration software	$632
Deltek	2016	ERP software for project-based businesses	$2,800
PowerPlan	2018	Data management software for asset-based industries	$1,100
Foundry	2019	Visual effects/3D software	$544
iPipeline	2019	Workflow software for life insurance industry	$1,625

Source: Roper filings, press reports

uation for an asset-heavy company with potential tail liabilities was not much less than the valuation for a software company. In fact, if the asset-heavy company had razor/razorblade characteristics, its valuation was often higher.

Jellison saw broad incompetence by M&A market participants. Investment bankers focused pitches on consolidating end markets and making easy-to-do deals where the value was in the synergies, like closing factories and corporate HQs. Boards wanted easy-to-explain combinations, regardless of whether the underlying business itself was good or bad.

He found it insane that a company like GE would sell a high-margin, high-cash asset like NBC Universal for 10x EBITDA (analogous to cash flow), only to turn around and buy capital-intensive and cyclical assets in oil and gas for prices exceeding 12x EBITDA. Capital-intensive semiconductor companies traded for the same valuation as low-capital-intensity software assets. Healthcare equipment was valued as highly as healthcare IT software. It made no sense to him.

Roper was in a position to exploit all those inefficiencies. With his typical deal profile, Jellison could pay off nearly all the debt from a transaction in as little as three years. All cash could go to service that debt, as opposed to building new factories, paying off an environmental liability, or financing a customer. That quick debt paydown allowed for stepped-up dealmaking. With the high-gross-margin profile of his assets, each incremental unit of growth generated outsized profits and cash, but he didn't need high growth to make his deals work. Jellison was willing to buy mid-growth.

Traditional software companies, like Oracle or Microsoft, generally favored internal new product investment. When they did do acquisitions, they wanted a high-growth profile—certainly above 10 percent, and rarely near the 5 percent ballpark that Roper was more than happy to take. Jellison found the biggest mispricings in less sexy, slower, but still solid growers. These were usually software companies in highly niche markets.

Software was in a different world from that of Roper's traditional businesses, and critics viewed the company as going down a path it didn't understand. But Jellison saw it more simply, starting with the basic fundamentals of the software sales cycle. Contracts were typically paid up front with the cash often received before the revenue was even booked, such as in a subscription model. Deferred revenue meant that Jellison could run his company on zero or negative working capital. That entire concept made him almost giddy. There were no factories to invest in, and there was very limited cyclicality to worry about. A large installed base made it harder to get disrupted, at least quickly. And most of these companies weren't all that well run, meaning Roper could help them to improve operations—in the sales and marketing organization, for example.

Jellison could take that 5 percent unit growth, and through operational improvement, he could translate it into nearly 10 percent profit growth. He then could utilize cash to purchase similar assets that would add another 5 to 10 percent to the top line, translating over time to 15 to 20 percent annualized profit growth. He did this without using equity and maintaining investment-grade debt. Few companies can sustain high-teens profit growth over time. Jellison was in that ballpark most of his 17 years as CEO.

The TransCore deal was the perfect beta test for Roper's unique M&A and governance models and would be the start of the modern Roper. The lion's share of transactions after 2004 was centered on high-CRI healthcare and software assets. The valuation spread between these assets and traditional industrial businesses was minimal. If we learn nothing else from the Jellison experience, it's that valuation mispricings can persist over a very long period of time. Even later in Jellison's career, he found reasonably priced software assets at valuations not much more than those paid for more asset-intensive businesses. We have seen those spreads widen over the last few years, in some cases exponentially. But for north of 15 years, Jellison was able to capitalize on a marketwide opportunity to invest in niche businesses that few would take the time to consider.

WALL STREET COMES AROUND TO JELLISON'S VISION

Jellison's early years at Roper coincided with my early years as an industrial analyst, and I have to admit struggling to fully understand his vision. He was good at describing the high-margin, high-cash characteristics of his assets, but he failed to communicate any tangible or repeatable growth algorithm to investors. He explained the CRI concept and his view that as Roper's returns rose, so would its P/E multiple. The problem, however, was that since each of his acquisitions came with a low asset base, almost by definition, the amount of goodwill created in each deal would be high. Therefore, his returns on a more traditional accounting construct like ROIC would actually go down each time a deal was closed. Then it would begin to rise after the deal, only to be deflated by another deal. For traditional investors, that was a challenge to understand.

To buy into Jellison's vision, you had to turn traditional accounting frameworks upside down and focus on the returns of the transaction after it closed—the returns earned on each additional dollar of investment. You needed a long-term view, because in the short term the deal would rarely look all that attractive. This was exactly the reason for the mispricing in the first place: deals just looked expensive, both to M&A bankers and to the CEOs and boards they advised.

Jellison's successes were often explained by critics as luck and pure financial engineering. In hindsight, too many good things happened at Roper over too many years for it to be mere accident. He bought good assets, seemed to run them better than they had ever been run, and developed a consistent growth pattern driven not just by M&A and R&D investments but also by high operating leverage within the assets themselves.

By mid-2004, I was convinced that Roper was doing something very different that deserved more attention. So I begged Jellison for an afternoon of his time and jumped on a plane. I discovered a different Jellison that was a far cry from his distant reputation. He wanted to teach, to mentor. He loved the job, and he loved the game overall, which he viewed as a competition. He wanted to beat the big guys—the GEs, the 3Ms, and the Emersons of the world. An outcast from that world, he was considered not polished enough, with opinions that were too strong. He had a chip on his shoulder. He wanted to win by having a better operating framework, proven by his sector-high margins. He wanted to invest cash at high returns and drive the stock price further up. He benchmarked his company against others, almost to a level of infatuation.

On that hot and sunny afternoon, I saw something unique, something powerful and inspiring. He stood for most of the meeting, writing on a board with multicolored pens. He went soup to nuts on his management philosophy, with increasing energy and fervor. He coached and taught. "This is how you run a company . . . This is how you lead people . . . This is how you grow . . . This is why we are different . . ." The passion was real, and time flew by. For an entire afternoon, I barely said a word. It was one of the greatest days of my business life.

I learned that Jellison wasn't just a serial buyer of assets; he was a visionary, an exceptional operator, leader, mentor, and person. I flew back to New York and upgraded the stock to Morgan Stanley's equivalent of a buy, a rating that I kept for 15 years and still maintain today. That stock went straight up nearly every year since then.

ROPER'S GOVERNANCE MODEL

The vast majority of Roper's acquisitions have been small to mid-sized assets, typically owned by private equity, but too small to IPO and off the radar of larger strategic buyers. Most good acquirers know the danger of overpaying, and overpaying almost always relates to having an overly optimistic deal model around the growth of the asset and the ability of its managers to deliver that result. Jellison's diligence sessions were skeptical, almost hostile. He wanted to know exactly what he was walking into, well before the deal was even modeled.

One of the lessons from the Danaher chapter is that in the M&A game, a certain amount of information always seems to get held back in diligence by the selling side. So much so that when Danaher closes a deal as the buyer, the first thing it asks is, "What didn't you tell us?" Common problems could be an unhappy customer, product-quality issues, or a product launch that's not going as well as reported. Sometimes the issues are very small, but if not fixed fast, they could become a bigger problem down the road. Danaher wants to know the issues as quickly as possible so it can prevent the "down-the-road" part. Danaher deals tend to be large, so there is always some element of surprise. This is just fine, given that much of Danaher's success comes from the management system it is applying to the asset, which often requires a turnaround.

Roper does smaller deals relatively speaking, does not do turnarounds, and wants no such postdiligence headaches, because when it closes a deal, it backs off and lets the company run as is, with new incentives usually, but with management intact. Roper wants all the pros and cons out on the table, well before it goes down the bidding path. Easier said than done, but Jellison had a way of finding problems up front and walking away from the transaction. This is perhaps why his hit rate was so high. There was extreme process in his diligence.

Although Jellison had an inner circle to assist him, he was hands-on from deal introduction onward. The corporate HQ of Roper has a grand total of about 50 employees, the usual legal, tax, HR, and IR functions and not much else. Jellison didn't want a big staff of internal dealmakers. The hard diligence, he believed, was with the people themselves, and he felt that only someone at the senior level could have much of a trained eye for management. He needed to be able to ask the tough questions, and that's the only way he was comfortable doing a deal.

Diligence with the management team was critical, because Roper deals have to include a management team that it could retain. Jellison wanted continuity. He didn't want the customer experience to change, and he didn't want the deal itself to be an excuse for leaders to cash out and leave. He wanted the team, and he incentivized the team members to stay and perform to a high standard. But he only wanted assets with A-grade management teams. The deals he turned down through the years were more likely due to management deficiency than the asset quality itself.

While Jellison and his senior team did diligence on management, he would outsource the actual business quality analysis to industry experts, firms such as Bain, McKinsey, or Boston Consulting Group. They may have been more expensive than internal staff, but Jellison wanted an independent view with customer diligence. In his experience, internal M&A folks were biased, wanted to do deals, heard only positive customer opinions, and dismissed the negative data points. And he didn't believe that Roper had time to do it all. The sale process wasn't long enough for his team to become experts in every facet of the company, so he paid up to have that analysis done externally.

That doesn't mean that he ignored the operations. With the company managers and experts in the room together, he asked tough questions. Roper companies often say that they learned more about their businesses after Jellison's interrogations, particularly because of his focus on a comprehensive value mapping of the product itself. Jellison wanted a detailed breakeven analysis on every product, an analysis that had a shelf life long past diligence.

Once Jellison was comfortable with the management team, product profile, and likely growth algorithm, he could sign off on a deal model that was clear on what price the deal would work at and at what price it wouldn't. After a transaction closed, we never saw Jellison worry about overpaying, because he knew exactly what he was getting. The Roper process seems to cut down the risk profile to an almost uncanny extent. Of the 50+ deals we observed Jellison do in his 17 years, we can name only a couple that didn't work out, and those were just modest disappointments.

The risk profile was also lowered, because there was no such thing as "integration risk." Roper assets are autonomous, never integrated. There are never social or cultural issues, because the existing entity is maintained. There isn't a mass exodus risk, because managers are locked down before the deal closes. This could be a bigger part of the deal success story than we give it credit.

After a deal closes, Roper focuses on a basic governance model: setting up incentives, doing the relevant benchmarking where it makes sense, and giving the business the tools it needs for success, including a healthy dose of Jellison teachings. Roper executives got paid very well but were expected to deliver results. Jellison demanded excellence and was hard to work for, especially if you were having a tough time growing the profit base. His biggest pet peeve was with underperforming managers who didn't understand why they were failing. And those who didn't ask for help when needed. The stars were left alone to perform as they were hired to.

There were a few common problems that Roper saw in its acquired businesses. The first was that high-CRI companies tend to underinvest in sales and marketing and overinvest in the product and in the back office. The high-margin structures helped hide poorly placed jobs. Jellison joked that he saw many companies with more accountants than salespeople, and he would self-fund sales expansion by cutting back-office roles down to the minimum necessary.

Many of his assets were so focused on "the product sells itself" concept that they would have only a few sales representatives, who covered only part of the United States. Many of these companies didn't even attempt to expand outside of large city centers or to think globally. Jellison raised the growth rate just by having more sales coverage.

He also did a lot of educating on the front lines on sales channel management, teaching the importance of increasing hit rates and maximizing existing client coverage. In the world of software, he saw salespeople inadvertently talk clients into postponing purchases because a new product version was coming out in six months. Since new products are often late, that six months could often become 12 months. That delay often ended up driving the customer to a competitor. He wanted sales incentives that maximized the sale of the existing product before anyone was even allowed to see or talk about anything new. He believed selling the current version of the product gave Roper a better chance at upgrades down the road versus "training" the customer to wait for the new product. (See Figures 8.4 and 8.5.)

Figure 8.4: **Roper's revenue increased 9x under Brian Jellison . . .**

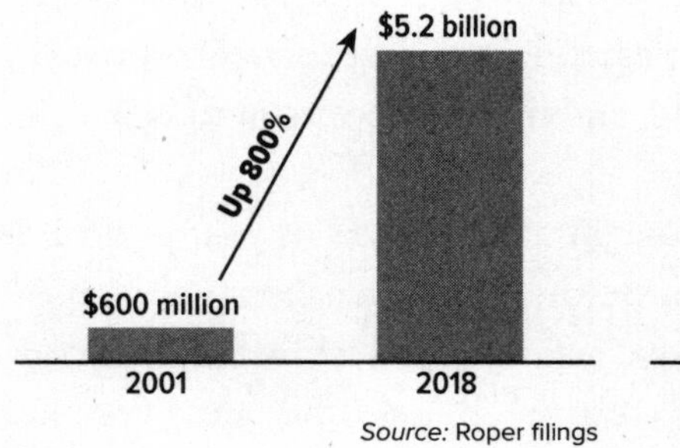

Source: Roper filings

Figure 8.5: **. . . while profits (EBITDA) increased by 14x as the portfolio shifted.**

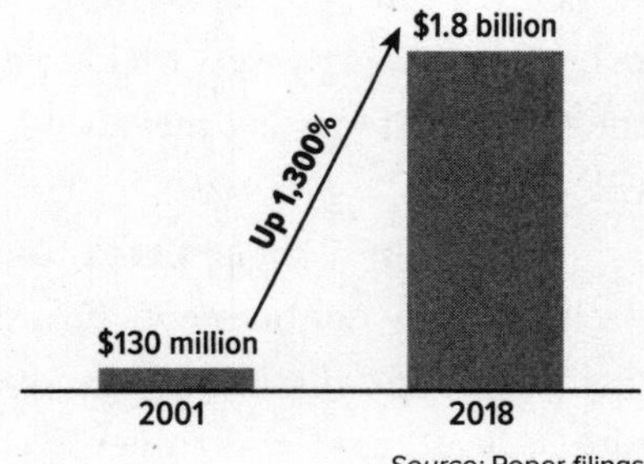

Source: Roper filings

For management teams within Roper, Jellison kept compensation schemes simple. Profit growth was his preferred metric, which made sense given the types of assets in the portfolio. One of the benefits of owning capital-light businesses was that Jellison didn't have to worry about measuring or paying for returns. As profits grew, returns compounded and profits were equal to or lower than actual cash. He didn't have to focus on one or the other; they went hand in hand. Jellison wanted simplicity and a common goal line.

One thing he never incentivized for was market share. He didn't want managers to push bad contracts to gain share. He gladly spent on R&D to develop best-in-class products, but the goal was always about compounding value. Because all his acquisitions were high gross margin and low capital intensity, paying on profit growth meant that managers really had to get only the top-line growth measure right. That was the most powerful lever they could pull. The incentive to grow with and above the market was already there.

POSTMORTEM

Jellison passed away in late 2018, but his legacy is alive and well in the Roper of today. CEO Neil Hunn and CFO Rob Crisci trained diligently under Jellison and use the same simple philosophies that worked for the company for nearly two decades. The concept of CRI may not work for every company or every asset base, but it works for Roper. If nothing else, it enforces discipline around the M&A funnel. High-quality assets that are asset light and generate cash rise to the top. That focus is time-tested, and there is no reason to believe it will change.

Roper is no longer a traditional industrial; yet its past portfolio decisions may not define its future either. Like Danaher, it has gravitated capital to the most attractive areas. Danaher saw the opportunity in healthcare, and Roper in software. But as other areas become more attractive, there is a clear pattern of willingness to adapt. For Roper, it's CRI that drives its growth focus.

Can Roper grow with this business model forever? Skeptics often say it's just a publicly traded private equity firm and will run into limits of growth over time. But the comparison to private equity diminishes the operating abilities and the culture of performance that have permeated the organization. There is a willingness at the very top to change, even drastically, if needed. In that spirit, there could be spin-offs and asset sales over time.

Either way, for the lessons in this chapter, what Roper looks like in 5 or 10 years doesn't really matter. What matters is the mathematical realities that Jellison exploited during his long and successful tenure as Roper's CEO—realities that form the basis for lessons that somehow get lost over time. At Roper, it's the simple mathematical realities that matter: rising cash flow, improving already high gross margins, earning a rising return on assets, and gravitating new investment toward better businesses. Rising returns on rising cash flow levels is the holy grail of compounding. It's not complex, but it requires patience for sure—patience rewarded with tremendous value creation.

Lessons from Roper

- Simplicity is underrated. Focus on a few basic drivers of value.
- Simple compensation schemes around profit and cash flow growth are usually best.
- Historical M&A patterns show large mispricings in niche assets. These can last a very long time.
- Incremental cash returns on capital are what matters—not the accounting definition, but in real money.
- High margins and low capital intensity are a powerful combination.
- Compounding works—it's a mathematical reality.
- New product cycles are tricky. Companies often "train" their customers to delay purchases.
- Entrepreneurs usually overinvest in product development and back office and underinvest in sales and marketing.

CHAPTER

9

TRANSDIGM

How to Turn a Million into a Billion

BY CARTER COPELAND

Wall Street has a tendency to oversimplify. Hours are long, and time is money; there's little room for complication. From the time a rising senior in college is working as an intern all the way through his or her eventual promotion to portfolio manager or managing director, the skill of delivering an effective elevator pitch is trained, retrained, and refined. If an investment thesis can't be distilled down to its key points in the time it takes to ride an elevator up or down, then it must not be worthwhile.

For TransDigm, a Cleveland-based aerospace parts company, the elevator pitch, since the time the company went public in 2006, has been something like, "It's a collection of acquired aerospace monopolies with outsized pricing power." These days, most of the publicly available content about TransDigm paints the company as an overleveraged and opportunistic price gouger. This is an oversimplification. Yes, TransDigm's story does include debt and the serial acquisition of companies with strong market positions. But it doesn't stop there. TransDigm would still be successful with a fraction of the price increases that the company has enjoyed over the years. This is because every day, from the factory floor to the C-suite, the people at TransDigm only focus on what truly matters for their consistent success.

This chapter is about an organization that compounds value at an extraordinary rate. It's about the power of a business model built on strategic and operating discipline and a relentless focus on the drivers of value creation for the company's owners—its employees and investors. It's about the optimization of internal and external investment as well as capital and cost structure. Many of the successful industrial companies we discuss in this book have very formalized businesses systems; TransDigm isn't one of them. However, any lack of formality is more than made up for by the company's strict adherence to its core principles of value-based pricing, productivity, and profitable new business.

GREAT BUSINESSES SITTING IN YOUR LAP

Anyone who's ever been on a commercial flight knows what an aircraft seat belt looks like and how it works. I bet you can picture the exact look and feel of the buckle and hear the flight attendant over the PA system saying, "Fasten the belt by placing the metal fitting into the buckle, and adjust the strap . . ." Why is it that almost every aircraft seat belt has a buckle just like the one you're imagining?

That's because almost no one but the maker of the original buckle has ever certified other designs with the Federal Aviation Administration (FAA). As a result, a company named AmSafe accounts for more than 95 percent of the global aircraft seat belt market.

How good a business is airplane seat belts? After all, it's only three pieces of metal and a spring. Well, you can ask TransDigm, which paid $750 million for AmSafe in 2012 and has generated a 20+ percent return on its investment. Aircraft seat belts are a fantastic business, especially in the right hands.

Look inside TransDigm's product portfolio, and you'll find thousands of other widgets that don't appear complex. Products incorrectly deemed "crappy" because you literally find them in the airplane restroom: lavatory faucets, drain assemblies, and door locks. Then there are overhead bin latches and extruded plastic vents that push cold air into the cabin, along with a litany of valves, pumps, cables, and connectors that all play a role in the flights of millions of people around the world every day. (See Figure 9.1.)

Figure 9.1: **TransDigm's product lines don't look particularly complex to the untrained eye.**

Source: TransDigm

These businesses are phenomenally profitable, and they're all owned by TransDigm, which has fully understood and maximized the returns from each of them. Through 2019, prior to the disruption caused by the COVID-19 crisis, the value created from these businesses made TransDigm the best-performing stock in industrials since the company's 2006 IPO, increasing by roughly 50 times over, including dividends. A company that started with an initial equity investment of $10 million 25 years ago grew to an enterprise value that was thousands of times larger (See Figure 9.2.)

Figure 9.2: **Prior to the disruption of COVID-19, TransDigm outperformed the S&P 500 by 4,900 percent since its IPO.**

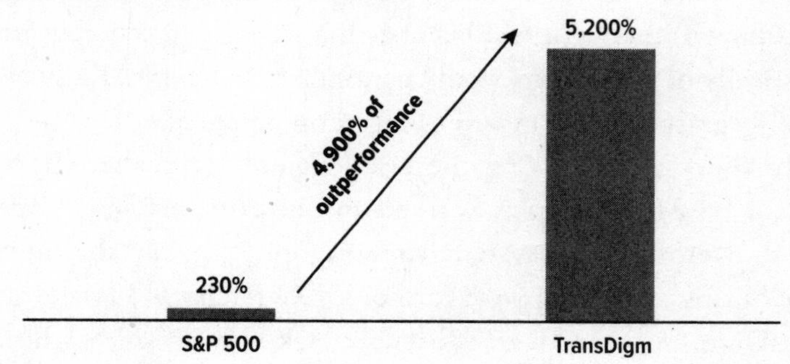

Source: Bloomberg

Note: Data is as of year-end 2019.

WHEN WALL STREET WAS SKEPTICAL

When TransDigm became a publicly traded company, Wall Street was initially more skeptical than optimistic. The company carried a large debt load, had changed hands in the private equity world three times, and had profit margins that were 20 points higher than any other aerospace company. When the company came to the public markets via an initial public offering, many didn't understand what TransDigm really was.

Investors are inherently skeptical toward most IPOs, especially for companies coming out of private equity ownership. Private equity firms have a reputation for gutting companies and overburdening them with debt before dressing them up for sale to institutional investors that they hope won't be able to tell the difference.

When TransDigm went public in 2006, it was the height of good times on Wall Street. IPOs were abundant, and investors could afford to be picky. As a result, the investment community was on the lookout for anything to dismiss an offering as imperfect. In the case of TransDigm, the combination of financial leverage, profit margins that appeared unsustainable, and the history of private equity ownership was all it took to generate skepticism. Few took the time to understand how TransDigm had been such a strong financial performer historically or why things would continue to get better. Early on, no one fully grasped the company's long-term potential.

In the years following the IPO, I gained a deeper appreciation for how the company worked and how its business model fit into the aerospace ecosystem. (See Figure 9.3.) My aha moment came during a meeting with former CEO Nicholas Howley and a TransDigm investor. In an effort to knock Howley off balance, the investor forcefully asked him why he should believe in the company following Howley's recent sale of millions of dollars of stock. Howley stunned me when he sat up in his chair, put his elbows on the boardroom table, looked the guy in the eye, and said: "This may come as a surprise to you, but I'm in this for the money. I haven't had many chances to sell stock under private equity ownership, and now I do. My wife wants a beach house. So we're gonna get a beach house. You can believe what you want, but I'm not going anywhere. I've got more money to make, and if you choose to, you can make it with me." This told me almost everything that I needed to know about TransDigm. The CEO was planning on making more money, but how exactly was he going to do it?

Figure 9.3: **TransDigm's history (1993–2019).**

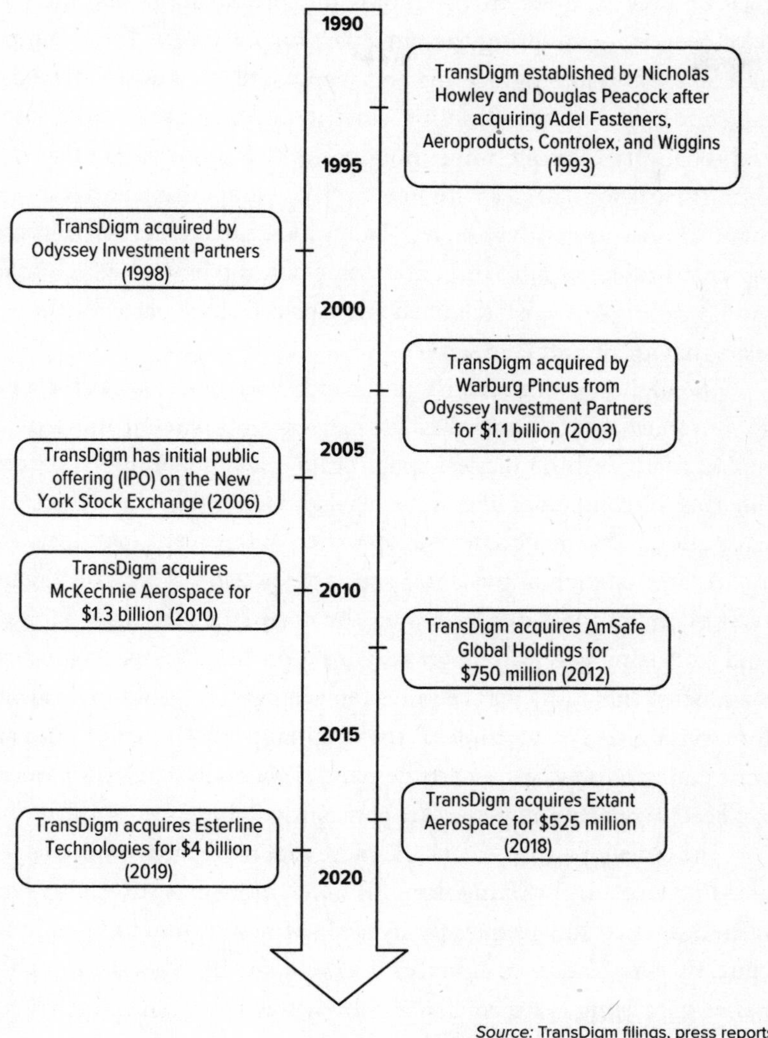
1990
TransDigm established by Nicholas Howley and Douglas Peacock after acquiring Adel Fasteners, Aeroproducts, Controlex, and Wiggins (1993)
1995
TransDigm acquired by Odyssey Investment Partners (1998)
2000
TransDigm acquired by Warburg Pincus from Odyssey Investment Partners for $1.1 billion (2003)
2005
TransDigm has initial public offering (IPO) on the New York Stock Exchange (2006)
TransDigm acquires McKechnie Aerospace for $1.3 billion (2010)
2010
TransDigm acquires AmSafe Global Holdings for $750 million (2012)
2015
TransDigm acquires Extant Aerospace for $525 million (2018)
TransDigm acquires Esterline Technologies for $4 billion (2019)
2020

Source: TransDigm filings, press reports

UNDERSTANDING TRANSDIGM'S MARKETS

Airlines have long asked themselves whether they want their spare parts to be safe or cheap. Unsurprisingly, safety and reliability always come first. As a result, today you'll find that for every part on a specific class of aircraft, there are often only one or two suppliers, and they have been manufacturing the same part for 70+ years. These companies build on prior engineering and manufacturing know-how, existing capital and certification investment, and track records of safety and reliability to create mini-monopolies that enjoy sales of specific aircraft parts for decades with low levels of competition and reinvestment. These competitive and regulatory moats make the aviation supply chain home to a lot of good businesses, the best of which make money selling low-cost, relatively high-priced spare parts for the ~30 years that an aircraft is in service.

The highest profit margins in the industrial world are in the aerospace aftermarket. General Electric makes 60 percent margins on replacement turbine blades; spare brake pads generate 70 percent margins for companies like Honeywell and United Technologies; and navigation software updates can approach 100 percent margins.

A large portion of the aerospace parts industry is built on a razor/razorblade business model, where the original equipment parts are sold to Boeing and Airbus for very little profit or a loss. Many years later, when that same part requires replacement, it is sold to an airline for a price that is a multiple of the original price charged to the aircraft manufacturer. Spare parts demand is generally stable, as parts are replaced regularly and planes are constantly flying.

The older an airplane gets, the more expensive it becomes to operate. This leads to shrinking fleets, as older, more expensive planes are retired or used less frequently in favor of newer, more efficient aircraft. By this time in an aircraft's life cycle, the likelihood of an alternative part being certified is increasingly low—new entrants struggle to justify the engineering and regulatory investment required to sell a new part into a shrinking market against an already established and trusted competitor. This allows the legacy manufacturers to push through annual price increases more aggressively. This pricing power more than offsets the declines in volume and justifies keeping production lines running efficiently, as incoming order velocity slows. These parts generate a ton of profit.

For most large aerospace companies, these highly lucrative parts are produced alongside far less attractive parts that don't earn anywhere near the same level of profit. Take United Technologies, where a super profitable brake business is tied up with metal landing gear, which is a capital-intensive and non-spare-parts–generating business with low margins. And that's just one example. The aerospace industry is littered with collections of good businesses alongside bad ones—except at TransDigm.

The average operating profit margin in the global aerospace industry is ~15 percent. TransDigm's is ~50 percent. (See Figure 9.4.) This is partially based on the purity of TransDigm's portfolio, which is made up solely of "proprietary aerospace businesses with significant aftermarket content." There are no bad businesses, which allows the company to enjoy the pricing benefits of being a sole source supplier without dilution from weaker business models. However, it's also a function of TransDigm's laser focus on its value drivers.

Figure 9.4: **TransDigm has operating margins 3x higher than that of peers.**

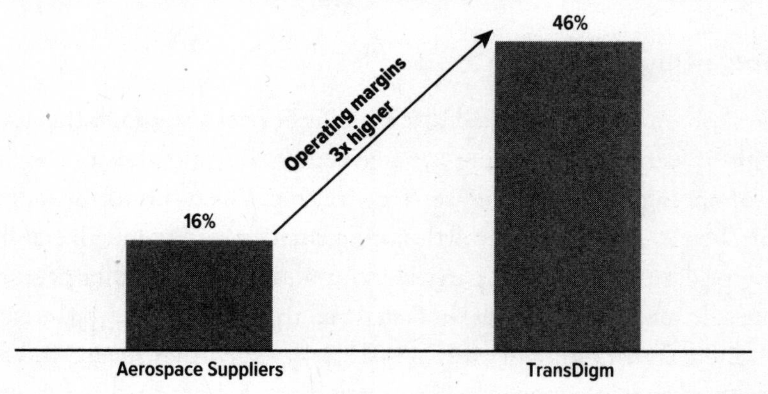

Source: Company filings

Make no mistake: it's unlikely that many businesses possess the same opportunity set as TransDigm, given the unique engineering and regulatory influences and brand/reputational entrenchment in the aircraft parts market. However, when you learn that many of TransDigm's businesses were actually acquired from the companies that make up the ~15 percent average, you begin to wonder what TransDigm has realized that everyone else hasn't.

TransDigm's core philosophy rests on a few key value drivers. They sound very straightforward and perhaps too simple to be true, but what makes them so powerful is how they have been consistently applied to a thoughtfully crafted portfolio of product lines and managed by an organization incentivized to maximize their value.

THE THREE VALUE DRIVERS

TransDigm is remarkably consistent in the application of what it calls its three value drivers: (1) value-based pricing, (2) productivity, and (3) profitable new business. It's a basic formula that requires masterful execution to get right. What's proved amazing over the years is how many levels of financial, strategic, and organizational discipline have been simultaneously layered on to achieve these seemingly simple goals to remarkable success.

Value-Based Pricing

For some that have looked at TransDigm over the years, the concept of value-based pricing is perceived as equivalent to leveraging monopoly positions to aggressively raise prices to unfair or excessive levels. However, it's worth noting that the company's overarching pricing strategy isn't particularly unique vis-à-vis other peers in the aerospace supply chain. In fact, when the Department of Defense audited TransDigm's pricing in 2018, it revealed that several industry peers were also raising prices on comparable products. Everyone raises prices; TransDigm just has a purer portfolio and is more focused on extracting appropriate value commensurate with the types of parts that it produces. For every part, TransDigm is maniacally focused on earning an appropriate economic return. That means that as older planes are retired and production runs of spare parts become less frequent and more challenging to predict, TransDigm demands that it be compensated, not just for the direct cost of the part, but for the costs of keeping production lines "hot" with skilled labor and working machinery. The company takes reliability seriously, and it expects to be paid for delivering a high-quality, usable part quickly. This mentality of driving an appropriate level of value out of every order is ingrained in the product line managers across the company. But how long can annual price increases approaching 5 percent really last?

TransDigm's pricing strategy remains sustainable because of three key factors: (1) regulatory, (2) economic, and (3) customer behavior. On the regulatory front, the time-consuming and costly FAA approval process for new parts creates a high barrier to entry. There are also the simple economic challenges of trying to compete against one of TransDigm's product lines. Many of TransDigm's parts are ordered in low and varying volumes and at infrequent intervals. Consequently, third parties often find the cost of investing in capital equipment and engineering expertise not worth the potential return. This dynamic is compounded by airline customer behavior. For an airline, the price points across TransDigm's portfolio of parts are relatively low. Seat belts cost a minuscule fraction of what a spare part for an engine costs, but an airline needs both in order to be cleared for takeoff. TransDigm's history of consistent on-time delivery and quality performance makes it rare for customers to switch providers. The risk isn't worth it. Airlines cannot afford to miss out on several hundred thousand dollars of revenue if flights are canceled because a $200 spare part is not delivered on time or to specification. In addition to having a smartly constructed portfolio of product lines that are able to bear consistent price increases, TransDigm is also one of the best companies at consistently wringing cost out of its businesses.

Productivity

TransDigm's productivity directive is focused on keeping annual growth in aggregate cost below inflation, year in and year out. This doesn't sound as revolutionary or as flashy as Lean or Six Sigma, but the general goal is easy to understand and communicate down to individual product lines.

Take a walk through any TransDigm facility, and you won't find anything extravagant. However, if you tour that same factory year after year, you'll find that the manufacturing footprint usually shrinks and the number of employees doesn't grow much, even as sales volume rises. Management consistently finds ways to eliminate employees who don't serve a value-creating function, and the company closes or consolidates factories to optimize TransDigm's broader manufacturing footprint. This reflects how dispassionately the company approaches evaluations of cost. When TransDigm acquires another company, it often relocates that company's manufacturing footprint into the space saved by previous productivity efforts.

Since the company's 2006 IPO, the company's sales have grown ~15x, and head count has grown by only ~13x, while floor space was tightly managed. This is a testament to the company's consistent push on improving productivity year in and year out. Despite pushing hard on both the price and cost front, TransDigm has not lost sight of the need to feed the business's long-term growth by winning profitable positions on next-generation aircraft platforms.

Profitable New Business

When it comes to pursuing new business, it is underappreciated how much time, effort, and money many companies expend chasing new opportunities that are unlikely to turn a profit. Many of the companies referenced in this book have employed teams of business development professionals who toil away at evaluations of growth opportunities with new customers or within new markets. However, their success isn't often judged by whether or not the opportunities result in *profitable* growth, merely sales growth alone. This is not the case at TransDigm. The company does not entertain business development efforts unless they offer a clear path to profits. There are no exceptions. Even with these strict principles, the company has been broadly successful in its new-business generation efforts. It has gained share on most next-generation aircraft and has done so with a tightly managed R&D and capital expenditures budget. Wasted effort is kept to a minimum.

TransDigm understands the difference between good parts and great parts, and it deliberately built a portfolio of companies that could compound the maximum amount of value over time. There are other aviation businesses that fit the TransDigm profile, but in many cases, they're not employing the same principles to the same effect. Often there are fantastic product lines within larger companies, but the manager that runs them is on autopilot because his or her business is an upper-quartile performer in a sea of mediocrity. TransDigm doesn't allow that to happen. All of its business units drive price, increase productivity, and win new business. The culture, the principles, and the compensation structure simply don't tolerate good if it comes at the expense of great.

NOT AS EASY AS IT LOOKS

A few years after TransDigm went public, the market gained familiarity with the TransDigm story, and the investment banking world was buzzing about a copycat firm running the TransDigm playbook in the private markets. The company was called McKechnie Aerospace and was nicknamed TransDigm 2.0 by investors. A McKechnie executive admitted to me that his company was simply trying to replicate TransDigm's success.

Before McKechnie ever had a chance to go public, TransDigm acquired it for $1.3 billion. At the time, the deal was the largest in the company's history, and many questioned how much value TransDigm could create since McKechnie was already a TransDigm "clone."

The McKechnie executive I knew was shown the door months after the deal closed, but he was there long enough to gain perspective on the differences between the two organizations. Shortly after he was let go, he told me that he was blown away by the TransDigm leaders. He said, "These guys are so much better than I ever imagined. . . . I totally underestimated how they do what they do . . . it's crazy, because every day we were trying to copy them."

Over the years, TransDigm's operational discipline has gotten far too little attention. And this discipline extends beyond the factory floor and the sales department. It touches so many other functions that amplify the value generated in the production facilities.

ALIGNING EVERYTHING AROUND VALUE MAXIMIZATION

TransDigm spent its first 13 years owned by private equity. With that experience came lessons that took the business model and put it on steroids. Private equity ownership certainly isn't without its problems. It's not uncommon for perfectly healthy businesses to be crushed under the burden of high levels of debt, cost cuts that run too deep, or decisions by owners who lack the operational or industry expertise to successfully navigate a business cycle. Other times, however, companies like TransDigm emerge from private equity ownership as more efficient organizations.

After it exited PE ownership, the company retained two core beliefs from its experience: (1) thoughtful cash deployment and a well-designed capital structure were tools for creating additional value, and (2) employees should think, act, and be compensated like owners.

With capital allocation and capital structure, TransDigm realized that a business built with a high degree of recurring revenue from spare parts, pricing power, low volatility in input costs, and limited capital requirements could shoulder a higher debt load than an average business. The extra capital raised could be deployed toward the acquisition of other parts manufacturers that fit TransDigm's model.

In the company's first 25 years in existence, it acquired more than 60 other businesses (such as AmSafe and McKechnie) and paid $7 billion in dividends. This was from a company that started with four small businesses and an initial equity investment of just over $10 million. (See Figure 9.5.)

Figure 9.5: **TransDigm acquired 60+ businesses since 1993.**

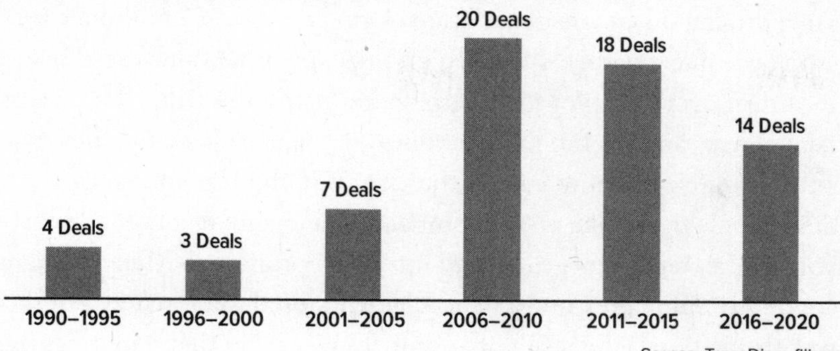

Source: TransDigm filings

The average company acquired by TransDigm had 20–30 percent margins upon deal closure, but within a few years TransDigm would often pull this up to nearly 50 percent, just by applying the company's operating model. The financial returns from these deals amplified the profits generated by TransDigm's core operations. Perhaps most importantly, TransDigm has never done an M&A transaction that strayed from its core competencies or diluted its overall portfolio of assets. In the event that an appropriate M&A deal is not available, TransDigm doesn't reach; it simply pays out its excess cash as a special dividend and waits for the right deal.

These elements are not top secret or unavailable to TransDigm's peers, but they are rarely utilized. This is mostly due to organizational constraints deemed too significant to overcome: capital structure limitations and broader incentive compensation plans that are a function of scale, a suboptimal business mix, or a focus on factors other than profits and cash flow.

WORK HARD, GET RICH

I've had the opportunity to be around the TransDigm culture for almost 15 years. The people there work harder, sleep less, and make more money than at any other company I've ever encountered. If you're a typical product line manager in an average industrial business, you likely take home $250,000 in annual compensation. That same product line manager at TransDigm can make $1 million. Every employee in every role is focused on the company's value drivers, and in return every employee gets to share in the rewards. The pace is demanding, and it's not for everyone—if you can't keep up, the company is quick to show you to the door. Of the top couple of hundred people that make up the company's leadership team today, nearly 90 percent were homegrown and internally promoted. Many of them are multimillionaires, and a handful are hundred millionaires. All this wealth creation is the result of a compensation plan that reinforces the desired outcomes.

TransDigm aspires to generate annual growth at a level that it characterizes as "private-equity-like." This equates to 15 to 20 percent over a number of years. The belief is that if the business can consistently generate that type of growth, sizable stock returns will follow. And at TransDigm, stock awards comprise a large share of overall employee compensation. The company is convinced that in order for the business model to work, those in charge of executing the strategy need to be compensated as owners. If managers effectively execute to the plan, they are compensated with stock that has the potential to appreciate well beyond the initial value of the bonus. I know TransDigm "retirees" who still have younger children and not a single strand of gray hair. They came in early, worked hard, were appropriately rewarded by the company, and then left with their riches.

WHY DON'T WE SEE THIS LEVEL OF SUCCESS ELSEWHERE?

I've had several conversations about TransDigm with an aerospace industry executive at another parts company. He often asks me, "Why do you like those TransDigm guys so much?" before criticizing the company's model as too aggressive on price and built solely on acquisitions—a Ponzi scheme waiting to unravel. I concede to him that while the company is not alone in its pricing posture, it does sit at the higher end of the peer group for the reasons noted previously. I also emphatically point out that this is just a fraction of its success story.

This executive manages his company differently from the way TransDigm is managed in several respects, not just pricing. His company's portfolio features products that are both darlings and duds, and his business employs countless people whose contribution to the bottom line is unclear. Employee compensation is tied to the success of other business units that have nothing to do with day-to-day operations. The business is managed top-down to protect large pools of profit derived from large customers, rather than to maximize the value from each aerospace part in a bottom-up fashion. It is a remarkably dissimilar approach. These divergent strategies are best evidenced by TransDigm's 2018 acquisition of Extant, a company that acquires intellectual property rights to "dying" lines of old aircraft parts that companies decide they no longer want.

Picture this: A business line manager at a large company looks at the list of products in her business unit and says, "I could grow this operation's revenues faster if I could get rid of the stuff that's shrinking." She finds products that go on older aircraft no longer in production, where inventory turns slowly and innovation is scant. If she gets rid of these parts, her business's overall growth rate goes up over time, and her inventory goes down. Depending on how she's being paid, which most often is by sales growth, she's a hero.

There's only one problem with this picture: these products often have the highest potential profit in the portfolio. They have the best pricing power, and they require little or no ongoing investment. The fact that managers were allowed to sell such product lines to Extant is crazier than anything TransDigm has ever done.

Many companies, especially those in the new economy, can learn an important lesson about value creation from the TransDigm/Extant example. At technology companies, growth is often emphasized above anything else. However, abandoning high-margin and high-return products when they slow or stop growing leaves significant value on the table. A lack of appropriate focus can push companies to make decisions that cause them to miss out on the full maximization and monetization of their previous efforts. This is a misstep that we've seen many companies make, and it's an error that TransDigm has taken full advantage of.

POSTMORTEM

To the untrained eye, TransDigm's collection of pumps, valves, and switches isn't particularly exciting compared with the product lines of other aerospace companies or those in the tech world. However, TransDigm has proven that even "boring" businesses can be extremely lucrative when focused strategic and operating principles are applied relentlessly.

TransDigm has consistently created value with every dollar of capital invested. Its persistent focus on price and cost, combined with secular tailwinds from growing air travel, has generated significant profits. Those profits have been diligently reinvested in similar businesses where the same value drivers can be applied, and waste is minimized. The business model is kicked into overdrive by the thoughtful addition of leverage and employees who are compensated as owners. There are always hiccups, but over any measurable period, value is consistently created.

The COVID-19 pandemic will inevitably put TransDigm to the test, as a lack of flying by the general public will hit aerospace suppliers hard in 2020. TransDigm will not be immune but the company's strong operational discipline and dispassionate adherence to its principles of value creation will almost certainly see it emerge from the crisis in a better position than peers. Over time, passengers will return to the skies and airplanes will consume spare parts. When that happens, the TransDigm model will again be on display.

At the end of the day, there is an ongoing debate about whether TransDigm is cheating through aggressive pricing or simply doing things much better than everyone else. While that debate rages on, TDG continues to succeed by knowing exactly where and how to apply effort, focus, talent, and capital. If nothing else, TransDigm has shown that even good businesses can often be much better. Good is simply not enough, and greatness often lives in organizing everything around the core value creation engine of a company. TransDigm is what great looks like. Other businesses and their leaders can be well served by understanding the discrete advantages of their end markets and product lines and designing an operating and financial system that aims to maximize those characteristics.

Lessons from TransDigm

- Even good businesses can always be better.
- Know your unique advantages and always focus on maximizing them.
- Simple goals create focused outcomes. Complex goals breed confusion.
- Cash and capital structure are often overlooked tools for enhancing value creation.
- M&A strategy should almost never stray from core competencies.
- Employees should think and be compensated like long-term owners.
- Bottom-up management can be far more effective than top-down management.

CHAPTER

10

STANLEY BLACK & DECKER

Adding a Digital Layer

BY ROB WERTHEIMER

Stanley Black & Decker (SBD) is a case study in repeated successes with one new edge. Two decades ago the company was in a place of weakness, a victim of the competition from China that was hollowing out much of industrial America. Its management team led the company through a remarkable, multistage revival: first a cost-focused turnaround, followed by the creation of a highly effective business system, and then acquisitions that levered growing expertise in operations. The new edge is how SBD has melded its high-functioning business system with the connections and opportunities of the tech world.

Few tech companies have mastered the systematic management of tangible assets. Apple is an obvious standout, but most have probably been too busy with innovation to focus on process optimization as much as older industries have been forced to do. Fewer still are the industrial companies that have successfully adapted to the rise of digital technology in the industrial sector. The systems of rapid innovation in the technology world are just too different, as are the networks of engineers, startups, and acquisitions required to keep pace.

Stanley Black & Decker's CEO since 2016, Jim Loree, pushed the company into its business system update. It's early days still, but the strategy shift is taking hold more quickly and effectively than is typical. The organization now has a defined purpose—"For Those Who Make the World"—and has hooks in different innovation networks, has recruiting designed to bring in fresh blood and ideas, and is on a path that can bring more profound changes to the production system through advanced manufacturing techniques.

WHAT IS STANLEY BLACK & DECKER?

Stanley Black & Decker is one of America's oldest companies, founded in 1843 as Stanley Works, a maker of bolts and hinges. It has paid a dividend for 144 straight years, longer than Procter & Gamble, Exxon, ConEd, or Coca-Cola.

SBD makes a wide variety of tools, from screwdrivers and tape measures, DeWalt drills and drivers, to high-end mechanics tools for auto and aerospace markets. Its consumer and contractor brands include the Stanley brand itself. The recently acquired Irwin and Lenox brands serve the electrical and plumbing trades, with a focus on drill bits and saw blades. Mac hand tools are for the automotive market, and Proto and Facom tools are for industrial markets. It has a commercial security platform where some advanced technologies are being tested. The company also has an industrial-facing segment that makes equipment for pipeline construction, heavy hydraulics, and fasteners, which include rivets, clips, nuts, and bolts, along with the systems for installing them.

Stanley Black & Decker has a history of innovation. Its products are mostly consumer-facing, so incremental features, updates, and variations have been longstanding parts of the marketing strategy—there's a deep internal competence around that. Those innovations have helped SBD as a whole, and its tools business in particular, grow faster than the typical industrial and stay ahead of the competition.

The company had long stretches of success and some stagnation in its 177-year history. The period from the late 1960s to the late 1980s was one of great leadership, growth, and expansion. By the 1990s problems had started to stack up. To reverse the slide, SBD made a GE executive, John Trani, CEO in 1997. He in turn recruited several executives from GE, including SBD's current CEO, Jim Loree. (See Figure 10.1.)

Figure 10.1: **The formative years at Stanley Black & Decker.**

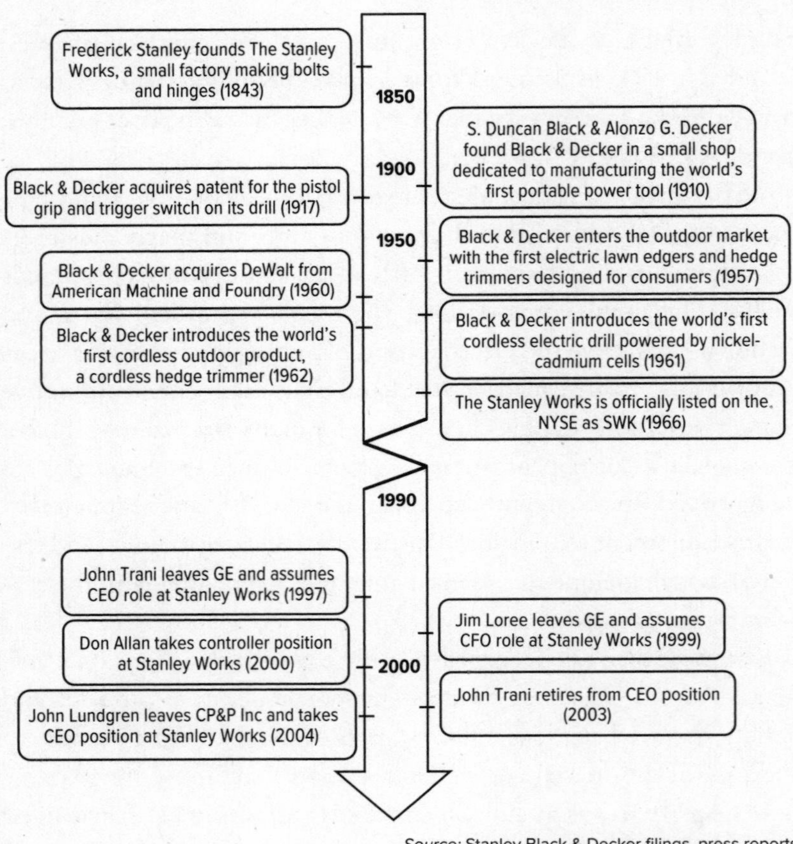

Source: Stanley Black & Decker filings, press reports

BUILDING THE BASE

Back in 1997, SBD was a different, weaker company, struggling with the same forces that led to many factory closures across the United States, forces that included the rise of Chinese manufacturing. Its operating margin fell below 10 percent and was slipping further. Its cost base was too high and its production too expensive, and it had no comprehensive competence in modern business systems.

The current top leadership came to the company during this challenging period. Loree had spent 19 years under Jack Welch, back when GE had one of the most well-recognized management systems in the corporate world. He started at Stanley Black & Decker as CFO and vice president. The company's current CFO, Don Allan, was corporate controller in 2000. Jeff Ansell, longtime head of the company's largest business, Global Tools and Storage, was a VP of sales. On arrival they found a business facing some major structural headwinds.

Some industrial companies are protected by a fragmented distribution channel, selling through thousands of small, disparate distributors and retailers. Consider how much easier it would be to sell to one large-scale customer, like Walmart, versus the intense sales strategy needed to get product into a vast multitude of independent convenience stores. In this way the rise of home centers like Home Depot and Lowe's made it easier for new tool manufacturers to scale up, driving out much of the older, diverse hardware store and lumberyard base where tools had been sold. However, the home centers also accelerated the move to lower-cost sourcing from China. (See Figures 10.2 and 10.3.)

Figure 10.2: **SBD's operating margin declined in the 1990s.**

Figure 10.3: **Low-cost tool imports from China rose sharply.**

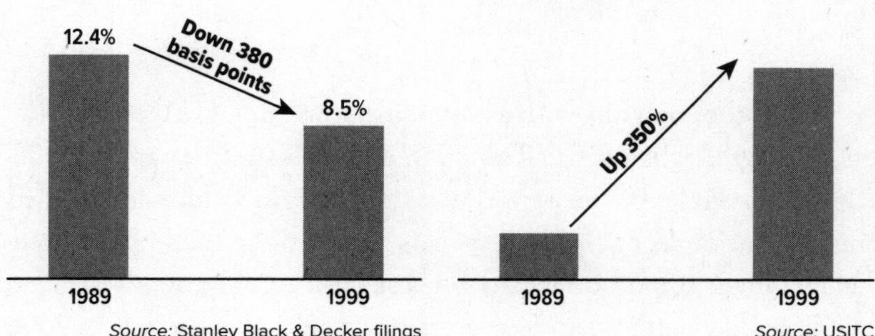

Source: Stanley Black & Decker filings

Source: USITC

These challenges came to a head with the recession that followed the dot-com bubble. The team responded with simple emergency cost-cutting, the only option available at that time. They closed factories in the United States and other high-cost regions and moved production to lower-cost countries, including China. From 1999 to 2002 SBD's sourcing from low-cost countries doubled.

More than 60 facilities were shuttered, and the company cut head count by 20 percent in the process. This was a difficult period: workers lost their jobs, strikes failed, and manager turnover was high. All that was painful but needed: it saved a long-lived company from terminal decline. The line between success and failure in a highly competitive space like tools is that thin. Revenue per employee rose by nearly a third, and profit per employee more than doubled as SBD pulled out of the recession. (See Figure 10.4.)

Figure 10.4: **Restructuring boosted productivity.**

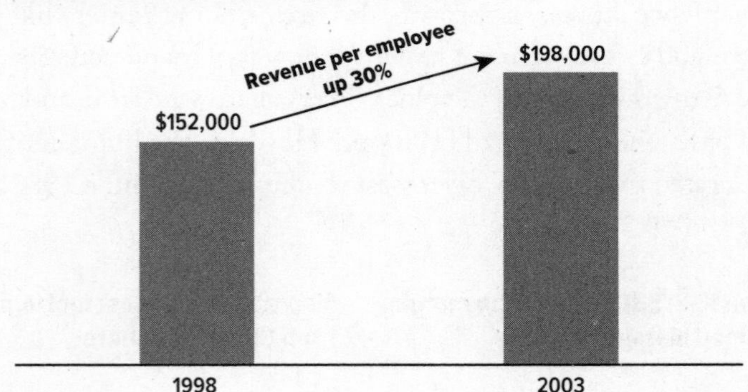

Source: Stanley Black & Decker filings

It left the company with a battered culture, though. Union workers celebrated when CEO Trani announced his retirement in 2003. Manager reviews of the period were also tough. Trani had churned through his ranks of senior managers, losing more than he retained. He had made important strides on cost-cutting, but notably little on building sustainable business processes or a culture of success. In 2004 the company brought in John Lundgren, and SBD began to build a strong base business system.

An early step was to implement Lean manufacturing, the foundation for any competent manufacturer. At SBD the move to Lean was the result of some hard lessons learned. The number of distinct products offered (stock keeping units, or SKUs) had steadily multiplied as the consumer-facing nature of the business drove an endless search for new and improved products. Customer focus is a positive, but the company didn't trim enough of the older lines: in 1998 it still had 140,000 SKUs, and 85,000 of them represented under 2 percent of sales. That is a mess of inefficiency and stale inventory. With so many different products, managers weren't using a pull-through system or even planning production for products individually; instead they applied large-scale guessing of overall tool demand. That led to too much money tied up in inventory and losses when stale products went unsold.

Lean manufacturing is the opposite of all that. The principles of Lean are simple: reduce waste, decrease inventory, and build what is needed quickly, rather than try to anticipate demand. Trying to predict how much inventory is needed results in compounding errors and lots of waste. Multiply that process times 140,000 different products, and you have chaos. Add in the worldwide move to low-cost Chinese manufacturing, and you have the exceptionally difficult predicament the company was facing in the late 1990s.

Systematic change requires systems, and SBD didn't have any at first. In those days, phrases like "brute-forcing it" came up frequently; relying on extra work and nonstandard processes isn't the ideal method, but moving in the right direction is critical. The company eliminated close to 10 percent of its SKUs in 2001 alone. Don Allan, the current CFO and controller then, was a part of the effort to introduce basic management processes that the company lacked.

Needing to create some of these systems from scratch, the company had to lean a little harder on managers like Allan. In practice, that involved monthly meetings at the CFO and CEO level and more frequent interactions down the line. Previously, SBD had operated without a formal sales and operations planning process. Creating that workflow helped immediately, with management of inventory and excess SKUs done in a data-driven way, as opposed to simply watching excesses build up and be chopped back down. Formalization created time to start actual process loops of continuous improvement.

Normal processes flowed without intervention, freeing up time to focus on anomalies or disputes, with the goal of finding and attacking the roots of problems to prevent recurrence.

It took a lot of work and time for these improvements to take hold, but after a couple of years, processes were working smoothly, and real continuous improvement accelerated. The company had run hundreds of kaizen events a year during the turnaround, adding a positive dimension to the dramatic acts of closing factories and cutting down the product line. By 2004 the company had laid the foundation for manufacturing excellence that would continue to grow. (See Figure 10.5.) Although the system was in better shape, it would still benefit meaningfully from some perspective from a board member.

Figure 10.5: **The evolution of Stanley Black & Decker.**

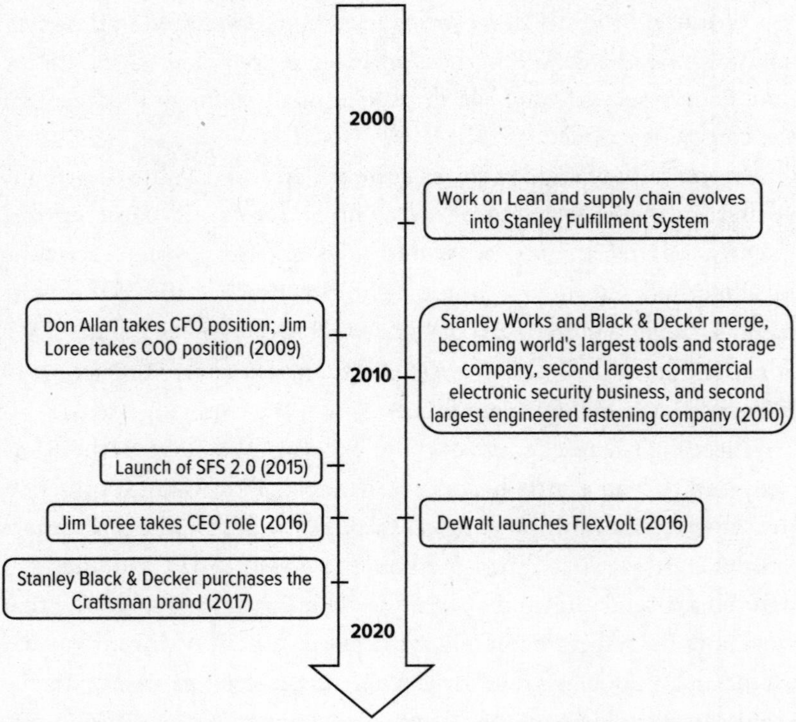

2000

Work on Lean and supply chain evolves into Stanley Fulfillment System

Don Allan takes CFO position; Jim Loree takes COO position (2009)

2010

Stanley Works and Black & Decker merge, becoming world's largest tools and storage company, second largest commercial electronic security business, and second largest engineered fastening company (2010)

Launch of SFS 2.0 (2015)

Jim Loree takes CEO role (2016)

DeWalt launches FlexVolt (2016)

Stanley Black & Decker purchases the Craftsman brand (2017)

2020

Source: Stanley Black & Decker filings, press reports

FROM TURNAROUND TO THE CREATION OF SFS: THE STANLEY FULFILLMENT SYSTEM

Emmanuel Kampouris had decades of experience in similar businesses, having been CEO of American Standard. Board members don't always add value to businesses, as with GE's board rubber-stamping mistakes in the Immelt era or CAT's board failing to ask incisive questions on the company's China coal mining failure. In the best cases, however, corporate leaders bring expertise and forceful challenges, and that's what Kampouris did. His push was a central part of what became the core business process: the Stanley Fulfillment System, or SFS. He challenged the company on the level of working capital it held even after making progress with Lean, arguing that it could make substantial improvements while providing better customer service.

Working capital is simply money that's tied up: inventory or accounts receivable (money not yet paid to the company), offset by bills that the company hasn't paid yet. It is an investment, just like building a factory. Over the course of the mid-2000s, the company took its working capital turns, or the ratio of sales to working capital, from around 4 up to close to 10.

That work unlocked about $3 billion extra that had been tied up in working capital—about the cost of building all its global factories. SBD directed the freed-up capital into acquisitions that compounded growth. The improved working capital was a major victory, but it was only one facet of a better operational system. Better customer service meant having the right products available, even while keeping inventory low.

If you walk into the tools department at a large home center or hardware store, you expect to see the product you want to purchase. If it's not there, you might buy it somewhere else, or you might buy a competitor product, or perhaps nothing at all. As a supplier, SBD's fill rates, a measure of what is on the shelf versus what should be if everything is perfect, were 93–95 percent at the start of the 2000s, which was just OK. Managing that "in-stock" presence isn't necessarily easy, and doing it while extending your supply chain out into Asia *and* remaining vigilant in managing working capital is harder still. Having lots of buffer inventory is one way to do it, but that's expensive, and you risk being stuck with stale or obsolete inventory if market preferences change, as SBD had already found out the hard way.

Effective fulfillment became a major push in SFS, supplanting the management of inventories on "feel." Production and inventory planning moved to a much more granular level, down to individual products. The company also used targeted changes to its compensation systems for an extra boost, effectively giving employees everywhere the chance to earn a double bonus if the fill rate target was met. The incentive had a galvanizing effect across the company and further strengthened the success of the new systems. Effective process along with employee buy-in drove better inventory turns as fill rates improved without needing to build excess inventory. Over time that fill rate rose to 98–99 percent.

The Stanley Fulfillment System highlighted the core importance of those efforts to improve the supply chain and deliver product efficiently to customers, but it's also a factory-based initiative. Throughout the early 2000s, the company was building on Lean and continuous improvement initiatives that were under way at the factories, with results equally as important as those seen with working capital.

If you ask the managers at any good manufacturer what they look at for a quick assessment of a company's manufacturing competence, the answers are often very similar: clean factories, high employee engagement, and, above all, good safety. There's sometimes a perception that manufacturers don't care about worker safety; there have been some shocking lapses in the coal mining industry, for example. But in the industrial world, nothing could be further from the truth.

Safety is a key indicator of a healthy factory with engaged managers and employees. It's also highly correlated with smooth operations. Stanley Black & Decker's safety trends suggest dramatic progress has been made not just in worker safety, but across the entire production chain. (See Figure 10.6.)

Figure 10.6: **Evidence of the progress in SFS in one simple chart.**

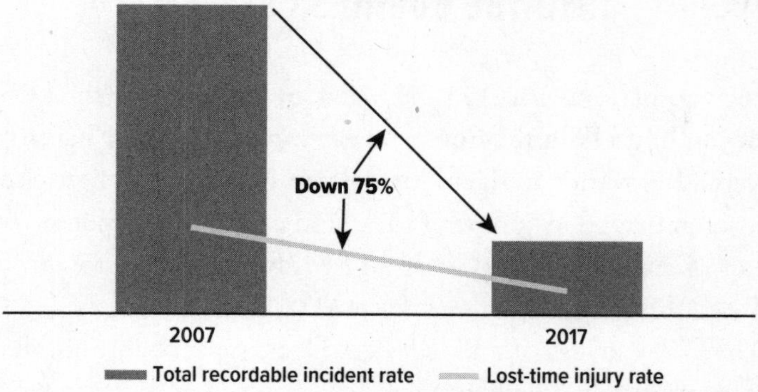

Down 75%

2007 2017

Total recordable incident rate — Lost-time injury rate

Source: Stanley Black & Decker filings

Developing the SFS business system opened up opportunities to acquire and expand. Money freed up from working capital went toward buying new brands or companies, to which SBD could add value across sales, innovation, and operations.

These efforts culminated in the 2010 acquisition of Black & Decker by Stanley Works, with the size and importance of this transaction leading to the company being renamed Stanley Black & Decker. Black & Decker brought substantial sales and marketing expertise to the company, but it was run more like the Stanley of a decade past, closer to seat-of-the-pants and gut feel than a well-tuned operational structure. SBD applied its playbook to the new assets, raising working capital turns and freeing cash, raising margins through better systems and management. The deal was a tremendous success, leaving the combined entity with better scale, systems, and products. Several deals that followed similarly levered the improved operations at SBD. Loree had led the M&A strategy at the company since 2002, a successful decade of diversification that, along with the operational improvement, transformed SBD from a toolmaker to an industrial leader.

INTEGRATING TECHNOLOGY INTO THE BUSINESS SYSTEM

Loree, who became CEO in 2016, led an evolution of the business system, adding a layer that most old economy companies haven't gotten to yet. Innovation in the industrial world, and everywhere else, has been supercharged by a flow of ideas and capital from Silicon Valley, instead of from old East Coast and Midwest factory towns. SBD embraced this shift, which was no small task.

The 177-year-old Stanley Black & Decker is probably not the first company most folks would have picked to become a leader in technology. Some might have said the same about its CEO, who drove this change. If you close your eyes and picture a corporate-looking CEO from Connecticut, you might get close to the actual Jim Loree. Loree attended Union College, one of the oldest schools in the country and located in Schenectady, New York, the home of GE's power businesses and United Technology's Carrier plant. Loree spent two decades at GE, the epitome of old corporate America, in a culture that failed in the 2000s and 2010s: disproportionately white and male.

At SBD, he and other leaders had executed well on the playbook of systematizing operations. Many companies fail to get that far. The next step, however, required a reinvention.

Loree saw the pace of change in the world increasing as systems that unlock growth and innovation stack onto each other—artificial intelligence, rapid prototyping with 3D printing, factory connectivity and automation. He wanted to push SBD ahead, to keep his workforce engaged, flexible, and filled with lifetime learners who can continually adapt to emerging tech and new challenges.

Loree spends a lot of time explaining the company's vision, and he's enthusiastic about it. We've never seen him happier, though, than when he spoke on the flow of diversity and new talent that the pivot toward advanced technology was bringing into the company. Novel ideas and an updated workforce are requirements for an old industrial trying to do something different. Stanley Black & Decker embraced those changes enthusiastically.

For context, the innovation ecosystem is dramatically changing for the old economy. Venture capital (VC) funding for industrial markets, under a billion dollars 10 years ago, exceeded $40 billion in 2018. Total R&D spent by all public industrial companies is now around $90 billion, so in a few short years VC investment has reached close to half that level. (See Figure 10.7.) Most of this influx of funding aims at disruptive innovations, while most standard R&D is incremental. Accordingly, the tech world is now outspending the industrial world on real disruption by a wide margin and with greater efficiency.

Figure 10.7: **VC funding has become much more important to the future of industrials.**

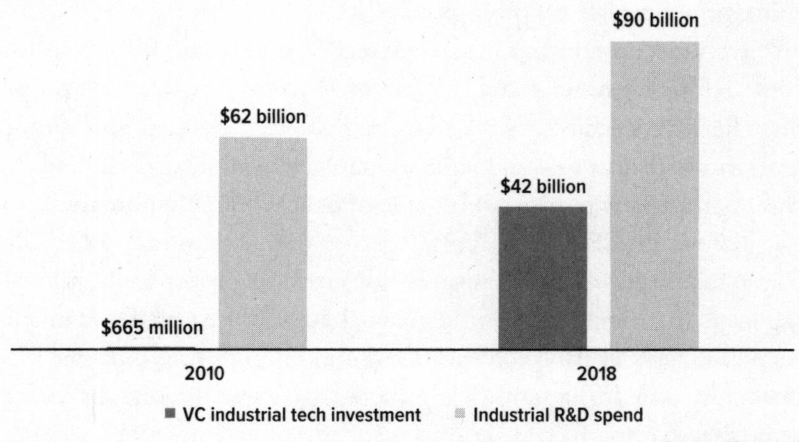

Source: Pitchbook

That sort of shift creates the sense of urgency that Loree was experiencing in 2014 and 2015. The risk of disruption is large, but so is the potential for leaders ahead of the trends. SBD took the base the company had built and systematically applied multiple different streams of technology integration to it.

STANLEY FULFILLMENT SYSTEMS 2.0: MOVING THE BUSINESS SYSTEM TOWARD TECHNOLOGY

The business system update was wide ranging, but the additions to the customer-facing innovation process might be the most important.

Stanley Black & Decker's legacy of innovation was excellent, but more incremental than transformational. Like other corporate initiatives, innovation went through a tightly managed process. Voice-of-the-customer studies brought direction, with set financial hurdles and a steady march toward go/no-go decisions. That process increases productivity and helps deliver what customers want, but it inhibits free thinking and true breakthroughs.

The work on innovation started in 2014 with a skunkworks team. It used different systems and had its own rhythm, with quarterly progress checks instead of tight management along a defined innovation path. It was kept small and agile to enhance flexibility. The mandate was to create new products with at least $100 million in potential.

The result, SBD's FlexVolt, far exceeded that hurdle. FlexVolt dramatically expands the options for cordless power tools, allowing users to choose between the normal 20-volt operation and much higher voltage levels. A 120-volt flow is enough to run tools that are normally corded. That option is a big deal on construction jobsites, as removing extension cords or noisy air compressors has clear benefits for productivity, safety, and quality of the work environment.

Fueled by this initial success, which saw FlexVolt sales rising 10 times as fast as prior innovations, the company formalized disruptive innovation as part of its update and expansion of SFS. It set up several teams outside its core offices, near universities and other innovation hubs.

One such breakthrough innovation center developed deep relationships with a German automaker. The automaker had an engineering challenge that wasn't directly related to SBD's product or expertise, but the teams knew each other, and the automaker knew of the new focus on outside-the-box thinking. A bit of collaboration solved the problem for the carmaker: fixing a troublesome hitch in the production process with an automated and consistent application. That led to much deeper engagement between engineering teams as they turned to solving larger problems that could bring both companies substantial benefit. Other early victories included automated welding on pipelines, a stud welder for rebar in construction sites that cuts time and labor by up to 95 percent, some exciting potential in solar pumps for irrigation in India, and more active projects that have yet to be released. These wins gave Stanley Black & Decker the confidence to continue.

EMBRACING A LARGER ECOSYSTEM

The company now had a robust internal product development system, and it had a culture open to delivering advanced new products to customers at a cadence much faster than industrials are used to. But SBD needed to engage with an external ecosystem as well. Tech advances too fast and with too much diversity to stay internally focused. This required a deliberate and wide-ranging set of changes all being folded into a finely tuned operations system, like new hires, new leadership, and new resources outside the walls of the company: venture capital and incubators. It involved redesigning incentives to encourage breakthrough innovation, piloting, and then expanding advanced factories. It was an ambitious plan.

A major theme was openness. The surge in startup funding made it more likely that substantial disruptions would come from the outside. Automakers saw those disruptions with Tesla, a startup that leapfrogged the industry. Tesla's Model S was launched in 2012. By 2020, it's still debatable whether any competing car can beat it. Typical corporate R&D processes are largely internal, with some cross-pollination via mingling engineers at conferences and trade shows, so a lot of activity stays within industry norms.

Stanley Black & Decker took multiple steps to get more ideas flowing in from outside. Stanley Ventures, its venture capital arm, is one such example. Most industrials aren't situated next to innovation centers: only one in five industrial companies has an office in or near Silicon Valley. That limits immersion in the buzz of innovation via employee networks, as well as opportunities for cross-pollination from hiring. Stanley Ventures aimed to sync with that ecosystem.

The company partnered with leading accelerator TechStars to create an external accelerator in Hartford, Connecticut, near SDB's headquarters in New Britain. The accelerator was focused on 3D printing and packaging, thereby investing in SBD's community and in advanced manufacturing at the same time. Internally Stanley Black & Decker created an Exponential Learning Unit in Silicon Valley, both to attract talent from that area and to serve as an incubator of ideas.

A look at the company's Facebook Workplace page will show a dozen activities and links showcasing the organization's openness: makerspaces, scholarships for students, sponsorships for vocational skills competitions, support for LGBT events, a women-founded 3D design lab. It's a much more creative and diverse set of events than other industrials offer.

A second major theme was infusing new talent into the company. In 2017 SBD brought in its first chief technology officer from the outside, Dr. Mark Maybury. Maybury had been chief scientist for the Air Force, where he guided a $5 billion investment stream, and previously he had served as VP of Intelligence Portfolios at MITRE Corporation, an entity that manages federally funded R&D centers for several large US government agencies. He was attracted by the opportunity to update an older company's operations and to have a direct impact on the real economy. That's proved an attractive pitch for many.

The goal was to avoid new tech businesses becoming islands; SBD wanted to diffuse some of the talent it was bringing in across the company. The structure set up to facilitate that was an internal digital accelerator, sited in Atlanta to take advantage of local engineering talent and a more favorable cost structure relative to Silicon Valley. Business unit leaders were given a year to come up with a digital plan, and the accelerator helped with that process. Those working in the accelerator didn't aim to be internal consultants for SBD, but rather a resource that teams could pull from and integrate. From an original staffing goal of around 15 people, the accelerator expanded to 60 by year two and 90 by year three, and it now has well over 100 team members, having seen many internal transfers along the way as other Stanley Black & Decker businesses absorbed some of the staff.

ADVANCED FACTORIES

Developing a deeper innovation ecosystem and digital capabilities are only part of what's changing. SBD is also working to bring advanced manufacturing into its factories, thereby lowering costs, localizing production, and accelerating product development.

The industrial world has an ongoing movement called Industry 4.0, which aims to bring manufacturing into the digital age. There are 30 or so advanced technologies in that broad concept, and SBD is aggressively pursuing several.

The first phase is deploying the industrial internet of things at scale. There's been lots of talk around IIOT for the past few years, and it's not always clear what it means or who benefits. Put simply, added sensors and technology on production lines bring an increase in visibility and the ability to respond to changes in volume or what's being made. On top of that, SBD is deploying industrial apps built internally and leveraging what's been built by others. The goal is full visibility into the production line.

Phase two involves predictive analytics and predictive maintenance, i.e., how to look at data in real time now that the factories are all connected. Value stream mapping, a basic tool of Lean, creates a visual map of production, its waste and value creation. It has some simple inputs such as taking a stopwatch and measuring how long it takes to complete a task. An advanced factory with software and sensors throughout can create that map and identify pockets of waste quickly and automatically. Visibility through a factory improves dramatically. After all, big chunks of Industry 4.0 are just tools to do current processes better.

An andon is a common visual signal in a factory used to indicate that something has gone wrong and needs attention. Andons often look like little traffic lights, with either the red or green lit up. A worker seeing something that isn't right pulls a cord, the signal light changes from green to red, and engineers and supervisors head over to fix the issue. Andons are highly effective, but still fairly basic. Modern tools such as iPads, software, and sensors tying together the whole production line can help identify and communicate problems faster.

With phase three come automation and robotics, thanks to the falling cost of robots and cobots (robots that work on a production line closely with humans). Cheaper, better robots sound exciting, but each one represents a fairly narrow savings, replacing one to three workers, while creating a more skilled job for a human manager. SBD and other manufacturers target substantial annual labor productivity gains, 6 to 8 percent at the factory level, translating to 3 percent or more for the total corporation with some reinvestment in R&D and marketing. The lower variability, higher quality, and steadier flow across the entire company gained by automating the whole production system will result in a much broader systematic savings—that's the exciting part of Industry 4.0.

Commitment and leadership are key to realizing those systemwide benefits. The investment takes multiple years to come to fruition. So far, many companies are experimenting with individual pilot plans but haven't yet rolled these out across factories on a systemwide basis. The reality is that it's very difficult, so much so that "pilot purgatory" has become a common refrain within the consulting community. Most organizations have considerable inertia, and part of the point of systematic operations is to drive repeatable work. Wide-ranging changes in customer-facing products, innovation, and factories are a major disruption to that existing flow.

There's another benefit beyond lower error rates and lower production cost. Automation allows companies to localize production. That can have brand benefits, as we discuss below in the case of Craftsman tools, while reducing supply chain length, working capital, and variability. In today's world, it also reduces tariff risk.

HOW TO GET IT DONE

We've seen corporate initiatives go nowhere beyond paper at many great companies over the years. What worked in this case was a combination of strong leadership and direction, infusion of outside talent and resources, and social networking tools that kicked off a feedback loop of successes and sharing. Here are some lessons in creating change.

Stars want to go where the organization is moving. A strong direction from the top draws in good people and frees them up to take risks; the best talent is attracted to new projects when folks know strategic priorities are clear. Lots of good ideas come through divisions, but it takes a major, public commitment from the CEO to get the organization moving in a coherent direction.

Early wins are hugely helpful. The success of FlexVolt led to more high-performing engineers and managers wanting to join the effort. It probably requires a bit of luck. But just as employee engagement is critical to any continuous improvement process, early wins help drive engagement in new initiatives.

Social media can reinforce change. Culture is an output of daily action and the vision behind it. Incentives matter a lot, and we've noted how Stanley Black & Decker pushed up its working capital turns partly through the power of incentives. It used small, targeted incentives for its tech teams as well. But we were surprised to find that the softer issues were cited more often as parts of the effort to push SBD's transformation forward. When we asked about incentives, several managers took the conversation in a different direction, to employee connectedness and engagement, facilitated by tools, rather than just different pay.

Stanley Black & Decker was one of the initial pilots of Facebook Workplace. Facebook actually resisted rolling it out with SBD, as it thought the product would work better with tech workforces than with an old economy stalwart, but the company ended up being one of the most dynamic users of the product. Workplace pushed connectedness and collaboration among teams: we saw folks commenting on projects and chipping in to help with expertise from another segment or another country.

Purpose is a powerful driver. That's a message I hadn't expected to hear, but it resonates. Part of the long process of designing and pushing through this change was some thinking on what employees want. Most of us want to do meaningful work in life rather than just punch a clock for money. I like to imagine I'm helping the global flows of capital drive up productivity, health, and wealth, rather than just picking one stock or another.

The factory closures and sharp reduction in the workforce of the late 1990s and early 2000s had damaged employee cohesion. Loree wanted to boost the sense of meaningful work and connectedness at Stanley Black & Decker. The company's new stated mission spoke to that effort: "For Those Who Make the World." Creating innovative tools for people who build. Large parts of the tech economy sometimes seem to boil down to "creative" ways to get consumers to part with their personal data. Working on better tools to make construction faster, safer, and more efficient has proved an effective draw for new talent.

COMPLETING THE FLYWHEEL WITH ADVANCED TECHNOLOGY

In 2017 Stanley Black & Decker bought Craftsman tools from Sears. That transaction is an excellent illustration of the virtuous circle of margin improvement and capital deployment that we have talked about, but with advanced technology adding another layer to the potential.

Craftsman is a historic brand in the United States that had fallen on hard times with the decline of Sears. Like Kenmore in appliances, it had a reputation for quality products and support. Craftsman benefited from a made-in-America image and from a lifetime guarantee. Walk into a Sears with a broken 40-year-old Craftsman wrench, and you could walk out with a new one under warranty. That was a powerful pledge for generations of home mechanics, contractors, and jobbers. In recent years, though, customers were complaining of quality slippage.

Sears started sourcing from China, and so American-made tools needing replacement were exchanged for cheaper ones made in China, with customers no longer feeling that Craftsman's price was warranted by better quality. That's the story of American manufacturing in many industries as factories moved to China, benefiting at first from lower labor and eventually from a stronger, diversified supply chain that reduces production costs further still.

SBD could have made Craftsman a success even before applying its advanced technology strategy. The brand folded seamlessly into existing relationships with channel partners, which had grown stronger with the company's increased competence over the years. The shift to tech, however, unlocked two additional ways to create value.

Advanced manufacturing allows Stanley Black & Decker to bring more production back into the United States. In 2018 it announced the opening of a factory in Texas to manufacture mechanics tools such as sockets, rachets, and wrenches, bringing 500 jobs to the region. The cost is expected to be equivalent to the cost of tools imported from China; this is made possible by SBD's innovative manufacturing strategy. That's a step toward restoring that brand promise of quality tools made in America.

Also, growing expertise in advanced innovation meant SBD could add disruptive potential to the acquisition. Among other things, Craftsman makes outdoor equipment such as weed trimmers, snowblowers, and lawnmowers. There is a huge opportunity to go electric in this space, at an even faster pace than with cars. The two-stroke engines of many lawn care products are inherently dirty, emitting pollution far out of proportion to their fuel use, because emissions equipment is too expensive on small engines. In 10 years, much of the lawn and garden tool products may be electric. Disruptive innovation teams are already working on the opportunity.

POSTMORTEM

Stanley Black & Decker took the flywheel of margin improvement and capital redeployment and added in a technology layer. The acquisition of the Craftsman brand exemplifies the synergistic opportunities that have been unlocked with SBD's transformation. The company's ability to improve margins and operational processes, coupled with its new innovation focus, gave management confidence that it could improve and revive this old brand better than others could. Sales results in the first years of the Craftsman relaunch have been far above expectations.

This is the culmination of two decades of steady improvement: factory closures and cost-cutting, implementation of Lean, and a decade of maturation, along with building SFS, leveraging its success with acquisitions, and finally adding the technology layer. The company continues to push its operating system forward, focusing on people and integration of technology, innovation, customers, and operational excellence. The result is a fully developed operating system, now called the SBD Operating Model, which continues to evolve. From a starting point behind most industrial companies, Stanley Black & Decker is now far ahead.

Lessons from Stanley Black & Decker

- Cost-cutting can be painful—it can create dislocations in the organization—but may be necessary to survive.
- Given sustained effort, even old businesses can be transformed. New challenges often demand it.
- Business systems can evolve to suit the needs of the time. SBD started with Lean, but it has pivoted toward innovation and technology.
- Stars want to go where the organization is moving. Clear signals from the top encourage the optimal allocation of talent.
- Embracing technology or new ideas requires openness, external networks, collaboration tools, and repeatable processes.

CHAPTER

11

UNITED RENTALS

Asset Sharing Done Right

BY ROB WERTHEIMER

Some companies start with a natural advantage, a breakthrough product, patent, or niche that drives abnormally large profits. Their success lasts for a while, until competition rises. Mature industrial companies are well past that stage, playing in a global marketplace where competition is widespread and ingrained. Such firms do spend on products and innovation, but more often they win and grow by focusing on operations. We've chosen an extreme example in this chapter to show a path to success *after* innovation has been commoditized.

Rental equipment is an industry in which even expert observers assume there's no chance to thrive. There are no obvious barriers: anyone with financing can start a company, buy equipment, and rent it out. Yet United Rentals, along with number two player Sunbelt Rentals, has built tremendous, compounding success through a feedback loop of scale and continuous improvement.

WHAT IS THE RENTAL EQUIPMENT INDUSTRY?

This is one of the least-loved industries of any we have studied. Rental yards aren't generally found in the expensive part of town. They are filled with products that get heavy use and often look worn after just a couple of jobs. In a rental yard you might find an excavator, a backup generator, or a selection of Porta-Potties in luxury and basic models. There are substantial economic and environmental benefits to renting. But investors see an ugly industry that consumes huge amounts of capital and has limited competitive differentiation.

The prevailing view is that the industry is a bit like the airline industry from a decade or two ago: the plane is expensive and going to fly no matter what, so you might as well sell tickets cheap to get all the seats filled, especially when demand falls. In a true recession, capital-intensive industries can be an exercise in who can take the most pain while others are shutting down. Rental equipment similarly doesn't make money if it's not rented, and rental has lower barriers to entry than do airlines.

United Rentals built a towering competitive advantage the hard way. In doing so it raised its margins substantially, widening the gap with competition, creating tens of thousands of good jobs, and professionalizing a scattered and entrepreneurial industry along the way.

There is a lesson for the new economy here. Designing a breakthrough software app at Uber created an industry, but managing an extremely large, asset-intensive chain is something else, and the costs of doing so poorly are creeping up. Uber may not own cars, but that doesn't make it an asset-light business model overall.

Equipment rental is asset sharing, old economy style. It differs in several ways from the recent versions created by Uber, Airbnb, and WeWork. First, it doesn't shy away from owning assets: it's a hardware management business, not just software. Second, the leaders employ people in good jobs with good training, instead of using contractors. Third, it is highly profitable. United Rentals and Sunbelt generate billions in cash to grow and expand, all while materially lowering the costs for their customers and making the economy more efficient. They do that by optimizing all aspects of the network: the asset base, the labor force, and even their customers' operations.

Mike Kneeland, the CEO for most of this story, transformed the culture and structure at United Rentals, building a connected company out of a series of independent branches and raising revenue and profits materially. Matt Flannery, the former COO and current CEO of United Rentals, made the company into a systematic, high-performing leader, with a culture of continuous improvement that keeps widening the competitive moat. They applied lessons in operations and improvement systematically throughout their enterprises in a way that most peers across the rental world, and industrials too, often fail to do. But to truly understand the company's pathway to success, some context on what the business is, and how high the hurdles were, is needed.

If you drive by a rental yard, you might see a collection of tall booms reaching two or three stories into the sky. Those are aerial work platforms, designed to lift a person up in the air (whereas cranes lift steel beams and other construction materials). They lift workers from one to more than fifteen stories, for jobs of all kinds: painting, doing construction or repair work, changing lightbulbs in factories, and so on. It is a versatile product that replaces ladders and scaffolds, which are far more dangerous. Aerials constitute by far the largest category handled by rental outfits, but there are many others, particularly at United Rentals.

Managing this variation requires the systematic improvements in operations that have been applied by the leaders, allowing for expansion into ever more categories. The smaller rental companies might rent a few dozen or a few hundred products; the larger ones, a few thousand.

One growing category for United Rentals includes pumps and tanks—dig a hole almost anywhere outside of a desert, and water seeps in, which needs to be pumped away so work can proceed. The company rents out steel shoring for worker safety in trenches. One of my last jobs in college, as a geology student, involved hopping down into a freshly dug trench, without such safety bracing. I can still remember the urgency with which the lead scientist wanted to take measurements and get the hell out. United Rentals rents out dehumidifiers for emergency drying after floods or hurricanes, preventing huge losses that might otherwise result. It rents out portable HVAC systems, saving patients in hospitals and allowing work to continue in buildings where the AC has gone out.

The business is built on the fact that renting is often cheaper than buying. If you use the equipment sporadically, a few days or weeks at a time, it makes no sense to own it. As rental companies get better at managing more categories, the reasons to rent multiply. Consider how the floors of any large office building in New York City are cleaned with a polisher several times a year. Owning the floor cleaning equipment might not be expensive, but it requires a closet in a place where real estate is expensive. It needs someone to maintain the equipment, to know where to get parts, to know how to fix it, etc. That's a hassle, and it represents a series of hidden expenses that companies increasingly don't need to own.

From the outside the business sounds simple: buy equipment; rent it out; collect money. But success requires good management of several different processes. It's a combination of logistics to pick up and deliver the equipment, repair and maintenance, customer service, customer acquisition, and fleet management. That process is magnified in complexity as the product offerings expand. United Rentals developed the tools and systems to manage that complexity as it grew from an entrepreneurial set of small businesses into the diverse industry leader it is today.

FORMATION AND EARLY YEARS

United Rentals was founded in 1997 as a roll-up led by Brad Jacobs, a serial consolidator and builder of businesses. Jacobs dropped out of Brown University in 1976, started an oil brokerage firm soon after, and then started an oil trading firm. He switched from that to running a successful roll-up of the garbage hauling industry, eventually flipping the company to what is now Waste Management. After leaving United Rentals, he transformed the logistics industry with a roll-up called XPO. These three companies are traded on the New York Stock Exchange today with a total market value of around $70 billion.

The early years under Jacobs's leadership brought more than 200 acquisitions of small rental companies, giving United Rentals economic scale. A simple benefit was in back-office savings—IT, accounting, billing, and so on—as well as the purchasing power that comes with scale. As the biggest customer of some of the equipment it buys, United Rentals can demand a lower price.

Until 2008, though, United Rentals operated as a collection of semiautonomous branches, each of which benefited from the network's scale advantage but had no real operational advantages. United Rentals didn't have technology, a cohesive culture, or a system of continuous improvement that could build a sustainable advantage in an industry in which perfect competition eroded profits. (See Figure 11.1.)

Figure 11.1: **The history of United Rentals.**

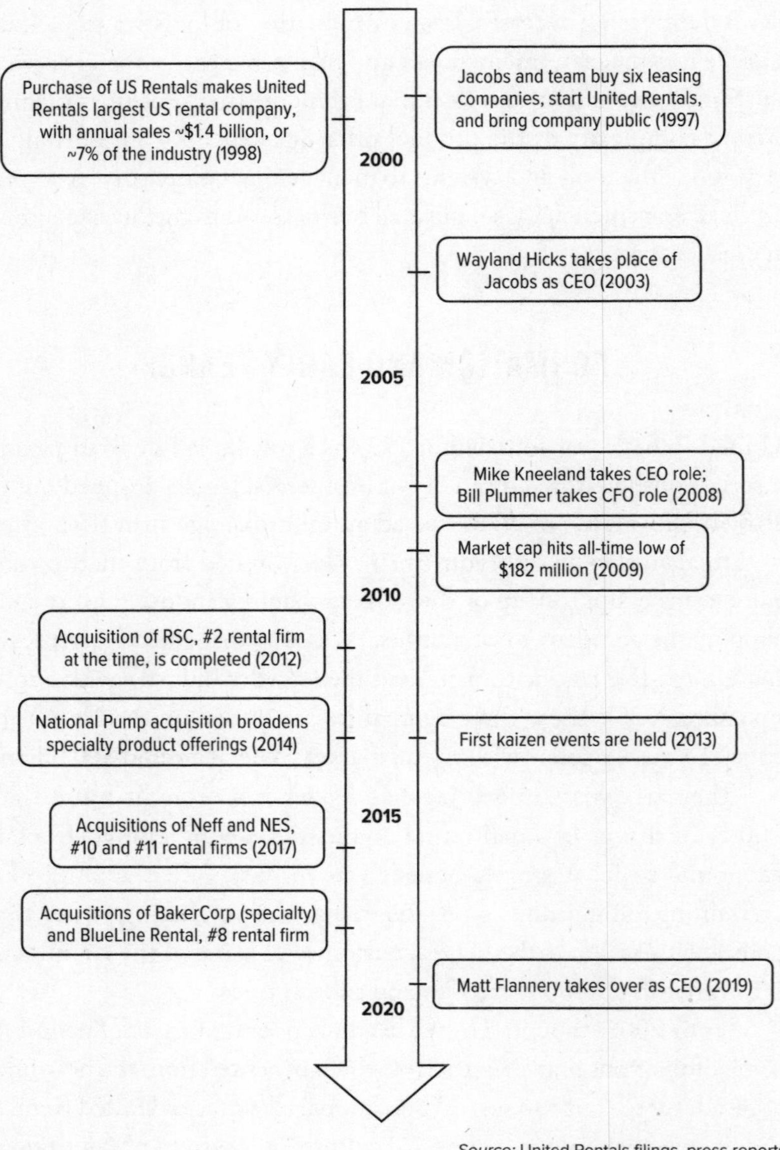

Source: United Rentals filings, press reports

THE ROOTS OF A CULTURE AND BUSINESS SYSTEM

Mike Kneeland took over as CEO in August 2008. The deck was heavily stacked against him, with the company having just come out of a tumultuous year and with the US economy about to nose-dive. A year earlier, in April 2007, the company had put itself up for sale, often a stressful time for employees. Its leaders left. The CEO at the time, Wayland Hicks, retired, and Kneeland was appointed interim CEO. United Rentals found a buyer in Cerberus Capital, which in July agreed to take United Rentals private. Jacobs left his position as chairman of the board in October, anticipating the sale to Cerberus would close shortly thereafter. But in November Cerberus pulled out of the deal.

On top of that, the financial crisis sent the booming construction economy into its worst downturn since the Great Depression. Remember that investor perception of rental as a capital-intensive industry prone to sharp price falls if demand dries up? Well, rental pricing fell by about 15 percent. To make matters worse, United Rentals had high debt, and the credit markets had gone cold. To shore up finances, the company had to sell off some of its fleet in a weak market for used equipment.

In short, Kneeland had multiple different messes to clean up.* From the start, though, he didn't think of his job solely as a crisis manager. He wanted to build on the company's leadership position and remake it into a unified operational leader.

Mike Kneeland is humble, always polite, and measured; his words and demeanor are never overconfident or excessively bold. That's not always the norm with corporate leaders. Kneeland projected calm, which was sorely needed. The recession was an ugly time. Operating margins fell from 17 percent before the crisis all the

* In addition to the obstacles already mentioned, United Rentals had also been under investigation by the SEC for accounting issues for the time period 1997–2002. The company eventually settled with the SEC and paid a $14 million fine in September 2008.

way down to 5 percent in 2009. The management team didn't waste the crisis, taking the opportunity to restructure and cut costs, but it was the next phase that would make United Rentals so impressive. Coming out of the Great Recession, the company needed only a few years to remake its operations and then reinvest the profits into bigger and more diversified businesses.

BUILDING A CULTURE

Kneeland's actions were anything but humble as he led United Rentals out of the recession. With its stock price having fallen from $20 to $3 (a sign that the market thought the company might restructure or go bankrupt), he started investing for the long run.

United Rentals had done a limited job leveraging its scale up to that point. It exploited its purchasing power, but it lacked cohesive operational techniques across the small entrepreneurial branches that it owned. For example, those formerly independent companies were reluctant to share equipment, something that might help the company overall but hurt individual-branch profits.

Kneeland began building a common culture by making structural changes to operations that forced a change in behavior and by revising compensation practices. The changes reflected a shift in focus to national-scale customers, which made collaboration among the branches serving them a necessity. The shift had other benefits, too: these customers had proved more stable during the 2008–2010 downturn, and the strategy made better use of the company's size and breadth. By becoming a one-stop shop for its customers, United Rentals locked in important customer relationships with efficient, comprehensive service.

The incentive changes were simple but powerful. The company's previous leaders hadn't come from the rental industry, and they probably hadn't thought deeply enough about how shared goals can overcome the bad practices and excessive autonomy of component businesses. Kneeland and Flannery were longstanding rental managers who knew the existing cultures and tricks and were thus better positioned to change them.

Charlie Munger of Berkshire Hathaway has been quoted as saying, "I think I've been in the top 5 percent of my age cohort all my life in understanding the power of incentives, and all my life I've underestimated it." In the case of United Rentals, the incentive puzzle wasn't hard. Managers had been compensated on growing EBITDA. In other words, they were paid for revenue and profit growth but were not charged for the fleet they owned. That promoted a simple, pro-growth decision: buy more stuff and worry about renting it later. It didn't encourage managers to wring utilization out of the fleet they already had, since buying another machine might be easier than trying to turn one around in the repair yard faster. This seems like an obvious mistake, but compensation practices are often surprisingly misaligned.

So was the lack of equipment and customer sharing among branches, meaning a core potential advantage for United Rentals was going unused. The new metrics were simple: "return on controllable assets" with a hurdle rate to reflect that assets cost money and need to generate a minimum return before any bonuses could be paid.

Flannery had also previously tweaked compensation in some regions to focus more on broader district results, which worked well. That approach was applied to the company as a whole. As a result, 70 percent of compensation for both branch and district managers was tied to district results rather than branch results, a move that immediately connected employees and encouraged collaboration.

STARTING TO BUILD OPERATIONAL EXPERTISE

The operational structures of the company, run by Flannery as COO, also improved dramatically. Kneeland had invested heavily in IT right out of the Great Recession, and it paid off in improved operational efficiency, from paperwork, to logistics, to pricing.

Pricing strategy was a substantial investment. For years, the industry had suffered from anecdotal, weak pricing dynamics. Jacobs and his successor had worked on better pricing, but it was still not systematic.

It can be a little startling to see how "informal" large parts of the economy still are. Construction is one the biggest tech laggards: contractors still do business on paper forms, over the phone, and in texts. Ten years ago the rental industry was even less formal. Sunbelt, now the second largest rental company, used paper notebooks to communicate pricing to its rental branches, while United Rentals used mobile devices instead of paper, but neither had real pricing engines. Branch managers felt the pulse of the local market and priced accordingly, communicating to their salesforce via email. Opinions varied from one branch to the next, and customers played the branches against each other. New systems, using external expertise in pricing and software, combined with an internal analytics team to gather the input of branches, made pricing much more rigorous.

Technology investment also dramatically improved the repair shop and logistics. Mobile technology brought huge efficiency: the FAST (field automation strategy and technology) project replaced paper forms with electronic documentation for order taking, contracts, and insurance. Subsystems optimized loads on trucks, including the order of loading and unloading. Driver logs went electronic, tracking safety, performance, and maintenance. Employees used mobile devices to take pictures of equipment at delivery, providing traceable condition reports. The company made good use of consultants like McKinsey and Bain throughout its reinvention and later found them to be a new source of talent.

United Rentals bought the software systems and mobile hardware from different vendors, as no comprehensive package was available. Designing and implementing the system put the company years ahead of the competition, and it paid off in margin. The company's operating margin had been 17 percent before the financial crisis and rebounded from 5 percent in 2009 to 15 percent by 2011. Two years later it was close to 22 percent.

TURNING ACQUISITIONS FROM A ROLL-UP TO A FLYWHEEL

Kneeland then went after acquisitions to push strategy ahead further. In late 2011 the company announced its acquisition of RSC, then the second largest rental company. That deal was financed with both new debt and issuance of stock. Leverage rose sharply, to over 4x debt to EBITDA, at the high end of what investors will tolerate in industrials. It was well timed, though, with the United States unlikely to go through another severe downturn right away. From 2011 to 2018, the company bought four competitors within the top ten in the rental industry and branched out into new categories, serving new customers.

CFO Bill Plummer helped the company to grow aggressively. He knew the improvements being made, and the flexibility and stability of the cash flow, and pushed ahead. Debt rose from $3 billion in 2008, when he started as CFO, to almost $12 billion by the time he stepped down in 2018. Profits and cash flow rose faster, though, making the larger debt load safer than the smaller one the company had previously. (See Figure 11.2.)

Figure 11.2: **United Rentals debt rose, but profits and cash flow rose faster.**

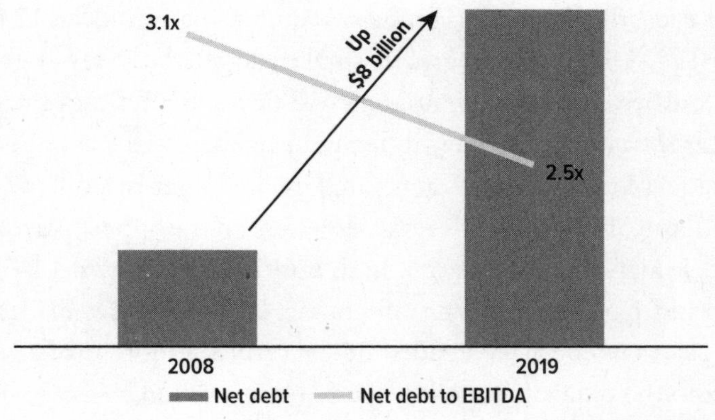

Source: United Rentals filings

We criticized Caterpillar for a big, aggressive acquisition right after the Great Recession, and now we're praising United Rentals for even more boldness. Indeed, there may be some luck at play in all of this. But United Rentals slotted the acquisitions into an increasingly capable business system in a fine-tuned, repeatable process.

Acquisitions did more than simply build scale. They also brought breadth: expertise in new product segments, business lines that could be used as platforms for even more growth. Without the investment in systems, the complexity would have been too great to manage. Without the focus on large customers with diverse needs, the company might have stayed stuck with a narrower product offering, missing out on niche profits. The strategy, systems, and capital deployment were starting to flow together in a positive feedback loop.

There *were* some notable hiccups. National Pump was a huge acquisition in 2014, with the purchase price of $800 million equivalent to roughly 10 percent of United Rentals' market value at the time—bringing an outsized exposure to the oil and gas industry. That led to some pain when oil prices fell by half, but the plan had always been to move from oil into the broader construction markets. Today pumps are a growing segment, despite the continued weakness in oil markets.

Other hiccups can arguably be found in the prices paid in some deals. Acquisition roll-ups can have a natural advantage in valuation spreads: the big public company acquirer might trade at 12 times the EBITDA it generates, and its smaller targets, with fewer growth opportunities, at a lower multiple, say 6 times. Sometimes the market folds the target's earnings indistinguishably into the acquirer, and the "value" of the EBITDA generated by the target is suddenly doubled. All too often, United Rentals experienced the opposite dynamic: the stock market didn't place a high multiple on its own EBITDA and would pay a higher one for its targets. Maybe fewer deals at lower prices would have yielded better results—more profit generated from the acquisition dollars spent—but it would have also been a slower process, limiting the rate at which the company's strategic scale advantage over the industry could grow. The cost of not compounding earnings as quickly must be considered as well; United Rentals redeployed capital with a high degree of efficiency all throughout a 10-year run. Most companies don't have enough opportunities to do that consistently.

ADDING CONTINUOUS IMPROVEMENT

While these successful acquisitions were building out scale and complexity, there was a separate effort going on internally to build more value from the purchased companies and create more sustainable competitive advantages for United Rentals as a whole. In 2013, the company began a series of kaizen events, a move pitched to Flannery by the employee base. This was the beginning of a formal process of continuous improvement and the creation of a true business system.

Although some of the methods of continuous improvement come directly from manufacturing, as a tool it can be applied to anything. In the end, anyone can still dump in capital and attempt to replicate some of the scale that United Rentals has built, though it's much harder now. However, the competitive edge afforded by doing thousands of things just a little bit better is hard to match.

It began with eight kaizen events at eight branches. The response was hugely positive. Employee engagement in the process was strong, and soon the company was running kaizen events in every district. Above all, continuous improvement fundamentally needs employee engagement, but it is also a managed process, implemented by line managers and unlikely to catch hold without strong support from senior leadership. All the district managers at the company spent 30 percent of their time in the first six months on kaizens and on managing improvement. That's a lot of time: rental companies take customer service seriously, and employees, managers, and senior leaders work long hours. Taking 30 percent of the day is a material shift.

As we have noted, many, maybe even most, moves toward Lean and similar tools falter and wither, as the discipline to keep up with continuous measurement and improvement takes tremendous focus. United Rentals had a culture that embraced the process from the start, and it had several early successes to keep excitement up, which it shared on Facebook Workplace, an important tool at the company.

Improvements in logistics provided several early wins. Imagine trying to route dozens of deliveries a day into Manhattan. This is a prospect that makes even experienced truck drivers with simple loads start to sweat. We read a fair number of trucking message boards, usually to see what truckers think of their equipment or what they think about the economy. Lots of drivers just say avoid New York City altogether. Traffic can force you to miss a turn and end up with an hour delay. Bridge height limits vary. A wrong turn can get you stuck or towed or add points on your license.

In equipment rental, the problems go far beyond simply finding that ideal route. Different pieces of equipment fit well or poorly on different trucks or in combination with other equipment. Traffic patterns change throughout the day. Customers want to keep equipment for longer, changing their minds when the truck arrives for pickup, or they ask for something different when the truck arrives for delivery. Equipment in the field breaks and needs maintenance. The business is far more complicated than it looks, and it's far more complicated than, for example, a FedEx style delivery system, which is generally a simple hub-and-spoke model.

United Rentals knew early on that addressing customer dissatisfaction with deliveries was a major opportunity. Late deliveries also brought excess cost and lost pricing. Rental equipment might be only 2 percent of the cost of building a high-rise, but if the equipment is not there or not working, dozens of other processes stop. High-wage workers stand around waiting, delays back up, and the customer gets angry at the rental company. An outflow of the early kaizen events was a visual fix for late deliveries. Did the order get taken correctly, with the customer specifying exactly what kind of setup was wanted on the 60-foot boom lift? Did the customer know exactly what was needed, or could the customer have benefited from a quick consult with an expert? Did the order include the phone number and backup number of the person who would take delivery on site? Is it a cell phone? Is the delivery address correct? If it is a large jobsite, what gate should the truck deliver to?

These are all simple issues, but a mistake on any one of them can lead to cascading delays and angry customers. Discounting price or other services are some of the potential results. The right solution isn't necessarily some complex IT project to drive better deliveries. In this case, the output of an employee-led kaizen was to put common mistakes on order forms on a wall, with a highlighter showing what to do. Visual management is basic and powerful.

Logistics isn't just order taking; rental companies have fleets of trucks and drivers to manage as well. A company that can run a truck on 15 routes a day is going to do better than one with only 5 routes. The assets are levered better, the revenue per employee is greater, the outside haulage cost is lower, and customer satisfaction is higher. For this issue the kaizens offered another simple approach: when a truck enters the yard, it lines up next to a painted strip with all the equipment to be loaded sitting there. Pick up the equipment, put it on the bed, and drive off. That saves time versus a driver wandering though the yard looking for the equipment.

United Rentals ran more than 500 kaizen events between 2014 and 2015. Flannery then took the initial success and embedded it in the business structure. The company wanted to have a common look and feel across its branches, for efficiency's sake and for customers who deal with many locations. Rather than have hundreds of separate evolutionary paths of continuous improvement at each branch, the lessons from the kaizens were incorporated into formal best practices. Regions that formerly had a VP and a sales and marketing director added an operational excellence director. Corporate now has around three dozen operational excellence workers, and the company has well over 100 working at branches, bringing the best ideas into the business system.

CULTURE BECOMES SYSTEMATIC

John Humphrey is regional vice president for the Mid-Atlantic region of United Rentals. I visited him after the closing of a large acquisition, BlueLine Rental.

Humphrey referred to United Rentals as a "machine" when explaining the integration process. That spoke to us; the system has become ingrained in operations and in the current employee base. He wasn't too worried about getting to the right place operationally. He *was* very focused on keeping people: the first concern was to not lose employees of the acquired companies, who might experience culture shock. The output of the kaizen events and other systematic improvements running back to 2008 made for a much more cohesive, teamwork-based culture and rigorous set of operations driving productivity at United Rentals. A salesperson at BlueLine might have had 500 products to sell, with a focus on the few most popular ones. At United Rentals, with the extra offerings enabled by geographic density, scale, and systems, that turned into 4,000 products. Accordingly, Humphrey's main concern was to keep good people from quitting in shock and work up their productivity over time as they internalized all the codified steps that keep quality, safety, and revenues high at United Rentals.

The extra product diversity is a huge profit driver, giving United Rentals more differentiated products to rent in an industry where most folks assume all the products are the same. Smaller competitors just can't compete. They don't have the right trucks, the right drivers, sales expertise, repair flow, mechanics, vendor relations, customer base, regional density, and so on. At United Rentals, the same people who couldn't manage the additional complexity at independents are equipped with the tools and processes to run a more robust and profitable business once absorbed into the company.

POSTMORTEM

Most companies we follow don't get the first step right for starting compounding growth: good operations, founded in continuous improvement, that drive a widening gap versus competitors. Margin expansion is great, but it only really counts if it is systematic and repeatable. Margins at United Rentals have improved by more than double the industrials group average over the past decade, through systematic improvements. (See Figure 11.3.)

Figure 11.3: **Margins rose by 7 percentage points, despite drag from acquisitions (average change in operating margin, 2007–2019).**

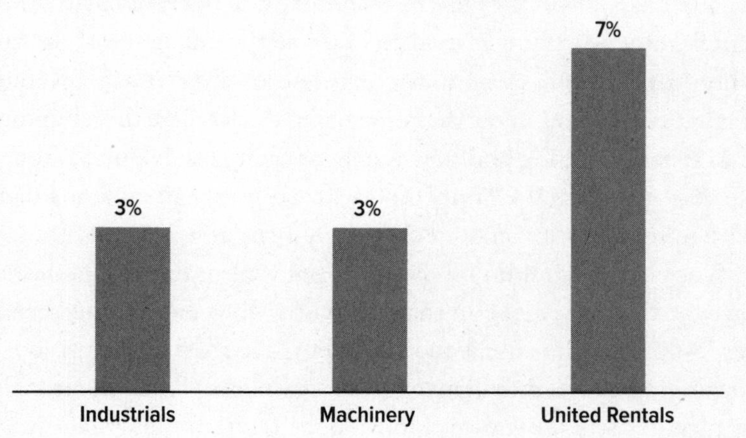

Source: Company filings

The second step is using the improved profits to acquire new assets. The fragmentation of the rental industry is fertile ground for acquisitions, and thanks to its operational strengths, United Rentals has both ample targets and plenty of cash to deploy.

Finally comes raising margins at the acquired companies, systematically, so the process can repeat in a virtuous cycle. Lots of companies do acquisitions; far too many in fact. There are reasons why most acquisitions fail to create value: trying to buy companies without a well-defined way to improve them consistently is an uphill fight. United Rentals has had a great deal of experience acquiring companies and integrating them into its system successfully.

The combination is rare: good operations, the ability to acquire repeatably and in a low-risk way, and the systems to consistently improve the acquired companies. Scale can get a company part of the way there, but the best bring benefits well past that.

LESSONS FOR OTHER ASSET-SHARING BUSINESSES

We started this chapter with a comparison to asset-heavy new tech companies like Uber; we want to end it with a suggestion that the lessons herein are applicable to future business models and may even be necessary for them.

There is a distinctive use of technology in operations at United Rentals. One workflow is used to increase the efficiency of the customers' operations, even at the expense of short-term revenues. Telematics data now allow the company to track where the equipment it has rented is sitting and how much it's being used. United Rentals calls its system Total Control, and its customers can look at a dashboard to see statistics on their own equipment utilization.

Maybe this shouldn't be shocking, but it turns out that customers don't use the equipment all that efficiently. They are renting because they know they don't use it enough to buy, but often on a large jobsite they forget it's even there, paying fees every month for equipment that has no purpose. One way to think about that from the rental company's perspective is, well, great. No maintenance, no problem—money comes in; costs are low. The United Rentals way is to tell the customer, "Hey, you don't seem to need this. Let us come pick it up and save you the cost." Revenue might be lost for a few days until the piece is rented again, but the customer is happy. And technology extends the efficiency benefits further into the system, making the whole jobsite better as opposed to just the operations of the rental company.

We only follow the new asset-sharing tech companies casually, but they don't seem to be driving lower cost and greater efficiency in the same way. Our own office for Melius Research started in a WeWork building, because it was a flexible way to start a business. We use Uber for seeing clients, with ease and real savings. Yet there are signs that these models are failing to create widening, sustained value. The companies might not own the assets, and they may not have employees. The assets are still there, though, and the "contractors" still cost money—if not for the business, for the customer. Outsourcing all the unpleasant and capital-intensive parts of the business is what makes it a tech play. But having the assets outside the system also limits the ability to optimize and raises the overall system cost, diminishing its attractiveness for consumers. You can't easily tell a contractor how to work more efficiently. You can't easily tell drivers to move away from an oversaturated area if they are independent.

Costs seem to be rising, and satisfaction seems to be dropping. One of the first Uber drivers I talked to was in London, sometime around 2012. He loved it. He took care of his daughter during the day and figured he may as well drive for a few hours while she was in school. He had a nice, basic Mercedes as a personal car, and so the opportunity was true flexibility.

Today the drivers don't feel the same. Uber driving is often a full-time job, for people with poor credit history and high costs. Drivers in New York City rent or lease the cars, with this expense plus insurance running up to $2,000 a month. Uber isn't effectively using its scale to lower system costs to the customer. Instead, it's simply pushing the capital-intensive cost onto people with the highest cost of capital, people with borrowing costs in the 15–20 percent range. Even bad, asset-intensive industrials borrow at under 5 percent these days. The source of profit to Uber is the desperation of its drivers, not superior systemwide efficiency. Probably not coincidentally, rates that seemed competitive with taxis five years ago in New York City are now often considerably higher. Uber launched with a no-tipping structure, with drivers making enough without tips. Now tipping is strongly encouraged, which is effectively another layer of price increase.

The physical assets still exist, and they are poorly run by many drivers. Right now, ride-hailing apps in New York have vehicles that run about half as many trips a month as do yellow cabs (and about a quarter as many as yellow cabs used to do before Uber came along). That's a substantially less efficient use of an expensive vehicle versus the use of the old yellow cabs. Lower efficiency is also adding to congestion, slowing down traffic for everyone.

It may not just be the management of the heavy assets that needs to be improved. Software isn't our focus, but from talking with tech execs and industrials that have acquired them, there is a surprisingly large void in process around software development. Tracking and continuous improvement are nonexistent in many cases. There are certainly efforts to make the process more systematic, e.g., Lean and "scaled agile" processes, but those are in their infancy.

We've heard dozens of companies adapt the lingo of continuous improvement and even some of the techniques. Most fail to make durable progress. Making an actual system work takes years of disciplined implementation. Software as a sector hasn't come up with differentiated and systematic workflows. For companies like Uber, that is an expensive problem: 3,000 software engineers and data scientists in a company expected to lose $3 billion in operating profits on less than $20 billion in revenue. This failure to build in rigorous continuous improvement is unsurprising and certainly not unique to software or technology.

As competition grows, winners will need a bigger moat. When Uber was founded in 2008, there were only a small handful of companies pursuing asset sharing. Ten years later, more than 200 startups received funding. The great successes of the companies in this book point toward a solution. If it works for an industry as hotly competitive as equipment rental, it has the potential to work for anyone.

Lessons from United Rentals

- Continuous improvement and operational excellence are as applicable to services or software businesses as they are to manufacturing.
- Developing an operational edge can be even more powerful in hypercompetitive industries, partly because it's so hard to survive in the first place.
- Incentives have to be tailored to the current needs of an organization—and then evolved over time.
- Feedback from employees can create a virtuous cycle. Those on the front lines are often a great source of ideas.
- There is a temptation in both the old and new economies to offload assets and become more "asset light." The reality, however, is that the assets are usually still there.
- Systematically leveraging your operational expertise into someone else's business through acquisitions is an incredibly powerful way to compound returns over time.

CHAPTER

12

THE IMPORTANCE OF BUSINESS SYSTEMS AND OTHER KEY LESSONS FROM INDUSTRIALS

There are real-world dynamics in our case studies. Each company we highlighted was faced with a unique set of problems, and each went down a unique path. Some did it with brilliant success, some with fantastic failure, and some with a mix of each. The data on the successful cases kept pointing us to three common drivers: a relentless discipline on costs, cash flow, and capital deployment.

The companies that rose to the top in our study used their high and growing cash flows to widen the moat within their existing businesses while gravitating investments to higher-return opportunities—and repeated these actions over and over. At that point, the power of compounding takes over and we get on the flywheel. Entire business books have already been written on this topic. But too many companies miss the point. They focus cost-cutting on the easy stuff, quick and abrupt fixes versus more cadenced and sustainable actions. We've seen more "one-time" restructurings in our careers than we can count. On the capital deployment side, "game-changing" acquisitions are far more frequent than a more disciplined and repeatable cash reinvestment strategy. These companies don't get themselves on the flywheel; instead they spin themselves far off it.

The most successful companies emphasize systems and processes over quick fixes, systems that incentivize and drive continuous improvement throughout the organization over an extended period of time. That almost always means being an excellent manufacturer, using tools such as Lean manufacturing. We've never come across a company that was bad at manufacturing and still managed to succeed in the long run. Those who manufacture brilliantly can get away with a lot of missteps. Those who do poorly have to rely on top-notch product development with increasingly impossible consistency. Or they have to do a lot of great M&A deals to overshadow the underlying weaknesses. But a slow couple of years or a couple of bad deals, and you're in trouble.

Operational excellence is absolutely critical to success. In almost every business case we've studied, success over the longer term is more often a function of factory floor excellence than of product differentiation. It's that excellence that drives above-average margins and the related outsized cash generation. Whether that cash is reinvested internally or levered through M&A doesn't matter, as long as the returns are high enough to stay on the flywheel. But without that cash flow, a company eventually falters, falling further behind peers each and every day. Said a different way, modest product differentiation isn't considered a game changer by nearly any real customer base. So unless the product differentiation is rather large, manufacturing cost and quality will reign supreme. This was a hard-learned lesson for industrials during their darker era, when globalization began to expose flaws. The ones that failed usually learned this lesson too late.

Lean manufacturing is the most common system on the factory floor. The principles of Lean originated with Henry Ford's revolutionary Model T assembly line in the early 1900s, but it was honed and popularized by Toyota in the 1980s. At its core, Lean seeks to eliminate waste in the production process. Done right, the result is faster production times to meet hard-to-predict customer demand, lower inventory levels, and higher product quality (fewer defects)—all of which lead to higher cash flow and profit margins. Of course, successful Lean companies get the benefit of free capacity as factory productivity typically improves at some level, often 2 percent per year or more, driving returns on capital higher in proportion to the intensity of the effort. Lean has grown far beyond the factory floor with inspirations throughout the entire organization. Even software developers have their own version.

There are other systems and tools (e.g., Six Sigma for quality control; economic value added, or EVA, for return focus), but none are as time-proven and comprehensive as Lean. The strongest industrial cultures that we have seen are Lean based, and the ones most committed to continuous improvement are Lean based. It's a tremendous focusing tool with very clear and measurable targets. And publicly available data sets help to continually dial in what exactly best in class looks like, with more than enough consultants out there to get anyone pointed in the right direction.

That doesn't mean just throwing money into a modernized factory. That can work for a while, but without some serious discipline, it can become a giant money pit and certainly does not differentiate from competitors with similarly deep pockets. Instead it is those with the most productive systems, those who practice continuous improvement and build culture through actions and incentives, that sustain success. Those are the ones we characterize as having factory floor excellence at a differentiated level. These companies are almost always far along the Lean manufacturing journey, and they benchmark internally and externally to best-in-class organizations.

The best of the best go beyond the factory floor. They apply systematic tools to all their functions, including R&D, sales, purchasing, distribution, and back office. Danaher, for example, customized the Toyota Production System and created (or borrowed) more than a dozen tools to focus its employees. Each function has its own toolkit and is empowered to lever that toolkit to its fullest. Increasingly, we see these best-in-class organizations also utilize metrics around employee engagement and turnover. They focus as much on filtering out bad managers as they do on elevating good ones. The same principle holds true for those providing services rather than physical goods, or even software, healthcare, and other high-margin-type offerings. The companies with continuous improvement cultures win out almost every single time. In the short term, "new economy" firms might neglect operations to maximize innovation or the customer base, but we see this as a mistake. The earlier a company can adopt Lean and embed a continuous improvement culture, the greater that company's odds of long-term success.

And it applies more broadly. We like to use sports analogies because they can have such amazing real-world relevance for businesses—particularly when it comes to studying teams who effectively use systems to help drive a culture of winning and comparing them with those who don't. Teams often have sharply different budget constraints. In baseball, we see this dynamic with the Yankees and Red Sox versus the Oakland A's and Tampa Bay Rays, etc.—where massive payroll differences between big-market and small-market teams bracket the top five from the rest (30 total teams). Yet, on average, the team with the sixth highest payroll has won the World Series over the past 25 years, including relative long shots like the Kansas City Royals in 2015 (thirteenth payroll rank) and Florida Marlins in 2003 (twenty-fifth payroll rank). A top-5 spender wins only half the time, driving home the point that big money hardly guarantees championships.

The General Electric chapters bring this exact dynamic to life. GE was on top of the world, winning in nearly every regard, but it eventually took winning for granted and stopped focusing on the little things. GE left its factories to starve, completely losing its cost focus, and had to make increasingly large financial bets to hide its decline. All while Honeywell and Danaher did the opposite and became two of the most respected companies in America. All three had deep pockets, all three could "buy" victories, but one failed famously.

To drive home this point even further, look at one of the toughest manufacturing businesses in America: automotive parts. It is a poster child for hypercompetition and demanding customers. History shows countless failures, and each economic down cycle seems to add more names to the list. But the ones that survived and thrived (the top 10 percent) have done so by investing in fully scaled manufacturing facilities, levering the best in robotics and automation technology. These are typically placed in strategic locations with a great cost base, close proximity to the customer, or both. They implement Lean manufacturing with enthusiasm and consistently benchmark to best-in-class companies well outside the auto world. They work on iterative product enhancements, solving small but important customer problems. They build cost-focused cultures, fully accepting the reality of their stingy customer base. They practice extreme customer service, knowing that it's hard to differentiate on product alone.

The ones that have remained disciplined have been rewarded with growth and margins well above the average. Their excellence also makes it hard for new entrants to get traction. In fact, their excellence leads to decreased competition, as those who can't keep up eventually drop out. And with outsized cash generated, these companies are able to remain committed to their factory assets while also allowing capital to find other efficient investments.

The lesson here is that even the worst businesses have examples of successful winners. Just as the best businesses, like software and the internet, have examples of failure. The commonalities are pretty clear, and it's rarely about having a uniquely disruptive product offering or someone else beating you to that next big thing. Instead, it's all about doing the little things right, with systems in place to ensure consistent focus, even as leadership changes or business conditions swing.

To get people to actually use a system, companies have needed effective leaders—first to commit the organization as a whole decisively to the system, which means excluding all the other seemingly attractive initiatives that get in the way, and then to promote and demonstrate that system relentlessly. Done right, the result is an organization that goes to work every day knowing what to work on. Done wrong, people learn to game the system, and the organization stops focusing on adding value for customers. The Danaher Business System may be the clearest example of the former. The Honeywell Operating System is another great example. These are world-class business systems that relentlessly focused their employees on adding value for the long term, and they are systems worth studying.

Business systems also help organizations focus on the main tenet of creating value. They focus on a simple question: What does the customer actually value, and how do we supply that at the lowest possible cost? Note that we say what does the customer actually value, not what you want the customer to value. That's basic stuff, but only half the companies that we have studied live that baseline principle with any real discipline. Voice of the customer is an important tool that is increasingly being adopted by the best companies to drive that very conversation. It's another way of driving focus—as long as you are actually listening to the customer in the spirit of "two ears, one mouth."

We've talked a lot about business systems in this book, largely because business tools like Lean manufacturing help an organization to find success at the very least on two of the most critical success drivers: costs and cash. But setting up a business system is hard work and takes amazing patience. You can't just copy the Danaher Business System; the very point of DBS is continuous improvement. Even if someone tried to copy it, it would already be an outdated version. However, the best practices are clear. Keep it simple: find what is critical to your organization's success, and then measure and compensate around those metrics. The payoff can be big. The flywheel effect itself assures some level of success, and if proper focus is maintained, it can be quite powerful. And whether you are running a company, searching for a better employer, or looking for investments, it's relevant for each.

DISRUPTION GETS TOO MUCH ATTENTION

There is a common perception that the companies that innovate the best, while getting the "other stuff" (like manufacturing) mostly or somewhat right, are the ones that succeed over time. That statement puts the emphasis on disruption and undermines the importance of manufacturing, marketing and sales, and capital deployment. But the reality is that meaningful disruption is rare and far more difficult to accomplish than perceived. Most companies do it once, providing the foundation for their existence, and then never do it again at anywhere close to the impact of that foundational event. Setting the expectation that an organization hits a home run on every innovation typically leads to no innovation at all.

Take 3M, the Minnesota-based maker of tapes and adhesives. Its most famous innovation was arguably the Post-it Note, a ubiquitous sticky-paper product, the sales of which continue to grow with high and rising profit margins. It was a disruptive product innovation from 40 years ago. But the curse of the Post-it Note is that 3M scientists have spent the better part of the last few decades trying to duplicate its impact. Achieving disruption of this magnitude while predicting future customer needs is extremely difficult, particularly when you consider that the Post-it Note, like many other top innovations, was created largely by accident.

After that celebrated innovation, the company became so focused on the next big thing that it often forgot to do the small things well. 3M is still an excellent company by most measures, but it has gone through meaningful periods underperforming its potential, with growth that hasn't exceeded that of far less innovative companies and costs that had a tendency to rise well beyond necessity. That said, there have been notable periods of brilliance, with two of the last five CEOs achieving remarkable results. The difference? The two CEOs, Jim McNerney and Inge Thulin, established two very common and simple mandates: the first was a hyperfocus on manufacturing excellence and included holding the line on costs in every part of the organization; the second established accountability for commercial outcomes in the R&D organization. Each of the CEOs made it very clear, via incentives and otherwise, that profit growth mattered more than market share and that developing new products (often incremental improvements on proven platforms) that customers were willing to pay a premium for today was far more important than shooting for the moon tomorrow. Commercial behavior took precedence over disruption.

And the results are clear. Despite representing just 10 of the last 30 years, these two CEOs created nearly all the shareholder outperformance in our study period. (See Figure 12.1.) Both were far more successful than most CEOs of their respective time periods, despite being in some very mature businesses. There is no evidence that any less disruption occurred during these time periods. Scientists who are focused on near-term commercial outcomes seem to be just as likely to stumble upon something big as those whose days are spent dreaming big.

The 3M example is more common than not. We use it because the disparate management models of five unique CEOs show such extremes in stock market performance. Sharply rising profits in the McNerney and Thulin eras were rewarded by investors with sharply higher P/E multiples. We could have used dozens of other large com-

Figure 12.1: **3M stock performed best against the S&P 500 under CEOs Jim McNerney and Inge Thulin, who focused the organization.**

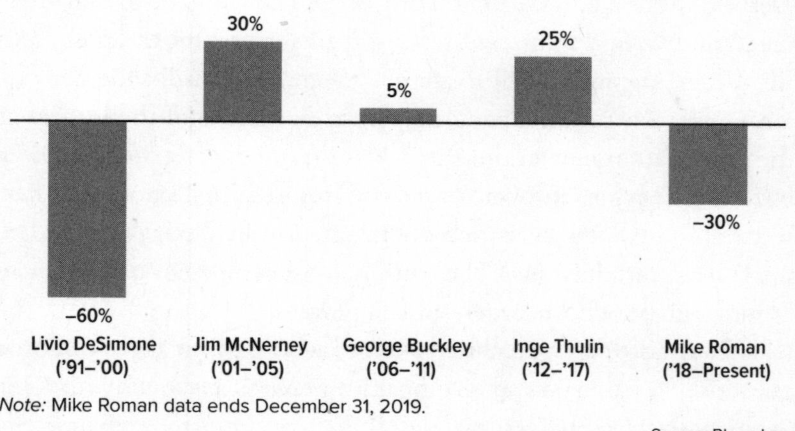

Note: Mike Roman data ends December 31, 2019.

Source: Bloomberg

panies to make the exact same point, however. Some far worse, in fact. GE under Jeff Immelt was a poster child for this dynamic. Its multi-billion-dollar foray into industrial software led it to develop "disruptive" products that customers had no actual need or desire to purchase. Billions of dollars wasted just because the company never bothered to ask, or listen if it did, to *what the customer actually wanted*. GE was a company absolutely fixated on disruption. Despite a near endless budget and a full decade to make an impact, little of commercial value was accomplished. Good money followed bad, perhaps the most common failing of the Jeff Immelt era.

The reality is that all businesses are founded on some level of disruption, but the vast majority of success comes in the years to follow as products are incrementally improved, manufacturing is dialed in, and markets are broadened or further penetrated. It's notable that the two most successful companies in industrials over the past two decades, TransDigm and Roper, have no mandate, desire, or effort at all related to disruption. Each has created tremendous value purely by focusing employees on growing the cash flow of the businesses and levering that cash flow by investing in niche, high-return assets.

TALENT MANAGEMENT

Despite all the evidence around process and benchmark-driven organizations, we find that management teams, investors, the press, and the public in general still fixate on "talent." Especially the personalities, histories, motivations, and strategic visions of the leaders at the top of an organization. But talent, in our experience, is more a buzzword that gets thrown around and misused. That's not to say that leadership by a few exceptionally talented individuals doesn't matter. It most certainly does. The truth is, most companies have a barely average subset of both leaders and employees.

Yet almost every executive team to whom we've asked a simple question, "What makes your company different?," responds with "Our people—we have the best people." But every company can't have the best people. Someone has to be average; in fact half of the companies by definition have to have below-average talent. It may be even more depressing than that. With so much current-generation talent gravitating toward just a few big technology companies in each global region, what's left for the rest may be far lower than historical standards. So it's actually disturbing that many leaders operate with the false belief that their competitive advantage is, in fact, their people. We are not suggesting that a company give up on the goal of acquiring the best people it can find. People are obviously critical to an organization's success. But there has to be a system behind the people at the top that drives the behavior of all employees, regardless of talent level. Otherwise, the success of the organization ebbs and flows in a rather volatile manner around the turnover or retirement of a small percentage of its talent.

If you look at most winning sports teams, the statistics show an interesting reality. A basketball or hockey team, for example, will typically have a few legitimate stars supported by several solid role players and others that can come off the bench and be somewhat helpful. What you find in the championship teams, however, is talent management at a different level. Stars typically perform as expected. They step up on the big stage. They perform exceptionally well in the big games.

That's not a surprise. The differentiator is the role players. In winning teams, those folks perform better than their salary would otherwise predict, and the players themselves coexist in a system that is amazingly efficient in maximizing each player's respective skills. They are often led by a coach who keeps everyone focused and distractions at bay, who is willing to make the sometimes unpopular decisions in ridding the team of a "destructive" player, who may have talent but doesn't fit in the culture or who otherwise brings down the performance of others.

In the business world, driving that similar "win" will require a few stars for sure (let's say the top 5 percent of head count), but the differentiator of a championship-level performance is similar. *Getting average people to perform at a higher level is the key*. And we find that "average" may be a pretty fat middle of employees, perhaps 80 percent. The importance of filtering out those who are destructive (the bottom 15 percent is quite possible) cannot be underestimated. And yet we find an unhealthy fixation on the stars and little attention otherwise, which not only makes no practical sense but makes no mathematical sense. Simple math shows that filtering out the destructive talent (15 percent) has three times the impact of protecting the top (5 percent). And getting the fat middle (80 percent) to perform at just a 10 percent more impactful level would have three times the impact of getting the top 5 percent to improve by 50 percent.

Factoring in the challenges in business overall, once the employee head count gets to a certain level and the sexiness of the business itself begins to fade, it becomes statistically even harder to acquire more than a fair share of stars. The interview process itself has shown to be full of all kinds of pitfalls, with many researchers arguing that it's more of a flip of the coin than most would think. There may be only a handful of exceptions to this rule, and sustainability is questionable. "Hot" companies like Google probably get the pick of the litter in the tech world today, prestigious firms like Goldman Sachs may get a lot of the top folks in finance, and McKinsey likely attracts the best people in consulting. If you are an aerospace engineer, Boeing would seemingly be a pretty darn good place to have a career, but even Boeing has gone from failure to success and back to failure with essentially the same workforce. Once upon a time, Arthur Andersen was the top recruiter of accounting talent in the United States, and it still went down the tubes with Enron in a massive managerial failure.

So do the people overall, and the stars among those folks, really make the difference? Not if they aren't focused. If they come into work every day and waste their talents, then the entire debate is irrelevant. And if a business depends explicitly on having the best people, it's probably going to be in trouble longer term. Eventually the industry itself is going to fall out of favor, and all those talented people who came to the business or industry because it was hot will go elsewhere.

In contrast, the most successful companies rely on a system and a group of leaders capable of getting ordinary people to succeed consistently over time while empowering the stars to perform as expected. The risk is that if you lose half your stars because an industry is out of favor or the company is going through a tough time, or you seat that rising star next to a time-sucking dud, or worse, you have her report to a total jerk, then the ratio of bad to good gets even worse. The bad ones never leave on their own. The good ones always have choices. As we noted in the Honeywell chapter, legendary CEO Dave Cote once said to us that he kept his stars by paying them not just for the job they did today, but for the job they would be offered tomorrow. Obviously, companies have to narrow down that small group of truly talented managers, or that strategy gets pretty expensive. But Cote did an amazing job of keeping his top talent on board, getting average folks to step up, and filtering out those who were destructive. The Honeywell Operating System was a big part of that success—perhaps because it exposed ineffective leaders earlier than they would have been exposed otherwise. Cote didn't make excuses for lousy managers; he simply got rid of them as fast as possible. The data he collected via the operating system were his guide.

When successfully applied, an effective system means that all employees show up to work every day understanding how their role contributes to the value creation engine of the firm, even if it's only a high-level understanding. This isn't just knowing how to do their job on a factory floor or in a back office but appreciating how they contribute to the goals of their team, their division, and thus the aggregate enterprise. People gain this understanding only from consistent messaging and from clear, coherent incentives. But a company must also be capable of shaping and shifting the focus and the messaging over time, as the demands of the external environment are not static.

What we've found time and time again in the industrial sector is that the most successful companies thrive under a team of well-placed leaders. By "well-placed" we mean those leaders who aren't the same type across various companies, nor are they the same type throughout a successful company's life span. They are the leaders who have the appropriate skills for an organization's needs at the right time.

After all, no leader excels at everything. In this book we celebrate some exceptional CEOs, all of whom also had notable weaknesses. They each delivered exceptional results by maximizing the returns on their particular talents, even if some potential return was lost as a result of their shortcomings.

It's notable that even great CEOs often begin to struggle as they get past a decade or so into their tenure at the top. Perhaps that is because their strategies don't cross over into different eras. Or maybe they just get increasingly distracted and struggle to maintain the message and focus. We've seen examples of both. The academic world has done studies on CEOs feeling isolated and disconnected and often reporting to boards of directors they characterize as dysfunctional. All these are real signs of burnout, particularly if these CEOs lack the energy or empowerment to drive the change they see as required. In that context, it is worth noting that the worst three years of most CEO tenures seem to be their first year and their last two. The first year they often struggle to get traction with a new message, and the organization gets stuck in a "pause." The final two years they often seem to be hanging on to the organization by a thread and cease to be effective. We could probably list upward of a hundred examples of this dynamic, including some pretty famous last-inning flops from some pretty talented folks. Even folks we celebrate in this book would have been better served had they exited a year or two before they did.

CULTURE IS AN OUTPUT, NOT AN INPUT

Culture is another notion we find many companies fixating on, but they often misunderstand what it represents and how to develop and sustain it. We've asked hundreds of executives to comment on their culture, and almost every time the answers were either aspirational (didn't match current reality) or, worse, made up of feel-good vagaries such as "customer-centric," "excellence," "ethical," or "inclusive"—qualities that are often tough to measure and more often than not do not match up with our observations. Whatever the leaders of these companies were doing, they weren't seriously promoting a real culture. (See Figure 12.2.)

Figure 12.2: **Culture is an output: actions of leadership and incentives drilled into an organization over time.**

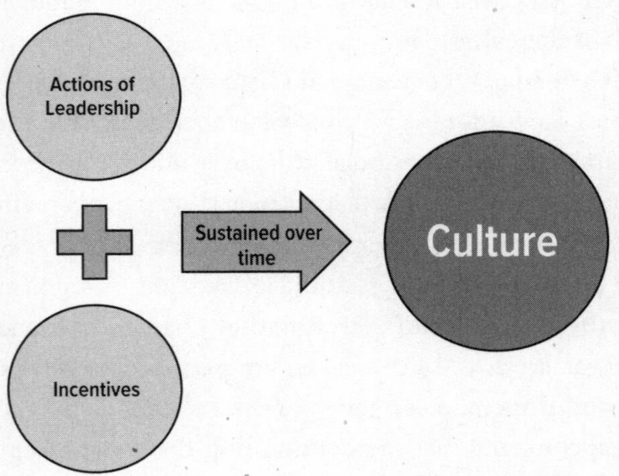

Source: Melius Research

Culture isn't something you can force or even actively promote using just words. It's purely a result of the concrete directions and examples you give to people. It's usually driven by whatever the leaders focus on, their actions and the incentives set around the organizational deliverables. Leaders can't impose a culture through just words, but if they embrace a system, use it consistently with their direct reports, and broadcast it to the organization, then eventually you get a culture pretty close to whatever that system encourages. The more consistent the message and the longer the duration of the effort, the stronger the culture. Culture and loyalty tend to go hand in hand. If bad behavior is stamped out and employees feel safe and empowered, that helps to define the very base level of the culture. If performance is fairly rewarded, that helps to define the more positive component of the culture. Both serve to underpin a culture with loyalty as an important by-product. We recently saw a viral post on LinkedIn that relates to this theme. It simply stated, "Millennials don't leave companies, they leave bad managers." Not sure who wrote this, but it sure seems accurate. And while culture takes a long time to develop, it can be lost in a nanosecond.

For example, if leaders don't embrace a clear system, then they're likely to adopt the flavor of the day. And the distraction of a constantly changing message alone can allow bad managers to flourish. As the struggling CEO of GE, Jeff Immelt described the company differently in nearly every annual report letter he wrote over his long tenure. (See Figure 12.3.) Could the company really change so much over those years, or was he just superficially chasing hot ideas? In the process of fixating on whatever was popular, GE managers, and by extension the employees, lost focus.

Part of the problem with the longstanding emphasis on culture is that analysts, journalists, investors, employees, and executives use it as an explanation for successes. But does culture drive performance, or does performance drive the perception of culture? We can't think of a failed company that at one point didn't describe its culture in glowing terms. GE and WeWork are good recent examples, with risk taking described as "entrepreneurial." They used powerful adjectives to make investors and other stakeholders think that their companies had some sort of special powers. But look behind the curtain, and you'll see that those cultures weren't much of anything real. It is important that Amazon and Facebook, among others in the tech world, don't fall into this trap. It is a slippery slope. Just ask Boeing alums; they lived that reality.

Figure 12.3: **GE's annual reports under Jeff Immelt were the poster child for "culture" platitudes.**

GE Annual Report Titles (Jeff Immelt Era)	
2002	"Only GE"
2003	"Growing in an Uncertain World"
2004	"Our Time"
2005	"Go Big"
2006	"Invest and Deliver"
2007	"Invest and Deliver Every Day"
2008	"We Are GE"
2009	"Reset . . . Renew"
2010	"Growth Starts Here"
2011	"GE Works"
2012	"GE Works"
2013	"Progress"
2014	"A New Kind of Industrial Company"
2015	"Digital Industrial"
2016	"Leading a Digital Industrial Era"

Source: General Electric filings

CAPITAL ALLOCATION, COMPOUNDING, AND THE NEED FOR REINVENTION

Future investment is essential, in ways people don't always understand. The key to long-term success is creating a powerful advantage over rivals, which is necessary for survival when the inevitable crisis hits. Whether it's superior quality in technically complex products, marketing prowess, or advantaged distribution networks, these don't come right away. Companies have to build a moat with sustained investments in competitively important areas. If done well, those investments should eventually yield ever-higher results. More profits, invested at the higher rate of return generated by the moat, lead to even more profits, and so on—the power of compounding—on the flywheel.

Companies can invest cash internally in operations and new products or externally in acquisitions; it depends on the opportunities available. The key is to generate returns on that investment, translated into cash flow, that show compounding growth in profits. Better yet, companies that master capital deployment (by regularly shifting in search of the highest return: organic growth, acquisitions, dividends, or share repurchases) win lower funding costs as investors pay up for that success and debt rating agencies see better execution. Lower funding costs result in greater compounding, which gives those companies the essential resilience to survive over long periods, particularly important in periods of unexpected disruption like the one we are currently experiencing with this year's pandemic.

As an illustration, suppose a company boosts revenues at the same rate as GDP, say 3 percent, and is competent at manufacturing. It could raise profits by 5 to 6 percent annually simply with disciplined operating improvements. But if the company consistently allocates the cash to opportunities with a solid return profile, then eventually it should start seeing profits rise by a meaningfully higher rate, say 8 to 9 percent annually. And if the company pursues businesses with a growth rate higher than the GDP, then it can achieve double-digit growth in profits. Double-digit growth is what puts a company well into the top quartile of a wide peer group, typically. A target worth pursuing.

That growth algorithm can prove particularly important in keeping investors interested during times of stock market distress. The spread between stocks that hold value and those that get punished severely becomes even more acute in tough times. And that's largely a function of the ability to hold profits and cash flow stable when conditions deteriorate. Compounders like Danaher, Roper, and TransDigm, even in their more cyclical pasts, were each able to limit downside during recessionary periods. And while we can't be certain exactly how they'll come through this most recent global crisis, we have confidence that they'll come out better than their peers.

Clearly though, the upside math is most compelling when business conditions are stable. An investment with 10 percent compounding growth, all else being equal, should double in value every 7 years, while one with 5 percent growth would take 14 years. The rewards of compounding growth are enormous, and there are many paths to get there. The main idea is to *treat cash as investors do*: dispassionately looking for the best return, not what builds an empire. Vanity deals never work. Deals done for defensive reasons are also usually doomed. And "game changing" is normally the path to "game over."

How can companies achieve compounding? Operational discipline is essential. If every employee and piece of manufacturing equipment improves by even just 1 percent a year, then returns will see an impact. (See Figure 12.4.) And productivity gains of 2 to 3 percent per year are often seen by those with true continuous improvement cultures. Those are the companies that really shine over time.

Figure 12.4: **Small deltas in compounding rates make big differences.**

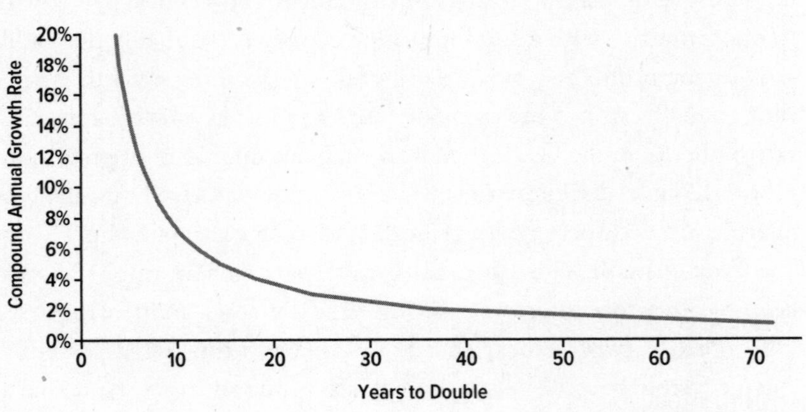

Source: Melius Research

Surprisingly, compounding is not explicit in the business model of many firms today. They prefer to work on strategic investments with highly uncertain returns, or they lack the organizational strength to act decisively and shift allocation in meaningful ways. They hide behind the view that "balanced" deployment is best. Balance may make some sense as it relates to risk control. Still, you get there not at any particular moment, but by heavily weighting one area over others when the time is right—such as outsized share repurchases or M&A during periods of stock market or economic weakness, or debt paydown and a tilt toward internal investment when deals are less interesting and valuations are high.

Some companies elect to change the complexion, business model, and collective mindset of the entire organization. We've seen companies that were once firmly planted in the industrial world migrated elsewhere. For example, Danaher pivoted from a legacy tools company to a healthcare company through bold spin-offs and opportunistic deals. Honeywell tossed aside its best-known business line, thermostats, to focus on warehouse automation and software. Roper transitioned from pumps to software. But these weren't pie-in-the-sky transitions. In each case, cash flow was deployed to a higher-growth, higher-margin, more defensible, and higher-return plan, executed over a long enough time period to better manage risks inherent in big change. These examples are less common, but they're emblematic of the lengths to which the strongest companies will push forward in pursuit of building sustainable competitive advantages.

BENCHMARKING FOR SUCCESS

We find that the most successful companies measure pretty much anything that can be measured but narrow their focus to match up with the goals of the enterprise. They benchmark to compare internal operations. They benchmark to best-in-class peers and to those outside their own industry. They allow humility to reign. There is always someone out there with higher margins, better growth, and a higher market valuation. In continuous improvement cultures, benchmarking can be highly motivational—where it makes sense, of course.

As for specific data that companies utilize, on average we find 8 to 12 fairly common metrics that the most successful fixate on. (See Danaher's list in Figure 12.5 as a good example.)

Figure 12.5: **Danaher has whittled its benchmarking down to eight key metrics.**

Financial	Customer	Talent
Organic revenue growth	Quality (external parts per million)*	Internal fill rate
Operating margin expansion	On-time delivery	Retention
Cash flow/working capital turns		
Return on invested capital		

* Refers to product defect rates.
Source: Danaher

At the highest level we find cash flow growth and profit growth to form a common base. Most of the best companies add an asset-return metric such as return on invested capital, but that can disincentivize investment and be manipulated, so it has to emphasize earning a return on new investment and allow time for that return to come to fruition. Good investments often take multiple years to really prove out. And ROIC doesn't necessarily fit at every level within every organization. Plant managers are prone to underinvest, for example, because they rarely stay in that specific role or location long enough to reap the benefits of a modernization project. So there is risk to a one-size-fits-all model. In any event, it's vital for senior leaders to be held accountable for investment decisions, particularly over the longer term. The best companies seem to have found the right push-pull on metrics, with the awareness that point-in-time targets conflict with continuous improvement and the flywheel. The last thing an organization wants to emphasize is the "sprint to the goal line" behavior that is now so common in business. It's just not healthy, sustainable, or culturally positive.

Danaher has one of the most focused sets of metrics that we have seen, perfected over many iterations. At its very foundation, Danaher is highly focused on cash flow. Two of the most celebrated CFOs in our studies, at Honeywell and Danaher, offer up cash flow as the single most important metric they fixated on day after day, quarter after quarter. That very focus, they believe, supported the success that their respective entities enjoyed. They both argue that a cash flow–focused firm typically has better risk controls, a sales organization with more price discipline, and a manufacturing organization with little choice but to embrace Lean principles. By contrast, we cite few examples of excellence in firms that focus on market share, particularly for companies well past the disruption stage.

In that context, goals for market share can be dangerous, as they often drive short-term behaviors (sometimes unethical) with long-term risks. Consider BlackBerry, which maximized sales of its handheld units above all else, dedicating its cash and management attention accordingly. Or consider GE: During GE's entire fall from grace, including near bankruptcy twice in one decade, it was a share gainer. Jeff Immelt cited share gains as proof that the strategy was working, all while the underlying foundation of the company was floundering. And clearly Boeing's race to beat Airbus and get the 737MAX out the door led to regretful oversights and mistakes.

In some fast-growing, immature industries, market share might make some sense, as when Google, Apple, or Amazon invests in growth to achieve network effects on its platform. But network effects are isolated to a few disparate examples where they can lead to outsized profits down the road. For 99 percent of businesses out there, pricing a contract at or below cost, or allowing a customer to defer cash payments, brings eventual pitfalls. We find few examples where the strategy actually works past a company's early disruption phase. Some industrials have succeeded with razor/razorblade models that warrant selling up front at just above cost. But these businesses require long-term service revenue streams protected by intellectual property. More and more, the bloom is off that rose. Network effects can prove fleeting, and the US government has threatened to investigate tech firms that have acquired outsized power with this strategy. Countries in Europe and Asia have promised to follow suit.

In the end, every company has its unique circumstances. Different levels of competition, different levels of maturity. But we find no precedent of long-term success for a company that is not highly focused (with incentives) around the cash flows of the business itself. And we find little pushback to the argument that even in the tech world, the top performers are absolute cash flow machines.

The best companies not only measure and compensate based on the most relevant metrics; they do so every single day with "daily management." A retired Danaher executive once told us, "Even in Danaher's best-run businesses we had challenges, literally problems that pop up every day." He went on to say that there wasn't one single day in his 25-year tenure that he didn't have to "fix something." Whether that was an unhappy customer, a supplier issue, a product-quality issue, or an employee doing something stupid, much of a leader's job is about finding and fixing those problems before they get bad enough to really hurt the company. The earlier he found the problem, the easier the fix. And he thinks that level of daily management is largely what differentiates good management teams from bad. You want a culture where bad news travels fast and leaders can solve issues quickly.

The National Football League offers a relevant study of cultural impacts on success versus failure. The league is littered with teams that win rarely, make the same mistakes year after year, and are forced to change coaches so often that consistency, process, and artful daily management have little time to take effect, even if they are implemented. You would think poor results would catalyze some serious soul-searching, but that hardly happens. Instead, excuses reign supreme, and coaches and players are increasingly paid on a lower set of goals and standards. It's interesting to note that the bottom half of NFL teams pay their quarterbacks about the same as the top half. Coaching staffs aren't paid materially differently either. *Losing teams just set lower standards and define their journeys in terms of "progress" as opposed to wins and losses.* They project an image that a system exists and that fans should be more patient, but over time it becomes clear that it's just not true. The virtual equivalent can be seen from factory managers (and their CEOs) in winning versus losing operations. There may in fact be progress, but the pace is too slow to close the gap with winning cultures and teams. Continuous improvement cultures raise an already high benchmark. Winning cultures tend to have amazingly honest conversations about success and how that will be measured, and about humility and how that tends to sustain the already high level of achievement.

The good news is that sports or business death is never all that sudden. The Honeywell case study is a perfect example of a company that got back on track after being on the path to likely failure. And although not illustrated in this book, Ingersoll-Rand, ITT, and Illinois Tool Works were each successfully managed out of the doldrums. 3M was struggling under a new CEO but became refocused during the pandemic and has risen to the occasion. It is very possible to turn around losing franchises, but it takes a healthy dose of humility and a period of relentless refocus.

RISK MANAGEMENT

Most corporate leaders are comfortable focusing on growth and profitability. That's what Wall Street uses to value companies and what the compensation for those leaders is normally geared toward. There are nuances in how to define those metrics, like cash flow versus profits or margins versus returns on capital. But in the end, compensation schemes need to be tailored to the challenges of that particular entity. Differentiation is often less dynamic than you would expect. Where we find few best practices, however, is around risk management and risk control. Leaders are often free to pursue strategies that offer sharply different risk profiles overall.

Ironically, professional investors tend to understand risk better than many of the management teams of the companies they invest in. Professional investors tend to have a "maximize gain while minimizing loss" mindset that identifies potential risks and expects to be compensated for them. This is a fundamental value driver that underpins the structure of almost everything in the finance world, and it's perhaps easiest to observe in bond ratings, where risk levels are assessed and assigned before securities are even sold. It's directly seen in stock valuations when you compare more predictable revenue models, like software, with less predictable ones, like financial services. There's a similar dynamic when you compare cyclical assets with less cyclical. The valuation differences relate completely to risk perceptions.

Inside many companies, especially once you get a few layers down into the organization, there's little such appreciation for risk. And incentive compensation systems often ignore risk entirely. Even in some otherwise well-managed firms, people are paid to boost revenues and earnings or to maximize cash flows, but these people aren't guided on how much risk to take when doing so. The result is a tendency toward risky decisions, especially when the potential consequences of those risks are well in the future and therefore another leader's responsibility.

To achieve growth and profits, both of which are outputs, businesses must contribute various inputs, and not all inputs are created equal. Some come with contingent costs, and others have timing consequences that skew evaluations of costs and benefits. In our experience, the most successful companies are consistently mindful of the inputs that best drive their desired outputs, and they find ways to limit the use of risky inputs. The outcome of this mindfulness is higher-quality growth, or returns that are less volatile and more sustainable over the long term.

Risk management is therefore a critical variable in our long-term analysis of success versus failure. And although investors are pretty good at discounting different risk profiles, companies are often very much asleep at the wheel. GE's near failure twice in one decade relates specifically to its failure to manage risks on more levels than we can even count: project risk, M&A risk, high debt levels, pension funding risks, cultural degradation risk, underinvestment risk, and the actuarial risk it retained with long-term-care insurance liabilities. Nearly every failure that we can identify has some element of an altered risk profile that went very badly, whether an ill-conceived M&A deal, or poorly made investments, or bad leadership allowed to linger far longer than warranted. Management flaws relating to risk control begin to show even in good economies but become particularly pronounced in recessions. (See Figure 12.6.)

Figure 12.6: **Returns are compounded by executing the flywheel.**

Source: Melius Research

CONCLUSION

All the companies we study have processes of some kind; that's not what's lacking. But much of that time gets spent on unproductive activities, such as budgeting, forecasting, doing capital planning, and fixing problems that were allowed to linger and grow. What works, instead, is an intense focus on three goals: containing cost—by reducing waste at every step; manufacturing for repeatable quality; and driving a high level of customer intimacy throughout an organization. It works when these are the goals of everyone at the company, and continuous improvement as a mindset becomes central to the culture.

At a bare minimum, the companies that effectively employ continuous improvement will gain opportunities through higher cash flow that could be spent on growth.

The best companies are those that have gone a step further and built something different and new, growth companies that are created around operational competence rather than around a product cycle. Danaher and Fortive operate a wide range of businesses arguably better than anyone else in the world, from professional tools to biotech. Roper transitioned from managing industrial assets to software. TransDigm is specialized, but with its tremendous focus on protected niches, it vastly outperforms even other well-managed aerospace suppliers. While it's not immune to today's aerospace woes, its track record of managing through challenges is well established. Manufacturing a quality product that customers demand matters, of course, but what really differentiates is the repeatability of processes, business systems that maximize effort and focus in every function. The flywheel of success comes when operations generate cash, which is used to invest in more assets, which are then improved.

Lessons on what to avoid are clear. Forecasting end markets many years out is a mistake in driving strategic decisions; it's a well-informed coin flip. GE bet heavily on years of uninterrupted growth in oil and gas industry spending and on spending for fossil fuel–powered electricity generation. Caterpillar believed spending in mining would grow exceptionally and for some time—and now US coal is in a steep spiral down to nothing. GE sold off NBC to make those ill-fated investments just before the media business improved. GE and Caterpillar are extreme examples, but outthinking end markets on growth 5 to 10 years out is a loser's game. To that point, no one could have anticipated either the timing or depth of destruction from the current pandemic. And if forecasting the top line is a remarkable challenge, then forecasting future profitability is even more so. It is a rare management team that would suggest margins will get worse due to market dynamics or their actions. Optimism is universal.

Management plays a critical role in setting goals for an organization and in reinforcing behaviors that support those goals. Incentives matter more than most managers think, and those incentives need to be tuned to the current strategy. The departure of a long-term CEO is an uncertain moment in a company's life, doubly so if the CEO is a legend, like Jack Welch at GE or George David at United Technologies. Investors often tread cautiously during such times, fearful of earnings "big baths" when hidden problems from the prior leadership are surfaced. The bigger danger is that things don't change. A strategy that's run its course, as at United Technologies, needs a careful reevaluation at the CEO and board level. United Technologies was one example, but there are a great many others. Managers who rise through the ranks during the 15-year run by a top CEO are going to be naturally supportive of the older strategy, and they probably have too much hesitation to break out of it. They've spent their careers implementing it, after all. That's one of the most impressive results of Dave Cote's long run of success at Honeywell; he chose a successor in Darius Adamczyk who took the company in a far different and yet still a positive direction.

The right questions definitely exist, for employees exploring their careers and for investors exploring ownership stakes. Management matters, often more than the business itself, over anything other than a short time frame.

We increasingly look for two markers of success. One is humility, a shorthand way of saying the ability to embrace feedback and change, benchmarking, and a method for generating quality feedback. The other is a well-established process for feedback, which enables continuous improvement, the core of any successful industrial, though one too often trapped on the factory floor rather than spread throughout the organization. Red flags are the opposite: arrogance, overconfidence, and a strategy of managing tightly to targets, as well as strong bets on end markets, or at least high confidence in making them. Shooting from the hip is dangerous in itself and probably a marker of something missing in its place.

Business books talk about strong leadership, but that often gets placed into military parallels, where larger-than-life, loud men shout out commands. That never seems to work in business. We define "strong" as the ability to plot a reasonable course, communicate the plan, and put people in place who can execute, all while incentivizing and rewarding behaviors that move an organization steadily toward long-term targets, with a continuous improvement mindset.

The best companies have strong cultures, but only as the output of years of sensible actions, disciplined processes, and incentives set by leadership. Every employee knows the mission and works toward some facet of it every day. It's a fairly obvious trait when you get to know it.

What does all this mean for the new economy? As industries age and competition deepens, newer companies that lack operational discipline will fall, just as hundreds of old economy leaders have done. Feedback loops and continual improvement work in any industry but seem to be lacking in much of the newer tech world. Big-idea cultures without daily management tools eventually go off the rails. Concept businesses and software companies are particularly prone to those risks.

Management of hard assets within the framework of an IP-based company is extra tricky; Uber and WeWork are good examples. Often the strategy seems to be to pretend the assets don't have a cost, so everything will work out over time. Sometimes the tech economy's crossover into physical assets seems an exercise in pushing as much pain outside the system as can be borne, rather than minimizing costs. That works only so long as there are enough desperate people to take the work, and it leaves itself vulnerable to an actual, profitable business. This is in addition to the clear ethical implications and likelihood that government watchdogs will take notice.

The lessons are not complex in theory: measure, develop process, apply incentives, correct as needed, and repeat. The further along that journey gets, the more robust and differentiated it becomes. The moat widens; the culture becomes ingrained.

It's critically important that an organization focus on the little stuff that keeps it on the flywheel. Adopt a business system that focuses the effort. Benchmark externally and to best-in-class organizations. Encourage a humble culture based on continuous improvement. And promote leadership that understands the critical importance of managing costs, generating increasingly higher cash, and redeploying that cash toward the highest returns. Not difficult at all, but somehow it gets lost with each generation of new companies that are so focused on near-term success, they forget that "long term" is often right around the corner.

FINAL THOUGHTS

The themes we've discussed in this chapter are the most notable of the best practices we have observed over time. But an exhaustive list would be misleading anyway. There is more art, and perhaps a bit more luck, to business success than we would like to admit. A commonality of most of our case studies is a lack of real-time popular appeal. Many readers, for example, have never heard of United Rentals; yet it has built up a business that could be called the Uber of construction equipment—but arguably with a much more sustainable business model than Uber's.

This is partially why we think the case studies are so valuable. They are off the radar screen but shouldn't be. Each case offers clear and common business problems and a set of solutions that either worked brilliantly or failed miserably. And while there are commonalities, there are also a lot of nuances and finesse. Without the context of the studies, the lessons we discuss here all fall pretty flat.

One thing we can guarantee is that beyond today's infatuation with disruption, these same challenges will emerge again. Many are happening already. WeWork needed emergency funding just a month after nearly landing on a windfall of an IPO. Facebook has been on Capitol Hill answering to legislators with increasing skepticism. Apple and Google are both facing challenges of operating in a global economy, where the rules are often different and the playing field hardly fair. And there is broad distrust of this new generation of success. Tech billionaires rank down with used car salesmen as related to public trust, and those perceptions will impact government policy for a generation.

Industrials have seen this movie already. We could have changed the names above and gone back 20, 40, even 60 years and made the same statements. In nearly every case, there is an industrial company that either solved for one of these problems or failed trying. Those who ignore history are doomed to repeat it. We don't have all the answers. Far from it. But we do have some, and those answers have implications for a broad audience: for those who invest, those who lead, those who still seek a career, and those who regulate—there is plenty to go around.

INDEX

D

N

O

ABOUT THE AUTHORS

Scott Davis serves as Chairman and CEO of Melius Research, where he is also the lead research analyst covering the multi-industry sector. He has 25 years of industrials equity research experience and has covered over 50 companies with an aggregated market capitalization of over $1 trillion.

Davis has led elite research teams for the past 20+ years, ranking in the top decile of all Wall Street analysts in nearly every time period. For the past 17 years, *Institutional Investor* magazine has recognized Davis as the number one ranked multi-industry analyst on six occasions and within the top three in most of the remaining years.

Prior to Melius Research, Davis was a Managing Director and Head of the Global Industrials Research Group first at Morgan Stanley for 16 years then at Barclays Plc for 6 years. He and his work have been cited in hundreds of publications, including the *Wall Street Journal*, *New York Times*, *Forbes*, and *Fortune*, and he appears regularly on CNBC, Bloomberg, Fox, and CNN.

Carter Copeland serves as the President of Melius Research, where he is also the lead research analyst covering the global aerospace and defense sector. In the dozen years prior to joining Melius, he was ranked in *Institutional Investor*'s annual survey of top analysts every year. He was also named the number one Aerospace and Defense analyst on Wall Street by *Institutional Investor*'s *Alpha* magazine. Copeland previously served as a Managing Director and senior analyst covering aerospace and defense at Barclays Plc and Lehman Brothers. Before beginning his career as an equity analyst, he worked as a research assistant at the Federal Reserve Board of Governors in Washington, DC, where he served as an assistant to the Federal Open Market Committee (FOMC) and conducted and published academic research on various topics in corporate finance, most notably pension management.

Rob Wertheimer is a founding partner of Melius Research, where he serves as the Director of Research and lead research analyst for the global machinery sector. He has more than a decade of industrial research experience and was recognized as a top three analyst by *Institutional Investor* during his time at Barclays Plc and Morgan Stanley.

Prior to Barclays, he led the machinery coverage at Vertical Research and Morgan Stanley. He started his career covering beverage and retail across Latin America as an associate on a top-ranked team. He also worked for several years as a strategy consultant for small businesses in manufacturing and retail. Wertheimer served in the Peace Corps in Niger, West Africa, where his work focused on agriculture, forestry, and water resources in a small rural village.

For more information, visit meliusresearch.com.